David Gallaher

THE COMPLETE RUGBY FOOTBALLER

ON THE

NEW ZEALAND SYSTEM

BY

D. GALLAHER AND W. J. STEAD

CAPTAIN AND VICE-CAPTAIN OF THE NEW ZEALAND TEAM
TOURING IN GREAT BRITAIN IN 1905

WITH THIRTY-FIVE ILLUSTRATIONS

METHUEN & CO.
36 ESSEX STREET W.C.
LONDON

206918

First Published in 1906

Ka mate ka mate ka ora kaora
Ka mate ka mate ka ora kaora
Te nei te ta nga ta pu huru huru
Na na e piki mai whaka white te ra
Hu pa nei, hu ka nei, hu pa nei kau
    pa nei white te ra.

Translation—

Together we live, together we die,
This man we bring is the murderous one,
He slew as long as the sun shone.
So shame on him! Shame on him!
Shame on him as long as the sun shines.

MAORI WAR-CRY

PREFACE

IF any excuse is needed for offering this work to those who are interested in Rugby football, we suggest that it is to be found in the widespread interest—without a parallel —evoked by the tour through Great Britain in the autumn and early winter of 1905 by the New Zealand combination of players, who came to be known as the "All Blacks" on ac ount of their sombre uniform. The reason for that interest was the wonderful record achieved by the team, who, though matched twice a week against all the most powerful combinations that could be brought to bear against them throughout Great Britain, only lost one match out of thirty-two, and that at the end of their tour when they were feeling the strain of their long campaign, and when they were opposed to the strongest international side that could be put into the field against them. Such a record was within the veriest trifle of perfection, and it has been freely prophesied that it will never be surpassed in our time. In such circumstances there was naturally some curiosity evinced as to the methods which made such success not only possible, but, if we may say so, almost easy; and there was a desire to study those methods.

Only half of our system, or perhaps not so much as that, could be discovered by the most careful student of it who merely saw it at work on the field of play. The remainder was secret to ourselves, and we conceived it to be to our advantage to keep it so until we had finished our engagements. For example, one of the details of our system—it was only a detail—that evoked most interest because it was most apparent, was our scrum formation, and, while many critics agreed that it had merits over other arrangements of the pack, they seemed to conclude that such success as was obtained with it must necessarily have been due to the mere arrangement of the seven men instead of eight, and incidentally the gain of a man outside. Thus, one constantly heard that it showed that seven men were as effective as eight. But while we considered that the arrangement was the best, it only partly accounted for the good work done by our pack. It was never suspected that one of the chief merits of our scrum was the way in which those seven men applied their power, for they never pushed straight in front of them as they were supposed to do. They would have been comparatively ineffective had they done so.

In the following pages we have told for the first time all about our game that there is to tell. One of the signatories to these remarks acted as the captain of the team during the tour and the other one as the vice-captain, and at home in New Zealand one is representative of the football that is played in the North Island and the other of that in the South Island. They are jointly responsible for all that is stated in the book, and have conferred together upon all the details before committing them to print. It may, however, be taken that each of the authors is more individually responsible for the remarks made upon those departments of the game in which he specialises, the captain having customarily played as wing forward, and the vice-captain as inside five-eighth—both positions being to a certain extent new to the players of Great Britain.

If it should appear that at times we lay stress on the superiority of our own system and our own methods as against those which prevail in Great Britain, it must not be taken that we are egotistical, and that we have no sufficient respect for the game as it is played elsewhere. We believe that our system is the best or we should not use it, and nothing has happened to shake our confidence in it, though we are not so foolish as to believe that anything like finality has been reached in the scientific development of the game. In this spirit we set out to describe our game, and to state its advantages, and in doing so comparisons to the disadvantage of other systems are inevitable.

We have introduced much useful matter into the Appendix, to which we may recommend the reader to give closer attention than he usually does to the contents of this section of a book.

We should like to take this opportunity, on behalf of ourselves and the other members of the team who were associated with us in our tour, of expressing our gratitude to all connected with Rugby football in Great Britain, players and officials, with whom we came in contact, for the efforts which were made to make our visit pleasant and enjoyable. We may assure them that these kindly and truly British efforts achieved the most complete success, and that it will be our ambition on some future occasion to prove that we are not unworthy kinsmen.

After all, the game of Rugby football—prince of games of its class—belongs to Britain. If we New Zealanders by our tour and by this work have accomplished some trifle in the way of its further encouragement and improvement in the homeland, we shall feel that this was an achievement surpassing any other record.

D. G.
W. J. S.

June 1906.

CONTENTS

CHAPTER I

IN THE BEGINNING 1

The object—Development of the game in New Zealand—Success of methods—How we came by the game—The Roman *harpastum*—Almost entirely a handling game—In the twelfth century—Monarchs forbid the game—Imprisonment for footballers—A splendid survival through persecution—Football to be "utterly cryed down"—Killed and wounded—A comparison with modern American football—Indictment by Sir Thomas Elyot—A strenuous game in Middlesex—Stubbes on "develishe pastimes"—Increasing popularity of the game—The Roman game in force—The annual match at Scone—A germ of Rugby—A decline—The public schools take up the game—Different methods of play—A mistake about Rugby—The boy who first picked up the ball—The game at the Universities—The real beginning of public Rugby—A football boom—Two kinds of football—A joint conference between dribblers and handlers—A majority for no handling—The birth of the Football Association—Lonely Rugby—The game in South Wales—Establishment of the English Rugby Union—More Unions—Absolute amateurism—More science in the game—Fifteen on the side—Changes of formation—Passing begins—Development of the three-quarter back line—Faster play—Spread of the game.

CHAPTER II

DEVELOPMENT IN NEW ZEALAND 17

"Anyhow" games in the sixties—A match against the *Rosario*—First tendencies towards Association—Formation of a club—Return match with the *Rosario*—A challenge to play for £200—A very scratch affair—Some difficulties as to rules—A strenuous engagement with the Goldfields—Shocking list of casualties—Some doubts about the future—A chaotic state of affairs—W. W. Robinson's enthusiasm—Development on Rugby lines—Shaping of the raw material—First match under Rugby rules—Interest and appreciation of the New Zealand public—The game spreads—Schoolboys take to it—Improvement in the play—Auckland goes on tour—A too trying programme—South Islanders victorious—Rivalry between the islands—Robinson plays two wing forwards against Canterbury—They win the game—The coming of the public schoolboys—Otago tour in the north—Inter-provincial football in 1880—Various formations—Characteristics of different centres—New South Wales send out a team—An odd formation—Establishment of the Auckland Rugby Union—A tour under its auspices—Australia sends another team—The study of the scrum—Lessons learnt from Stoddart's team—The fruits of knowledge—Variations in passing movements—The New Zealand Union—The ambition of the colony.

CHAPTER III

ORGANISATION AND EFFICIENCY 35

Necessity for a complete national organisation—But the simpler the better—The nursing of the player—Local government—The system of decentralisation in New Zealand—Attention to the schoolboys—The Auckland model—The Union for the schools—Towns divided into districts—One club one district—Players' clubs chosen for them—Advantages of the system—The residential qualification—Three fifteens in each club—Competitions for each class—A strong feature—Security of the seconds and thirds—No first players in second teams—The greatest encouragement to young players—Promotion by merit only—Sometimes very quick—A notable example—A system worth copying—Teams not made by money—The system of the common ground—Union takes all the gate money—Ladies always free—The influence of the fair sex—A very important stimulus—Better behaved crowds—Better matches on neutral ground—Fairer tests—Union pays back the funds in kind—Limited incomes of the clubs—And limited expenditure—Automatic insurance of every player—The system of the training halls—A valuable feature—The centre of each club's activity—The country unions—The sole selector—Mistakes seldom made—Arneil's fine record—Tours in the provinces—The Ranfurly Shield—Union must take the initiative—Conservatism a bad fault.

CHAPTER IV

THE IDEA OF THE GAME 53

General principles governing the play—Goals and tries—The off-side rule—Limitations in ball propulsion—Elementary methods in olden days—The inevitable advantage of scientific play—The three groups of methods—Combination—Moral and actual advantages—Backing up—Infinite variety of passing movements—Short and sharp work for the individual—An object of strategy—The gain of

CONTENTS

a man—Slight odds against attackers when forces are equal—Men not gained in tackling—Two men to be drawn to one place—Two attackers and only a back to beat—Individual effort—Opportunism—A difficult and thankless task—Success the only justification—A possible charge of selfishness—"Unofficial and very guarded approval"—The ruse—Neglected possibilities—Ruse must be good—The double edge—Necessity for a side to adapt itself to circumstances—Large stock of variations advisable—The placing of the team—Backs and forwards—A comparison between the British and New Zealand formations—The wing forward and the flying half—The virtues of the five-eighths—Great possibilities for developing an attack—The advantage of the extra line of defence—Capacity to strike in many ways.

CHAPTER V

QUALIFICATIONS OF PLAYERS 68

Need for versatility among backs—Should be able to play in any position but with one speciality—Examples in the New Zealand team—Wealth of variety in attack and defence—Qualifications of the back—A necessity in the wing three-quarter—The advantage of private practice—Punting and fielding—Methods of practice in New Zealand—The donkey man of the team—The work of the half back—The magnificence of Roberts—Methods of the half—His prospects of scoring—His cunning and strategy—Doing the unexpected—More definite qualifications—The five-eighths—Quite indispensable to our system—Attacking movement begun much more expeditiously—An Oxonian's appreciation—Five-eighth must be a quick-witted man—Harmony between the scrum half and the five-eighth—The necessity for a code—The colonial system—The weak spot of the enemy—Some points in tactics—The three-quarters—Forward in attack, back in defence—The centre—Necessity for unselfishness—Fast men wanted—New Zealand's best—The full back—A trying position—Great possibilities—Points of the back—Little of the orthodox—A difference in methods—The forwards—What is wanted in them—Must keep their temper and not talk—Always to be in the pink of condition—Dribbling—And when to dribble—Expensive experiments—The fine footwork of the Irish forwards—Combination among the pack—Need for the exercise of common sense—Speed a requirement.

CHAPTER VI

IN POSSESSION OF THE BALL 85

Science in passing the ball—A man out of action—Compensation wanted—Pass must not be made a moment too soon—Hold to the

ball until the last second—Opponent bound to tackle—Passing at
the moment of contact—The flick pass in Britain—A pretty thing
but rather uncertain—Must be made before the opponent is reached
—The New Zealand style—A low swing pass just at the time of
collision—No danger of failure—How we receive the ball—Taken
with the hands outside and hugged to the body—A very reliable
method—The man with the ball—Swerves and cuts—The best
swervers born, not made—The time for swerving—Reserve of
pace—How it is done—Gliding out of the arms of an opponent
—Hunter's corkscrew swerve—How Smith beat Scoular, with
Scoular not to blame—A good thing for the wing three-quarter—
Cutting is to be acquired—Necessity for constant practice—The
point of perfection—As little pace as possible must be lost—
Practising starts—A firm foothold wanted—See to the studs—
Dodgery—Comes by instinct only—Gwyn Nicholls—A great
Welshman—On tackling—Energy wanted—The man must be
brought down—Half-hearted tacklers a danger to their side—
Tackle low down, just below the hips—Little danger of accident—
Watching the man—A battle of wits—When to go for the ball
and not the man—Points in place-kicking—The methods of Wallace
—Constant practice of all kinds—Drop-kicking and punting.

CHAPTER VII

WORKING THE SCRUM 100

Seven forwards in the scrum—The British formation—Advantages of
the New Zealand system—The Wedge formation—Particular places
allotted to each man—Particular qualifications—The hookers—The
lock—A heavy man wanted—The side-row men—Two fast men
in the back row—How they all push—Pressing towards the
centre—One foot behind the other—The resultant of the seven
forces—Immense driving power—One of our secrets—Waste of
power with the British formation—Facilities for getting the ball
out quickly—An open line from the front to the back—Quickness
and cleanness—Backs run off their legs—The necessity for the wing
forward—The half could not get back in time after putting in—
Referees in doubt—Alleged bias on the ball—An absurd suggestion
—How the hookers hook—How we screw the scrum—The British
system—A comparison—Advantage of the man holding the ball
between his knees—When our forwards " heave "—When the back-
row men break away—Opponents prefer the scrum to the line-out.

CHAPTER VIII

THE WING FORWARD 115

His duties—A thankless task—An unprepared public—British teams
must try him—A surprise—Our usual game—The origin of the

CONTENTS

wing forward—Arneil and Mackenzie—An earnest pupil—Variations in different parts of the colony—The spare man—A matter of names—Inevitable errors—A necessity to a system—The commision given to the winger—What the half back tries to do—Too late—Qualities necessary in a good wing forward—He should be tall and fast—Keen eyes—Good at reckoning up a situation—When the ball comes out at the side of the scrum—Ready to receive it—As to obstruction by the winger—No basis for argument—An addition to the science of the game—The winger makes the game faster and not slower.

CHAPTER IX

PLAY FROM THE LINE-OUT 122

Possibilities not realised—What we did with the line-out in Britain—Too limited idea of the possibilities of forward play—Two situations when we do not attack from the line-out—In our own twenty-five and when the weather is wet—A simple and effective method of procedure—Mistake of putting the scrum half to throw in—One of the short hookers is the man to employ—The unmarked man—Not difficult to obtain in practice—Attackers do not need to mark men—Everything in their favour—The unmarked man knows he will receive the ball—Others in ignorance—How the men are disposed—The gap between the thrower-in and the other players—Attackers make the gap to their own size—The scrum half and the unmarked man—The unmarked man may go off with the ball if permitted—The usual course of procedure—A pass to the scrum half—Something that referees do not always understand—An attack upon stereotyped lines—Tries scored with backs standing still—Where the attackers lead others must follow—A lively form of attack—The Gap government—Pure bluff—How it is worked—The open space—The wing three-quarter who is ready to rush in—Others in ignorance—The ball thrown short—A fast sprint—A good example by an over-eager three-quarter—A limit to tactics of this kind—A puzzled opposition—Defence on the line-out—Tactics for the time—The loose ruck—Heeling out the ball—A man to the good.

CHAPTER X

ON TACTICS IN GENERAL 135

Nothing like good tactics—Mere combination is not tactics—A refinement—The need for study—Hall or class-room is a good place for the purpose—Dummy players—Tactics not rules—The need for novelty—No finality to the study—Good to study the old tactics and adapt them—Trifling changes afford complete alternatives—

CONTENTS

Great variety of tactics wanted—Special methods for special occasions—Forwards must be good—Tactics spoiled when front rank is weak—On pulling a match out of the fire—Everything to be sacrificed to attack—Playing a gambling game—All possible play wanted out of the ball—Every forward must become a back—Course of procedure when points up—Every man is a defender when time is approaching—The high kick up the field—How the taker may be hustled—On a wet day—Backing up—Insuring against accident—Extra confidence given to the man with the ball—A little drudgery, but it pays—On clinching an attack—All possible energy and resource wanted at the last moment—Full back who goes to the three-quarter line—When the wing three-quarter is jammed on the touch line—Man in attendance an absolute necessity.

CHAPTER XI

TACTICS—COMBINED ATTACK ON THE OPEN SIDE . . 145

The standard form—Diagram explained—The need to gain a man—The functions of the inside five-eighth—Takes stock of the situation—Scrum half instructed by code word—How the scrum half receives the ball—Ball taken at top speed—Attitude of the defence—Probabilities of the situation—The opening for the attackers—The next pass—The importance of not passing too soon—An alternative in defence—Adaptation of the attack—The man gained—The advantage to the attackers—Setting a trap for the defence—Useless passing without gain of ground—When the five-eighth cuts in toward the scrum—An adventurous movement—When unnecessary it can only be justified by success—The other backs mere spectators—No rule against it—Prospects of success—A tight corner—Possible help from the wing three-quarter—A lob pass under difficulties—When the opposition know too much—Leaving five-eighth out of the movement—A dash round by the scrum half—Better on the blind side—An alternative—A pass direct from the scrum half to the outside five-eighth.

CHAPTER XII

TACTICS—ATTACKING ON THE BLIND SIDE, AND OTHER VARIATIONS 158

Two methods—Defence turned into attack—A commission to the wing three-quarter—Only serious difficulty the full back—The five-eighth on the blind side—Bluff is wanted—May be left with an open field—The pass-in—The rule in Britain—An excellent variation—A splendid chance given on the pass back—The advantage of surprise

CONTENTS

—Another movement which is all surprise—A punt over the heads of the opposition—The duty of the second five-eighth—He knows beforehand—Successful ventures when on tour—A useful manoeuvre when the defence is good—A complete novelty in attack—The Taipu movement—The second five-eighth cuts in to the right—The ball transferred behind his back—Opposition taken off their guard—Opening an attack from opponent's drop-out—Object is to bustle the taker—A dash into the open—Two courses open to the taker when pressed—He may pass or take a line kick at a good angle—Another advantage — Opposition will take precautions — An adventurous alternative—Pure bluff in tactics—The man without the ball—A daring but sometimes successful manoeuvre—Demoralisation of the opposition—A cross punt forward and a chance to the outside three-quarter—Tactics in defence—Advantage of numbers—Assistance from the back-row men in the scrum.

CHAPTER XIII

ON EQUIPMENT AND TRAINING 173

A first-class constitution wanted—Visit the doctor—Good digestion and good eyesight—Unfit men should stand down—Must feel well to play well—Good jerseys—A strange delusion—Knickers, stockings, and shin guards—Another delusion—Gloves for the back division—Players with too heavy boots—The shape of the buttons—How to make them bite—The care of the boots—The importance of training—Irksome and unpleasant methods—An undesirable reaction—A system in which we do not believe—Differences of opinion—No training, no play—Men who are always in condition—The polishing process—The system of the training halls—A busy centre—Men in large cities and towns—A sharp run before breakfast—A strict rule—An evening walk—The advantage of companionship—Backs' cultivation of their speed—The question of diet—The rival schools of thought—No belief in special diets—Eat what you like—Advice of a great surgeon—When on tour—Smoking and drinking—The day of the match—A midday meal—Beauty sleep—The danger of being overtrained—Recipe for a rubbing oil—The common-sense life—No such thing as special training.

CHAPTER XIV

ON CAPTAINCY 188

A hard man to find—A list of necessary virtues—His relations with the team—A crude team but fine material—The captain's duty—Must see that his men are in agreement—Knowledge of the rules—New ideas—The omniscient captain—A human compendium of football law—The peculiarities of the fifteen—Little differences—The proper pegs in the proper holes—The place for the captain on the field—Wing forward or five-eighth—What to do in emergencies—Possible changes in the arrangement of the side—Advantage of knowing his men—Filling sudden vacancies with the smallest loss—The weakness of the one-position man—Practise men in different positions—Studying the other side—A valuable mental file for reference—The captain's tactics—On listening to the advice of others—On resource—Hope to be sustained—Some points in tactics—When the toss has been won—Fatherly superintendence over the team—A priceless man—Good captaincy worth more than good play—The pride of the old general—The greatest honour that a footballer can ever gain.

CHAPTER XV

GOOD RULES 201

Discuss the plan of the game—Don't be late on the field—Practising specialities—Watching the ball—On codes—Codes should be changed—On new ideas and inventions—The reliability of old-fashioned things—The selection of a ground—Advantage of sandy soil and coarse grass—The methods of your opponents—Bad temper—Quack medicines—The possibilities of a new position—The mark—Removing wet things—The incidents of the match—A day off and the best way to spend it—The half-hearted player—Justifiable blame—An injured opponent—Allowances cannot be made—Talking to opponents during play—Don't play if you don't feel well—If chances do not come your way—Playing to the whistle—On shouting for a pass—After the match—Ask questions—On playing to the gallery—Quickness of decision—Attention to the boots—Be spick and span—The studs—Play a clean game—On speculation—When hurt in play—When you have missed your man—Never be idle or neglectful—On guarding a vacant position—Backing up a colleague—"My ball."

CHAPTER XVI

TWO DANGERS TO THE GAME 211

Referees and refereeing—The independent critic—Blame on the official for declining popularity—A game that is being strangled—Splendid opportunities for Rugby—A grand game—Its local patriotism—Advantages over the Association game—Not so attractive as it might be—The game is made too slow—Fast play in New Zealand—Tedious play in a great international match—Disappointment of Association spectators—Referees who are too fond of the scrum—More free kicks should be given—Little things that might be overlooked—Different interpretations placed upon the law—The need for conferences of referees—Neglected points—The off-side rule—When the ball goes clean through the scrum—Why order it to be put in again?—Do referees like scrums?—The referee's attire—Does it conduce to efficiency?—Laggard referees—They must keep up with the game—A rule that would be wise—But it is easy to blame the referee—Difficult duties—People who could always perform them so much better—On arguing with the players—Answering a captain's civil questions—Concerning professionalism—Our own status—Players out of pocket—The New Zealand Union's risk—The best principles—Professionalism in the Association game—Does professionalism necessarily mean better play?—The Northern Union—Some of its captures—The game must be made more attractive—The size of the scrum—On future developments.

CHAPTER XVII

PROSPECTS OF EXPANSION 225

The "games of the world"—Spread of the British games—The games of the future—Their features—Climatic conditions—Rugby football in France—An increasing aptitude for the game—In Europe generally—Cricket as a universal pastime—Its disadvantages—Needs to be bred in the player—The advantages of football—The superiority of Rugby—The value of tradition—Its colonising properties—An amateur game—Simplicity of organisation—Bad examples—The evils of red tape, and their consequences—The status of Association football—Bright prospects of Rugby—An Imperial council—Rising colonies—The game in Australia—Customs in Sydney—The next menace to the supremacy of the mother country—The game in South Africa—Excellently suited to the country—Football in the United States—Suffering from want of good tradition—A very bad state of affairs—Description by an authority—A change required—A chance for Rugby.

CHAPTER XVIII

HOW THE "ALL BLACKS" PREPARED FOR THEIR TOUR . 239

A dream of old—A previous effort—New Zealand not united—Opposition from Otago—English Union would not entertain the proposal—All for the best—The colony united—Visit to Britain arranged—Excitement in New Zealand—Selecting the team—Trial matches—An avalanche of criticism—Eleventh hour selections—The team's last matches in New Zealand—Embarkation on the *Rimutaka*—Conferences on tactics—Methods brought into line—Entertainments during bad weather—Some disquieting experiences—The calm—Monte Video—Hard practice on board ship—Training rules—The daily programme—A very thorough system of preparation—Forwards and backs hard at it—Huge appetites—Tropical heat and cessation of work—Players in the stoke-room—Prizes won at the ship's sports—Arrival at Plymouth—A little nervousness—Headquarters at Newton Abbot—We witness a match—More confidence—Hard practice on the field—An Englishman's prophecy — How we won our first match — Welcome back to Newton Abbot—The British sportsman—The campaign begun.

CHAPTER XIX

THE GREAT CAMPAIGN OF 1905 252

The match against Cornwall—Another easy victory—Third victory at Bristol—Good work by our halves—At Northampton—A criticism—169 points to 4—The Leicester match—Gift of boots—In London—The Middlesex match—Anxious to make a good show—Points of our play—Engaged against Durham—A hard game against the champion county—The Hartlepools—A gigantic score—One try every five minutes—A telegram from Mr. Seddon—Ordeals before us—The Northumberland match—The men who scored the tries—Gloucester—Good combined attack—Wallace's fine run—The game against Somerset—Devonport Albion—The first team to attempt to play a winning game—Backs short of pace—The Midland Counties—A good lot of forwards—The thirteenth match—The Surrey match at Richmond — Too many free kicks—The Blackheath match—A team of many internationals—Seven forwards in the scrum—The University matches—Richmond—Bedford collect a side—Necessary change in our plans—The international match against Scotland—Trying conditions—Scoular not to blame—An unfair accusation against us—West of Scotland—Gloomy prophecies—Staleness in the team—A great responsibility—An enjoyable visit to Ireland—Tactics in the international—Splendid forward play by the Irishmen—Match with Munster—The international match against England—A great crowd at the Crystal Palace—Disappointing conditions—A poor game—Could England have chosen a stronger side?—Entertained by the Rugby Union—At Cheltenham—The match against Cheshire—Against Yorkshire—Northern Union spectators—The great match against Wales—Staleness prevalent—Dashing play by the Welshmen—Most of our backs off colour—The only defeat—Glamorgan opposed at Swansea—The Newport match—A remarkable match at Cardiff—A narrow escape at Swansea—All over—Return to London—A trip to Paris—A great time—Happy remembrances—Great British players—British sportsmanship—Hopes for a future visit.

CONTENTS

APPENDIX

	PAGE
Plan of the Field	271
The Laws of the Game	272
Bye-Laws of the Rugby Union	279
County Qualifications	282
Regulations for the County Championship	283
Bye-Laws of the International Board	285
Delegation of Powers	286
Rules as to Professionalism	287
Bye-Laws of the New Zealand Rugby Union	291
Regulations for the New Zealand Referees' Association	295
Decisions of a Conference of New Zealand Referees	297
Suggestions to the English Rugby Union	299
Opinions of the English Committee	299
New Zealand Union's Delegation of Powers	300
International Board's Recommendations to Players and Referees	301
Case Law	304
British Team in New Zealand, 1888	313
British Team in New Zealand, 1904	314
Native Team in England, 1888–89	314
New Zealand Team in Britain, 1905	315
Teams in the International Matches	316
The Record of the "All Blacks"	317

LIST OF ILLUSTRATIONS

	PAGE
DAVID GALLAHER . . . . . . *Frontispiece*	
From a photograph by BOWDEN BROS.	
NO DOUBT ABOUT IT (New Zealand v. Middlesex) . . .	20
From a photograph by BOWDEN BROS.	
THE NEW ZEALAND TEAM IN BRITAIN, 1905 . . .	34
From a photograph by E. KELLEY, Newton-Abbot.	
COMBINATION UNDER DIFFICULTY (New Zealand v. Somerset) . .	58
From a photograph by BOWDEN BROS.	
THE PROPER TIME TO GIVE A PASS.—AT THE MOMENT OF BEING TACKLED	88
HOW THE BALL IS PASSED AND TAKEN	88
WALLACE ADJUSTING THE BALL TO SUIT THE CIRCUMSTANCES PREPARATORY TO A PLACE KICK	94
From a photograph by BOWDEN BROS.	
BALL PLACED FOR AN ANGLE PLACE KICK . . .	96
BALL PLACED FOR A PLACE KICK IN FRONT OF THE GOAL .	96
TYLER'S PLACING OF THE BALL IN WET WEATHER . .	96
THE PROPER WAY OF HOLDING THE BALL PREPARATORY TO PUNTING	98
THE PROPER WAY TO TAKE THE BALL ON THE FULL . .	98
HOW THE HOOKERS (ON THE LEFT) PLACE THEMSELVES IN THE SCRUM	104
SHOWING THE HOOKERS IN THE ACT OF HOOKING OUT THE BALL .	104
HOW THE SIDE-ROW MEN IN THE SCRUM PLACE THEMSELVES AND APPLY THEIR POWER	106
THE SCRUM (New Zealand v. Middlesex)	110
From a photograph by BOWDEN BROS.	
LINE-OUT PLAY (New Zealand v. Devon)	126
From a photograph by BOWDEN BROS.	

LIST OF ILLUSTRATIONS

	PAGE
ANOTHER GOOD EXAMPLE OF PLAY FROM THE LINE-OUT	129
From a photograph by BOWDEN BROS.	
PASSING PRACTICE (R. Deans and G. Gillett)	178
From a photograph by BOWDEN BROS.	
WALLACE CONVERTING	200
From a photograph by BOWDEN BROS.	
GOAL! ONE OF WALLACE'S CONVERSIONS IN THE DEVON MATCH	224
From a photograph by BOWDEN BROS.	
TACKLING PRACTICE BY THE NEW ZEALANDERS	248
From a photograph by BOWDEN BROS.	
"ALL BLACKS" ATTACKING (New Zealand *v.* Middlesex)	254
From a photograph by BOWDEN BROS.	
NEW ZEALAND AND WALES AT CARDIFF	266
From a photograph by BOWDEN BROS.	
THE WELSH TEAM THAT DEFEATED THE "ALL BLACKS"	268
From a photograph by W. H. STEPHENS, *White House Studios, Newport, Mon.*	

IN THE TEXT

COMMON BRITISH FORMATION OF SIDE	65
NEW ZEALAND FORMATION OF SIDE	65
THE SWERVE	91
BRITISH SCRUM FORMATION	101
NEW ZEALAND SCRUM FORMATION	101
THE GAP	131
STANDARD FORM OF COMBINED ATTACK ON THE OPEN SIDE	147
FIVE-EIGHTH'S VARIATION OF ATTACK BY CUTTING IN	154
WING THREE-QUARTER'S ATTACK ON THE BLIND SIDE	159
FIVE-EIGHTH'S ATTACK ON THE BLIND SIDE	161
ATTACK OPENED FROM A DROP-OUT BY OPPONENTS	165
STRENGTHENING THE DEFENCE FROM THE SCRUM	171
PLAN OF THE FIELD	271

RUGBY FOOTBALL

CHAPTER I

IN THE BEGINNING

The object—Development of the game in New Zealand—Success of methods—How we came by the game — The Roman *harpastum*—Almost entirely a handling game — In the twelfth century — Monarchs forbid the game — Imprisonment for footballers—A splendid survival through persecution—Football to be "utterly cryed down"—Killed and wounded—A comparison with modern American football—Indictment by Sir Thomas Elyot — A strenuous game in Middlesex—Stubbes on "develishe pastimes"—Increasing popularity of the game—The Roman game in force—The annual match at Scone—A germ of Rugby—A decline—The public schools take up the game—Different methods of play—A mistake about Rugby—The boy who first picked up the ball—The game at the Universities—The real beginning of public Rugby—A football boom—Two kinds of football—A joint conference between dribblers and handlers—A majority for no handling—The birth of the Football Association—Lonely Rugby—The game in South Wales—Establishment of the English Rugby Union—More Unions—Absolute amateurism—More science in the game—Fifteen on the side—Changes of formation—Passing begins—Development of the three-quarter back line—Faster play—Spread of the game.

IT is our object in this work to show to what point of development we have brought the playing of the game of Rugby football in New Zealand, and to indicate what are our principles and practices and the details of our system, the advantages of which were conspicuously displayed during a recent period. Generally speaking, it is, of course, the same game as that played in Great Britain at the present time. It is played by the same number of men in very much the same way, and according to precisely the same rules, the suzerainty of the mother country in this matter being gladly acknowledged. Up to a certain point the histories of the game in the two countries are common; but from the time when it took root in New Zealand, it has, while conforming to the rules laid down at home, pursued a line of development which has been largely its own. When they first began to play Rugby football and to understand how splendidly was this noble sport adapted to the spirit and the conditions of the people, and the climate of the country, the New Zealanders took the game as they found it; but thenceforward, as was almost inevitable, they began to study it independently, taking not much heed of the course of development that was being followed at home, except in so far as it became necessary to conform to change of rules. At all events, they did not feel it to be obligatory to adopt the same changes of method and system.

It happens in other departments of life that a young colony, beginning things afresh, infuses more energy and thoroughness into its business, and displays a greater fertility of invention and resource than its parent; and whilst in the matter of its football New Zealand fully and gratefully recognises its debt to the mother country, and admires the spirit of progress which has animated some sections of players there, it thinks that, as the natural result of its semi-independence, it has possibly displayed a greater keenness in perfecting the science of the game. At all events, it was generally admitted in the course of the tour of the New Zealand team through Great Britain in the closing months of 1905, that the visiting players exhibited methods of achieving their object which were more expeditious and more certain than those of most of the sides to which they were opposed; and it is a matter of history that those methods were rewarded by more striking successes than attended the efforts of any other combination in similar circumstances. This tour was the great justification of the

New Zealand system, and is the excuse for this present work of explanation.

It is often found that the "new ideas" of our advanced civilisation are merely the old ones of our forefathers polished up and adapted to the needs of the time. Napoleon's advice to those who would study the art of war, was to read and read again the history of the great campaigns of the great generals of the past; and though indeed one must admit that on a careful survey there seems little to learn from the records of what transpired in the early days of Rugby football, or in those still earlier times, almost prehistoric, when the evolution of a game of football was in slow progress, still it may not be without advantage, and will at all events be of some interest, to consider how we came by the game that to-day finds such warm support among thousands and tens of thousands of people in different parts of the world. One may appreciate the efforts of modern players in Great Britain and New Zealand the better for having some knowledge of what has gone before. Therefore some slight sketch of the history of the game is here presented.

And the first thing to be said about football generally is that it is one of the oldest of all games. In view of its essential simplicity this is almost inevitable. A game which in some particulars resembled that which we play to-day was indulged in both by the Greeks and the Romans. The games which the Greeks played with a ball which was called the ἁρπαστόν, and the Romans with the *harpastum*,—a ball of cloth or leather stuffed with flocks,—which were evidently similar to each other, appear to have borne some resemblance in general principle to the Rugby football of these times; and here one would point out that the greater antiquity is clearly on the side of the handling game as against the dribbling. The game with the *harpastum*, as its Greek derivation indicates, was to seize and handle the ball, and we are told in a standard work of reference that it was played in much the same way as we play, but by a greater number of persons, divided into two parties opposed to one another. We are indeed informed that when playing with the *harpastum* the Romans were divided into two companies, and strove to throw their ball into one another's goals, these being the points of gain and victory. The *harpastum*, we see, was solid; but the Romans also played with another kind of ball called the *follis*, and this was an inflated bladder of skin. In this case also it was a kind of catching game, and the only thing against a fairly close comparison between the game of those far-back days and that of the twentieth century, is that the feet appear to have been very little used in the course of the play, if indeed they were used at all. There is very little doubt that it was the Romans who taught the Britons to play.

The first distinct mention of a game of football having been played in this country was by William FitzStephen, who, writing on or about 1175, makes reference to the custom of the young men of the city once a year going out into the fields after dinner to play at the well-known game of ball. It is strong evidence that this game had something in kinship with our modern football, that for many centuries (and even to-day in particular places) there were local football festivals, when immense sides were formed, with the object of forcing a ball to one end or other of the main street of a town or village. Generally it was the middle or lower classes who indulged in this sport, and not until quite modern times did the gentry give football any amount of patronage. From time to time in the early days of its development it came in for the censure of the authorities. Thus we find that Edward II. in 1314 issued a proclamation forbidding it to be played, on account of the "great noise in the city caused by hustling over large balls, from which many evils might arise, which God forbid." The penalty for disregard of this proclamation on the part of any too-zealous enthusiasts was nothing short of imprisonment. At last we find the game plainly called football by Edward III., who, without any intimation that he had anything against the game in itself or against the methods by which it was played, nevertheless took strong exception to it, on the ground that it had a tendency to weaken his armed forces, since "the skill at shooting with arrows was almost totally laid aside for the purpose of various useless and unlawful games." The sheriffs of London, to whom he had this message conveyed, were ordered to suppress "such idle practices."

Football can claim that it has survived and flourishes after such a lengthy period of determined persecution as was the unhappy lot of no other game, and it says much for its intrinsic merits even in its most primitive forms, and for the grit and persistence of the class of men who played it, that it came scatheless, so to speak, through this ordeal of centuries to command the devotion and respect of thousands of people of all classes in the most enlightened age. Forty years after the third Edward had banned it, Richard II. found it necessary to renew the prohibition, including it in a mixed list of "tennise, football, and other games called corts, dice, casting of the stone, kailes and other such importune games." But the successors of this monarch had likewise to renew their threats against the footballers, so that it was clear that the love of the game was stronger in the people who were attached to it, than their obedience to the law; while in the meantime in Scotland, where it seems to have taken firm root from early days, accounting perhaps for the great proficiency which the Scots have always displayed in playing it, a determined attempt was being made to kill it. In the middle of the fifteenth century, James III. decreed that displays of weapons and reviews should be held four times a year, upon which occasions "footballe and golfe be utterly cryed down and not to be used"; and the next monarch to sit upon the Scottish throne also decreed that "in na place of this realme there be used futeball, golfe, or other sik unprofitable sportes." It is evident that the constant fear of those in authority was that love for such sport would interfere with the practice of arms; and another point to be noticed from these ancient records is the constant association in these acts of tyranny and suppression of football with golf, games which in the twentieth century, no longer linked by adversity, have each an almost unequalled hold upon the people, so that the sovereign adds to his popularity when he himself participates in them, even though in the one case it is only passively as a spectator.

Having thus, as it were, definitely arrived at the establishment of football of a kind in Britain, we may glance lightly over the period intervening between then and that part of the last century when it emerged from the shadows and came to be regarded as a national pastime worthy of encouragement and support. During these centuries it continued under the ban of the authorities and respectable people; but whatever may have been the case in earlier times, one is forced to the conclusion, after a careful study of the records, that there was a good deal to be said for the unkindly feelings with which it came to be regarded by all peace-loving folk. Successive monarchs continued to denounce and prohibit it, and with good cause, for not only was it shunned by the better classes and confined almost exclusively to the rough and ignorant, but the game itself became one in which so much ruffianism and brutality were constantly displayed, and the sport that it contained so seemed to be one of the least important considerations to those playing it, that frequently there were severe injuries and even deaths sustained by the players. It has been pointed out that in the most advancd civilisation there is sometimes noticed a tendency to "throw back" in manners and habits to those that obtained in times when the development of the race was in a comparatively elementary stage, and, when looking over these lists of killed and wounded in the football as practised in the middle period of British history, one cannot resist a comparison between such results and those that have recently been obtained from the playing of a very "advanced" kind of football in the United States of America, about which something more may be said in subsequent pages of this work.

Sir Thomas Elyot spoke his mind very freely about the game in the *Boke, called the Governour*, mentioning "foote-balle wherein is nothing but beastlie furie and exstreme violence whereof procedeth hurte, and consequently rancour and malice do remain with them that be wounded, wherefore it is to be put in perpetual silence." There is a record of the fact that in the reign of Elizabeth the Middlesex grand jury on one occasion found a true bill against a collection of country persons, who "with unknown malefactors to the number of one hundred assembled themselves unlawfully and playd a certain unlawful game called foote-ball, by means of which unlawful game there was amongst them a great affray likely to result in homicides and serious accidents." Some years later a coroner's jury in Middlesex sat to consider the death of one of the footballers of the period, and the particulars of the proceedings which are vouchsafed to us cast a very serious reflection on the way in which the game was then conducted. The dead body which the jury had seen was that of Roger Ludforde, described as a yeoman. Between three and four o'clock one afternoon Roger was taking part in his game of football at "Evanses field at Southmyms," and two other players were Nicholas Martyn and Richard Turvey, who, like Ludforde, were described as yeomen. It appears that presently some feeling was introduced into the game, and when Ludforde and another player of the name of Simon Maltus were brought to the ground, the former called out lustily "Cast hym over the hedge." He made it clear that the man he would thus have summarily removed from the field of play was Nicholas Martyn, and it was perhaps not unnatural that Nicholas should resent the suggestion, and should for his own part suggest that if anyone was to attempt to put him over the hedge Roger Ludforde was clearly the man indicated for the task. So he called out, "Come thou and do yt." Roger, however, seemed to have thought that the matter had better end at this point, and accordingly he at once got up and made for the ball as if to kick it. It would have been better for all concerned if the game had then been allowed to proceed, but "Nicholas Martyn with the fore-part of his right arm and Richard Turvey with the fore-part of his left arm struck Roger Ludforde on the fore-part of the body under the breast, giving him a mortal blow and concussion of which he died within a quarter of an hour." The conclusion of the jury, after being satisfied on all these points, was that "Nicholas and Richard in this manner feloniously slew the said Roger."

But probably the most dreadful picture ever presented of any sport or game except bull-fighting was that set forth by Stubbes, the author of the *Anatomie of Abuses in the Realme of England*. Poor Stubbes indeed came to the conclusion that the world was not so very far from its end in his day, so wicked were the practices of the people, and one of his foremost reasons for this belief was that football playing and other "develishe pastimes" were practised on Sundays, this being near the end of the sixteenth century. According to him—obviously prejudiced to the last degree—the men who took part in the football of these times were always either killed or injured. "Sometimes," says Stubbes, "their necks are broken, sometimes their backs, sometimes their legs, sometimes their arms, sometimes their noses gush out with blood, sometimes their eyes start out, and sometimes hurte in one place, sometimes in another. But whosoever scapeth away the best goeth not scot free, but is either forewounded, craised or bruised, so as he dyeth of it or else scapeth very hardlie; and no mervaile, for they have the sleights to meet one betwixt two, to dash him against the hart with their elbowes, to butt him under the short ribs with their griped fists, and with their knees to catch him on the hip and pick him on his neck, with a hundred such murthering devices." One may well believe that if football were played upon a system anywhere near approaching to this, then "brawling, murther, homicide, and great effusion of blood" were the results, as the good Stubbes tells us they were. And King James I., in his *Basilikon Doron*, remarks on football being "meeter for laming than for making able the users thereof."

The legal enactments against the game remained in force, but they do not seem to have been put in practice except when a serious public disturbance or injury to life or limb ensued as the result of the play. Meanwhile all over the country the game increased in popularity, though almost exclusively confined to the lower classes. It was played far north in Scotland, and in the south of England, and in Cornwall in the west it flourished exceedingly. Yet nowhere does anything in the nature of a code of rules appear to have been framed, and play continued upon the most primitive lines. As we now distinguish the games of to-day as being Rugby or Association, we may call the football that was practised throughout these centuries, up to the time when it began to take other shapes in the playgrounds of the English public schools, as Roman, for, as far as one may discover, there was no substantial difference between it and the game that was obtained with the Roman *harpastum*. Goals were selected at each end of the playing arena, which might either be a field or a street, and these goals were of no particular shape or size. The number of players on each side was not limited, and the object was to get the ball through the goal in any way possible. It happened that the hands were more used than the feet, and that the game was really more a game of handball than of football; while in the case of the peculiar game that annually took place at Scone in Scotland between the bachelors and the married men, the players were positively forbidden to kick the ball. The description we are afforded of the play that took place on these occasions states that "he who at any time got the ball into his hands ran with it till overtaken by one of the opposite party, and then if he could shake himself loose from those of the opposite party who seized him, he ran on: if not, he threw the ball from him, unless it was wrested from him by the other party, but no person was allowed to kick it." There seems to have been a germ of Rugby football in this game at Scone.

The old-fashioned football was most in vogue when it was roughest and was the sport of the commonest people. The tendency during succeeding generations was slightly in the direction of refinement, and at last towards playing by rule; but as the game improved in these respects there became less of it. At the beginning of the nineteenth century it had sunk to a very low point in the favour of any section of the public, even though there is evidence that by this time something in the nature of a real and well-defined game was emerging from the chaotic methods of the previous centuries. Strutt wrote at this time that "football is so called because the ball is driven about with the feet instead of the hands. When a match at football is made, an equal number of competitors take the field and stand between two goals placed at a distance of eighty or an hundred yards the one from the other. The goal is usually made with two sticks driven into the ground about two or three feet apart. The ball, which is commonly made of a blown bladder and cased with leather, is delivered in the midst of the ground, and the object of each party is to drive it through the goal of their antagonists, which being achieved the game is won. The abilities of the performers are best displayed in attacking and defending the goals; and hence the pastime was more frequently called a goal at football than a game at football. When the exercise becomes exceeding violent, the players kick each other's shins without the least ceremony, and some of them are overthrown at the hazard of their limbs." It is clear that while the play was still very rough at times, the fury and danger of the earlier game had largely departed, and that there was as yet no science in the play adequately to compensate for the loss of the previous excitement. The Shrove-Tuesday football festivals, once so numerous and popular, had almost entirely died out by 1830.

Thus may be said to have ended this one long era in the history of football, and it was succeeded by the public schoolboy era, for during many years following the game was scarcely played anywhere save at the great public schools. Each had a different way of playing it, and here it was that some kind of a science of football was being evolved, which in course of time led to the outside world of grown-up men being attracted by it, and to the beginning of the third era of the game, which is being continued at the present time. At the schools, too, there came about such decided differences in the methods of play as to permit of the different styles being somewhat loosely classified as either dribbling or handling. There appears to be little doubt that these variations were not the result of the special predilections of the different communities of boys, but that each was rendered necessary by the character of the play-ground upon which the game was played. Thus where space was very limited the dribbling game was the one that was usually favoured, Charterhouse and Westminster, and in a lesser extent Harrow, adopting this system. At Rugby alone was the real old-fashioned game, according to which the player could pick up the ball and run with it, in force. The prevailing idea that the succession of this game from the old times to Rugby was complete and unbroken, would appear, however, to be mistaken. It has been argued that the picking up and running remained always the game at Rugby, because there alone among the public schools was there plenty of room for such a game. But it has been proved that picking up the ball was not allowed at one time, and there is very clear evidence of how on a celebrated occasion the rule, which was possibly enduring a threatened existence, was contemptuously ignored by one player, who thereupon struck the first blow for the great revolution which attached Rugby to the handling game. Mr. Matthew Bloxam, in the report of a sub-committee of the Old Rugbeian Society on the Origin of Rugby Football, points out that towards the end of 1823 during a game at Rugby "William Webb Ellis picked up the ball, and for the first time, disregarding the existing rule, rushed forwards with the ball in his hands towards the opposite goal." This famous deed is commemorated by a tablet set up in Rugby School Close, and there appears to be little doubt that it was to Master Ellis that the real Rugby football was primarily due, all unconscious as he may have been of the momentous nature of his action. His fellows did not at once agree that he was justified in his action; but there were no such elaborate rules, and no referee with his whistle to stop the game, as made it possible for any punishment to be inflicted upon a player or his side, save that which could summarily be administered to him at the first opportunity in the form of a vigorous hacking, and this the player who picked up the ball and ran with it had for a time to endure; but by and by the innovation was sanctioned, and it became the Rugby system.

Of the kind of game that was played at Rugby in those days, and of the enthusiasm that it evoked, we are given a fine description in *Tom Brown's School Days*. Gradually one kind of football or another became the usual thing in the winter time at most schools, both great and small, and it naturally followed that when these boys went to Universities, and after their education was complete, they should still have a fondness for the game to which they were bred; and this is really the whole story of how the third era was opened, and bit by bit the new and refined game of football began to take hold of the people, first for the simple playing of it and then as a spectacle.

Some kind of football, partaking of the dribbling variety, was played at Cambridge in 1855, and then three years later some old boys of Rugby and of the Blackheath Proprietary School started the now famous Blackheath Club. A club made its appearance in the north of England at about the same time, and in the following year the Richmond Club was organised. Shortly afterwards something in the nature of a "football boom" was commenced, clubs springing up everywhere, and Sheffield being made a strong centre of the game. But the feature of this sudden enthusiasm for the game was the greater popularity of the dribbling style than the picking up and running of the Rugbeians, and by 1863 there were the two kinds of football being played everywhere, which was not regarded as a desirable state of affairs. Now, at the beginning an effort was made to effect such a compromise between the rival schools of play as would enable the game thenceforth to be played universally under one code of laws. The attempt was made in London, and the compromise proposed was that running with the ball should be allowed when it was caught on a fair catch or on a bound. But simultaneously the old Etonians, the old Harrovians, the old Westminsters, and the old Carthusians who were up at Cambridge called a meeting of their own, and drew up a code of laws upon which they all agreed, and according to which all running with the ball, tackling, and the distinguishing features of the Rugby game generally, were excluded. The London dribblers wavered from their attitude of compromise when they heard of this movement, and it was soon agreed that there should be a joint conference of the London and Cambridge committees. At this meeting the Cambridge representatives insisted upon the attitude they had taken up, and, being willingly joined by the London dribblers, there was a great majority in favour of no handling. Here at this time and place the

Football Association was formed in 1863, and the faithful little band of adherents to the rough and tumble Rugby game, which they loved better than any other, drew away and went off on their lonely path.

Still Rugby football prospered. It came to be played before long in Scotland, Ireland, and South Wales, and from the beginning the people of the last-named part of the country showed great enthusiasm for it and great skill in the playing of it. But good progress was difficult without any definite and universal rules, and, the time now being ripe for a controlling authority, the English Rugby Union was established in 1871. A code of rules was drawn up, practically all the clubs in England gave the new Union their allegiance, and in March of the same year the first International match between England and Scotland was played at Edinburgh. Two years later the Scottish Rugby Union was established, in 1880 the Welsh Union came into being, and in the following year Ireland founded a Union for itself. In due course an International Board brought all these Unions into line, and made it possible for them to exercise concerted action in all matters. In one respect the Rugby Unions proved themselves superior to the Football Association, which was carrying all before it. They remained staunch and true to the principle that games are games and should not be trades, and that they should only be played for the love that the players have for them. If in the ordinary course of events the people who do not play manifest a desire to see their games, let them come to see them, and if the players may derive an advantage from these sight-seers that will facilitate the playing of their game, well and good. But the game was to be the thing, and the playing of it was never to be subordinated to the spectacle, while the amateurism of the players was to remain absolute. These principles of sport were abandoned by the Football Association. The time came when the canker of professionalism began to eat also at the heart of the Rugby game; but in the crisis the Unions were brave, and they cast the professionalism away from them. The result was a secession of the advocates of professionalism and the establishment of the Northern Union in 1895, which now controls a game apart from all others.

From the time when the first Union was formed the scientific side of the game underwent a quick process of evolution. From the chaos of the old run-kick-and-shove game something like order was rapidly brought about. At the beginning there were twenty players on each side, instead of the unlimited number which had formerly obtained; but after a few years' experience it was agreed that even these were too many, and accordingly in 1877 it was decided that fifteen should be the numerical strength of each side. Fifteen it remains to the present day. With a definite and constant number of players on a side, and strict rules in force, it naturally followed that much time and care were given to the study of how to get the utmost attacking and defensive power out of this fifteen, and experiments were made with different combinations. Two great features of the game, as it is played to-day, were left out of these early calculations. Efforts were either individual or made up of rushes, as there was practically no passing, and the advantages to be gained from an arrangement of the side which would bring the three-quarters into operation had not been suspected. However, the new rule which was made to insist on the ball being put down immediately it was held, which had followed on the more open style of play that had come in with the reduction of the side from twenty to fifteen, had gradually resulted in the strengthening of the three-quarter back division. There were two three-quarters with two full backs, and then one of the latter was brought in front to make a third three-quarter. Then passing began; but at first only a system of short passing was in vogue, although Blackheath and a few other clubs brought it to a high pitch of perfection. In 1882, however, the Oxford fifteen began a new system of long low passing among both forwards and backs, and it proved so wonderfully successful that it soon became a universally recognised system of play. Eventually there was a further development of the three-quarter back line, Wales proving herself the more resourceful in ideas for the improving of the game, and rendering the combination of the players more effective. Four three-quarters, two half backs, one full back, and eight forwards became the rule, and at one time the experiment of seven forwards and five three-quarters was tried. The result of all these changes was to make the game very much faster to play and more interesting alike to both player and spectator.

These were the developments in Britain, the home of the game. But in the meantime Rugby football had spread far beyond the confines of these islands. It was played on the continent of Europe; in India, America, Australia, South Africa, and New Zealand. In some of these places it was old established, and had been growing up to some extent independently of the game at home. New Zealand was one of these places, and the result of this independent and partially unfettered existence in our country may best be considered in a separate chapter.

CHAPTER II

DEVELOPMENT IN NEW ZEALAND

"Anyhow" games in the sixties — A match against the *Rosario* — First tendencies towards Association — Formation of a club — Return match with the *Rosario* — A challenge to play for £200 — A very scratch affair — Some difficulties as to rules — A strenuous engagement with the Goldfields — Shocking list of casualties — Some doubts about the future — A chaotic state of affairs — W. W. Robinson's enthusiasm — Development on Rugby lines — Shaping of the raw material — First match under Rugby rules — Interest and appreciation of the New Zealand public — The game spreads — Schoolboys take to it — Improvement in the play — Auckland goes on tour — A too trying programme — South Islanders victorious — Rivalry between the islands — Robinson plays two wing forwards against Canterbury — They win the game — The coming of the public schoolboys — Otago tour in the north — Inter-provincial football in 1880 — Various formations — Characteristics of different centres — New South Wales send out a team — An odd formation — Establishment of the Auckland Rugby Union — A tour under its auspices — Australia sends another team — The study of the scrum — Lessons learnt from Stoddart's team — The fruits of knowledge — Variations in passing movements — The New Zealand Union — The ambition of the colony.

THERE is some mystery about the introduction of football generally into New Zealand, and the only thing that can be said with absolute certainty is that one of the "anyhow" games was played there before the real Rugby was tried in the colony, and that it was played there in the sixties of the last century. Mr. W. W. Robinson, the well-known Anglo New Zealand player, has told us that he remembers seeing a small black football punted about by a crowd of all sorts and sizes and of both sexes one afternoon in 1868 when he went to the Auckland Domain, a public recreation ground, a Sunday-school festival of some kind being in progress at the time. A year later there was quite a stir in Auckland on the occasion of a big match that was arranged between a side of Aucklanders and a team drawn from the British warship *Rosario*, which was at that time lying in Auckland harbour. This match may have been of some slight consequence as marking a beginning at the game in the province, and therefore credit for the idea must be given to F. Whitaker, an old Westminster boy, who approached the captain of the ship, Moore by name, and enlisted his interest in the encounter. But the influence of the Football Association had not yet penetrated to New Zealand, and the Rugby Union was as yet unborn; so, when it came to deciding how the match should be played, there was little definite choice to be made, a free and easy shove-and-kick sort of game being mutually agreeable to the opposing sides. There was no offside and no holding, and it is to be noted that no picking up and running with the ball was allowed, so that clearly there was nothing of Rugby about this match, which was not surprising having regard to the origin of Mr. Whitaker. It happened thus that the first tendencies of New Zealand were apparently towards the Association game, and they were somewhat strengthened by subsequent proceedings; but later on, as will be shown, there could be no doubt as to which code the New Zealander naturally leaned when given the opportunity of making a fair test of both, and weighing up their several points. Auckland at this time does not appear to have possessed either goal posts or a football of any kind, such was its state of darkness in respect to the game, and even the sailors on a roving warship were better off than these colonists, and brought ashore with them the necessary impedimenta for the match. It was a very wet day when the match was played, and nobody seems to remember what happened.

The match, however, certainly stimulated some enthusiasm for football in Auckland, and one of its immediate consequences was the formation of a club. Nowhere in New Zealand was a ball to be discovered, and one of the

DEVELOPMENT IN NEW ZEALAND

soccer variety had eventually to be obtained from Melbourne. W. L. Rees was chosen as captain of the side, and the game that was played was a kind of Association as adapted in Australia and according to Melbourne rules. The players of the warship were challenged again, and a second match was arranged. It would seem, however, that by this time the game had not obtained much vogue in the district, for some difficulty was experienced in making up the side to the necessary numerical strength, and at the eleventh hour an Irish odd-job man of Irish extraction, who was coachman footman, boots, and other things at the house of an Auckland gentleman who had some near relatives in the team, was drafted into service. The result was that he was too late that evening to hand the dishes round at table, and earned a reprimand in consequence, his answer being "Shure, the young jintlemen said they would rather go widout their males than be bate by the footballers from the *Rosario*, and shure I was the man that would prevent them from being bate." Whether it was the Irishman (who was certainly very fleet of foot, and subsequently achieved some distinction as a runner) who mainly brought about the victory or not, it is certain that at the end of the game it rested with the Auckland side.

The Irish in Auckland at that time were disposed to be pioneers of football in the province, for there were crowds of them working as miners at the Coromandel mine, and, hearing of what had been taking place, they sent along a challenge to the Auckland side to play them a game with no fewer than a hundred players on each side, one goal to be at one goldfield and the other at another a long way off, and the game to be played for £200. This was a rather too sudden reversion to the old methods of semi-barbaric football, as already explained, and the challenge of the miners was not accepted. In 1870, however, a match was arranged between the Aucklanders and a Thames Goldfield side, and a very curious affair it was. When the field was taken, one of the sides found itself to be four or five men short, and the obvious way of filling up the vacancies, as most of the chosen players were of a very scratch variety, was to go round the ring of spectators and ask for volunteers. A policeman, a bushman, and two or three Irishmen stepped into the breach, and the side was made up. A motley and unbusiness-like side it looked, for while the bushman was in his scarlet shirt he appeared more like a footballer than any of them, most of the men originally chosen thinking fit to turn out in linen shirts, waistcoats, light boots devoid of bars and buttons, and even retaining their watches and chains during the play. They were chiefly stockbrokers and clerks. When both sides were on the field, and everything was in readiness for the fun to begin, there was still a doubt as to what kind of a game was going to be played, and a consultation was held for the purpose of coming to an agreement in the matter. One side proclaimed that it usually kicked between flags and underneath a tape, and that it disregarded all rules of offside. It allowed handling within limits, that is to say a man with the ball could run with it for five yards, and could proceed with it for another five after bouncing it and so on, this being one of the Melbourne rules. This method of play was agreed to at once by the others, and the game began. A very rough and tumble sort of game it was, with plenty of fierce earnestness introduced into it. The players had no idea of combination, and they closed together all in a heap and scrambled for the ball as best they could. There was difficulty at an early stage over the rule limiting a player to running with the ball for five yards at a time; and when it was alleged that various too enterprising men carried it for long distances in sublime disregard of this important condition, there were angry disputes, and once or twice they nearly developed into fights. The Irish players were a great force. They tripped and hacked to their hearts' content, and, when told that it was not the thing, they usually sheltered themselves behind the excuse

NO DOUBT ABOUT IT
(NEW ZEALAND v. MIDDLESEX)

that their tripping was very neatly performed and was very effective.

This match was drawn, and so was another in the following year between Auckland and the Goldfields, when an attempt was made to play more strictly according to rules, those brought out for the occasion having a greater resemblance to those of the Association code then in force at home than to any others. Credit must be given to the players for treating the game as a more definite thing, and for trying to stick to the rules which they understood; but nevertheless it was clear that they could not disabuse their minds of the feeling that football was a game for brute strength, and that the side that could show most of it was the most likely to be successful. Therefore this game was very rough, rougher in fact than the one of the year before, and when the play came to an end there was a shocking list of casualties. A man named Bull had two of his ribs broken; another named Dunlevy was severely kicked in the groin, and had to be carried to the hospital; a third of the name of Cussin was knocked insensible, and a fourth left the field with many fewer teeth than were in his possession at the time of the kick-off. If the game had been enjoyed in a way, it was nevertheless evident that something different from this would have to be introduced if the peace were to be preserved and Auckland was to retain any reputation for civilisation. Nobody seemed to know exactly on what lines to continue with their football, which in its essentials seemed to be very much the kind of sport that was wanted in the colony. The Rugby game was proposed, but the suggestion did not immediately meet with favour. Play according to the Melbourne rules was also suggested, but neither did this seem to meet the needs of the situation. These circumstances are recited to show the chaotic state in which football was at its beginning in New Zealand some thirty-six years ago, just at the time when the game was coming out into the strong light at home. These early movements were practically confined to the North Island, although some kind of football of even simpler character was being played in the south in a haphazard kind of way. It was on such a rough basis that the pioneers of the Rugby game in New Zealand set about its establishment, and within a very short space of time succeeded beyond their best hopes.

Mr. Robinson was one of the first to show enthusiasm, and in the course of a visit to Auckland he made a determined and not unsuccessful attempt to establish a kind of Rugby game there. His idea was to make the game as much as possible like the Rugby that he knew at home; but he had no rules at hand, the proceedings of the new English Rugby Union not by that time having circulated so far. Some rules, however, were necessary if any successful attempt were to be made to rescue football from the chaos in which it then was, and so a completely new set of thirty-three was drafted, partly from memory of the game at home, and partly with the assistance of an old Lillywhite's annual. George Dunnett, the brothers Whitaker, and other well-known men were among these pioneers, and those who did not understand the game were coached in a room at night. They showed some aptitude and a desire to improve. There was much practising of scrums, tackling, and so forth; and here was the nucleus of the first New Zealand Rugby side; but in numbers the players were very disappointing, and on this score the success of the venture at one time seemed doubtful. At last, in 1872, the first match under Rugby rules was played in New Zealand, the contesting sides being Auckland and the Thames Goldfield. There were only ten players on each side, and the game ended in a draw. Auckland, indeed, scored a try, but tries only did not count at that time. This was the beginning.

As it turned out, only such a start was necessary in order to grip the interest of the people generally. They immediately appreciated the points of the game that had been introduced, and other clubs were formed, with the result that in the winter season Rugby football was soon being played on three grounds in and around Auckland. Then it spread all over the country. At Taranaki, Otago, and Wellington it was adopted with enthusiasm, and at Canterbury there was a little colony of British old public schoolboys, whose services were much requisitioned for coaching purposes. Thanks to them, Canterbury soon began to show considerable form. It was one of the best signs of all that the schoolboys, who were much in need of what they might regard as a national game, took to it at once, and manifested a great earnestness to play it well and scientifically. The Rugby boom had begun. The interest of New Zealand sportsmen was fired, and those who could see far prophesied a great future for the game in our colony. We had the best physique; we had surely sufficient sense; and we had, best of all, a solid determination, which arose partly, no doubt, from the fact that we had few other loves in games, and that we were beginning at the beginning with this one, and had a considerable ideal to realise.

An eye was now kept on what was going on at home; but, in the early stages at all events, it did not appear to the New Zealanders that they were likely to gain much from a slavish attendance on such movements as were in progress in Britain. Between 1872 and 1876 great progress was made, the quality of the play improving all over the country, so that when in 1874 Auckland and the Thames Goldfield again met, on the latter's territory, a really good game was the result, and as there was no score of any kind it ended in a draw.

In the following year there was a most important event, although the issue was not so successful as had been desired. Auckland was disposed to take the initiative in most of these matters, and a proposal was put forward that a representative team, or one as nearly representative as was possible in the circumstances which obtained, should visit the South Island, and in the course of a regular tour should play a number of matches with all the clubs that were to be found. The management of such affairs was, however, in these early days very imperfectly understood, and the elementary mistake was made of imagining that merely fifteen players would be quite sufficient to go through the whole business, no allowance being made for accidents, staleness, or any other contingency. Moreover, five matches were arranged for a fortnight, and in between the players had to journey from the scene of one encounter to another in small boats along the coast. Whatever had been their normal superiority over the South Islanders, it may easily be imagined that they stood very little chance of showing anything like their true form under such conditions, and as it turned out not a single match was won. It is to be noted that in the course of this tour a new method of scoring was introduced. It was generally felt that the old system, by which only goals counted, was weak and really unfair, since a side which were morally victors were quite frequently losers; and accordingly it was decided that matches thenceforth should be decided by a scale of points, six points being given for a goal, two for a try, and half a point for a touch down, or force down as it was called.

The following year, 1876, was again a most important one, and a very definite advance was made in New Zealand football. The north and the south began to display the kneenest rivalry, and there was a marked improvement in the science of the game, the study that was being made of tactics thus early bearing good fruit. The possibilities of different arrangements and combinations were constantly exploited. The event of the year was the visit to the north of an excellent team sent up by Canterbury, captained by W. F. Neilson, an old Rugbeian. Great arrangements were made in Auckland for the match. The resources of the province were carefully considered, and the country players were brought up to headquarters overnight. Mr. Robinson was chosen as captain of the team, and on him devolved the task of arranging the formation of the side. Among his followers was J. Wood, a half who had learnt his game at Blackheath, and who, with a fellow-clubmate from the Waikato district, named Cox, made a very good pair. An old Cliftonian forward was instructed to be up always, to put the ball into the scrum, and keep the scrum together. Robinson, having sized his men up very exactly, came to the conclusion that he had a fast lot, and that it would be better to depend chiefly on fast dribbling with running and a little passing than on solid scrum working, particularly as he was aware that his visitors were very strong forward. His ultimate decision in this case was to play two wing forwards.

Thus in their most primitive form we had these players, about whom there was so much discussion in Britain last year, no fewer than twenty-one years ago. And it was certainly not claimed for the innovation at that time that it was a real novelty, for in fact it was merely an old idea revived; and this gives some point to an early observation in this work, that it is possible to gain something even in these advanced times from a study of methods which were long since regarded as obsolete, but which nevertheless are capable of adaptation to modern needs. In this case Robinson had had experience of the wing forward game as a boy, and knew of its advantages in certain circumstances. The opposition had no wing forwards, and as it happened the wing forwards won the game for Auckland. One was a man who had played a good game of soccer at home in England. His name was Dacre, and his colleague in the wing forward game was J. Nolan, who at that time was the amateur champion hurdler of the province. In passing, it may be remarked as a coincidence that the New Zealand team that toured in Britain last year also included a champion hurdler. No class of athlete is so likely to be able to adapt himself thoroughly to the needs of Rugby football as the man who is an expert runner and jumper.

Dacre got a try straight off from the kick-off, and Nolan obtained another in the second portion of the game. This second stage, however, was not the concluding one, for a match of this importance was not arranged in New Zealand every day, and all were anxious to obtain as much football as was possible, with the result that it was agreed to play for two hours, and to split up the game into four spells of thirty minutes each. Auckland won the match by seven points to three. It was a good, fast game, and it did much for the encouragement of Rugby football in New Zealand at that time.

By this time all the provinces were eager for the improvement of their game, the spirit of rivalry was in the ascendant, and each club was on the alert for new colonists arriving from home who had had a public school education and were players of the game. The services of such as arrived were eagerly solicited, and some very good captures were made by the different clubs, old boys from Rugby, Marlborough, Clifton, Wellington, and other schools being drafted into the different teams. One of the best discoveries in this way was C. B. Mercer, an old Wellingtonian, who was a beautiful drop-kick, and could accomplish most perfect work with either foot from practically any position. He was one of the finest exponents of drop-kicking who had ever been seen in New Zealand, and he left his impress on the style of many a youngster beginning at that time and for some years afterwards. There was no doubt about the individual quality of many of the men who came out during this period. When they came out to New Zealand they constantly seemed to develop a new enthusiasm, and one greater than they had experienced at home. Those who had imagined they had done with the game for ever on sailing from England, found in some cases, shortly after their arrival at the other side of the world, that they were really only at the beginning of what promised to be the most lively and interesting period of their football careers. At this early period it was also very gratifying to notice that the youngsters in the native schools were showing signs of becoming very clever little players. They were taking to the game quite naturally, and the capabilities of the majority of them in the way of kicking, tackling, and swerving promised well for the future of Rugby football in the colony; for it was upon these that the success of our game would ultimately depend, as we very well knew.

The game was going very strongly in the south, and in 1877 the players of Otago decided that they would send a team to tour in the northern provinces. A very good combination was selected, and when they had got used to each other's play they displayed some very clever passing, while their tactics generally were thoughtful and sound. They had a very good pack of forwards. Against them Auckland played seven men in the scrum, with two wing forwards, Nolan again being one of them, and there were two half backs, three three-quarters, and one full back. Robinson was again captain of the side. Otago had no wing forwards, but their scrum work was very effective. They pushed the New Zealand scrum everywhere, and their forwards went through with the ball at their toes, only exceptionally fine tackling saving the home side from very severe disaster. As it was, they kept them from scoring, and the game ended in a draw, although Auckland claimed a try. It is worthy of note that Joe Warbrick, the captain of the Maori team who visited England in 1889, first came out as a provincial player on this occasion.

In 1880 there was no important tour, but there was some good inter-provincial football. Wellington played Auckland, and adopted a novel formation, consisting of eight forwards, without wings, two quarter backs, two halves, one three-quarter and two full backs. Auckland, thinking there was something in the idea, imitated it and forsook her wing forwards—to her undoing. It is noteworthy that at this early date precisely the same system of scoring as that which is universal now, was in operation in New Zealand; that is to say, the original scale had been remodelled, and five points were now allowed for a goal from a try, four from a dropped goal, and three from a try. In the following year inter-provincial games were the leading events, and everywhere there was keenness in evolving new formations and tactics the principles of which seemed to be sound. One of the most notable evolutions was the five-eighths, though they were not called by this name at once. A scrum half and two fly halves was the original idea. Attention was particularly directed to the development of the wing-forward game. As it was practised at first it was evidently effective; but the system was immature, and the duties of the winger were not so clearly defined and were not so extensive as they became later. In course of time, however, some very fine wingers were bred, their characteristics varying according to the province whence they came; for then as now there was by no means unanimity in New Zealand as to what was the most effective manner of employing the winger, though all provinces were and are agreed that in one way or another he is necessary, although a conference of referees once suggested that he should be abolished. In Auckland two wing forwards were the rule, and a fine, fast forward game was the result. J. Arneil, originally a three-quarter, came out as a specialist at this game, and was without doubt one of the best wingers who have ever played, and one who has left his mark in this department. Wellington soon decided to use their winger in the same way as he was used by the New Zealand team on their British tour last year. Otago fancied him as a pusher in the back row, to break away at the right moment. In other respects the different provinces showed marked characteristics of their own at this early period, and there was very little imitation except when some certainty was felt that the thing imitated was the best possible. Each knew that perfection was a long way ahead, and that the shortest cut to it was by originality. Also, the class of colonists varied in the different provinces to a very marked extent; and this circumstance had considerable influence on the style of game that was cultivated. For example, in Otago they were largely of Scottish extraction, and there were big, powerful forwards here; while in Canterbury, and particularly round about Christchurch, there was a large proportion of old public school players, whose methods were a little more delicate and reminiscent of the play on their native grounds. Wellington was producing very fast forwards. Taranaki was famous for its halves. Everywhere a high standard of sportsmanship was being set up, and if the prospects of the game from the playing point of view were good, it was also clear that its tone was sound and healthy. The Maoris had taken keenly to the game, and there were many of them in Hawkes Bay who could play it as well as anyone.

Meanwhile the game was being cultivated in Australia, and there also they were setting themselves seriously to the study of its science, and experimenting with all kinds of formations. Eventually, in 1882, New South Wales, which was the stronghold of the game on this adjacent continent, considered itself to be sufficiently advanced to go on a foreign tour, and a team was sent over to New Zealand. It was a good team, not much inferior to those we could put into the field; but generally it lacked cohesion, and while on tour there was a considerable indecision as to arrangement displayed, and drastic experiments were tried on important occasions. A tour of this kind is hardly a time for trials, and it was not surprising that the results were unsatisfactory. Even if our New Zealand arrangement had been unsuccessful in Britain last year, we should hardly have been likely to remodel it to any considerable extent. If a side's own game is not good enough—that to which it has been brought up and understands as it understands no other—it is little use trying to learn that of the opposition in a week, and to risk it in a pitched battle at the end of that period. The

Australians, however, may have felt that the very great difference between their arrangement and that of ours, and the non-success that attended the former, necessitated some move of this kind. The formation that they first came out with was certainly peculiar, and at the first glance did not seem to promise well against that to which we were accustomed. They put into the field six forwards, three quarter-backs, two halves, one three-quarter, and one full back, and the merits of such a formation were certainly not self-evident to the New Zealanders. The latter adhered to their own setting, and though that of their opponents generally puzzled them at first, it did not usually give much trouble when its points of strength were understood and the necessary measures for counteracting them were adopted. For example, when the visitors came to Auckland, the latter adhered to the kind of game that she was playing at that time, having her customary wingers, three halves, one three-quarter and two full backs. Nothing was scored in the first half; but in the end Auckland won by seven points to nothing. After that the visiting side went on its tour in the South Island, and when it came back its formation was completely changed, ten forwards now being put into the pack, with a quarter, three halves, and one full back. Auckland changed her constitution only to the extent of bringing one of her full backs forward to make a second three-quarter, and against her the tourists with their huge pack were very ineffective, and were beaten by eighteen points to four. They lost more matches than they won in New Zealand, though they were certainly not without some conspicuous successes.

So far there had been no serious attempt made at organisation, but in 1883 a Rugby Union was formed in Auckland, and the other provinces quickly followed suit, affiliation to the English Union being sought in due course and obtained. There were only five clubs in the Auckland Union when it was established, but many more soon gave their allegiance to it. The advantages of the new movement were quickly made apparent, and a great impetus given to the game. Under the auspices of the different Unions, club matches were arranged on a more definite system than had been possible in the old unorganised days, and competition became keener, while now there was a piece of machinery in existence which enabled inter-provincial engagements to be more easily and frequently carried out; and the teams, not being so much of the scratch variety as they had often been before, the honour of being chosen for a place in them became more appreciated. Undoubtedly the Union system was a great advantage to New Zealand football, and marked a new epoch in the history of the game in the colony.

One of the first things done by the new Auckland Union was the selection of a side to make a tour in the southern provinces under the management of the Union, where it beat Canterbury by a goal and a try to a try. The uncertainty that was felt as to what was the best formation in the back division was again exemplified on this occasion, for Auckland reverted to two full backs and one three-quarter, though she stuck to her wingers. It is worth noting that Canterbury had one full back, three three-quarters and two halves. When she was pitted against Otago, Auckland adopted the arrangement of her late opponents—one full and three three-quarter backs. Both this match and that against Wellington were drawn. Such was the success of the Unions, that in 1884 they combined to send a team to New South Wales, and a very fine selection was made of the available players from the different provinces, W. Millton being appointed captain, while Warbrick was one of the side. It gave the best exposition of New Zealand football that had ever been put forward up to that time, and in the course of its tour it did not lose a single match. It was clear at this time that New South Wales were not progressing at the same rate that we were.

However, two years later, our plucky Australian opponents sent another team out to play us. By this time they had abandoned their early eccentricities in arrangement, and had gone in for wing forwards, two being played in the matches of the tour. They had three three-quarters and a full back. They were a very useful side, and the same fifteen, if it had been in New Zealand three or four years before, would have gone home with a very fine record of victories. But by this time we had made more progress, and the result was that our opponents did not do so well as previously.

This was nearly twenty years ago. New Zealand football was then in a fairly advanced state of development, and it was natural that future progress should be slower, and should be mainly in the direction of improved combination and a study of the finer arts of the game. The best constitution of the back division was still something of a puzzle. The forward arrangement was less troublesome; but from now onwards for several successive years the utmost attention was given to the perfecting of one department of the game where it was evident there was considerable waste of power and in which great gains were to be made from the adoption of the right methods. It need hardly be said that this remark has reference to the scrum, the inefficiency of which in its crude state was obvious. By dint of thought and experiment there was slowly evolved the two-three-two formation with the hookers the lock, the side row men and the back row men, with every player chosen for his particular aptitude for a particular place, and special duties assigned to them all. Instead of being simply a disorganised lump of a team doing its work in a haphazard manner, the scrum under the new system became a perfectly fitted piece of machinery, working with the precision of a clock. It was a long time before anything like the satisfactory system that was practised during the recent tour in Britain was arrived at, but there was constant improvment.

Combination tactics were what New Zealand was most short of. Hitherto play had been almost entirely individual, and superiority depended very largely on individual physical strength and skill. The artful dodger, the strong fending runner, and the bullocking forward were the ideal players of the day. It was left to Stoddart's British team to show Maoriland the fine points of the game and the vast possibilities of combination. The exhibitions of passing which they gave were most fascinating and impressive to the New Zealander, who was not slow to observe the advantages of these methods. One may safely say that from that season dates the era of high-class Rugby in the colony. Many new formations were born and died, and another British team that came out to us in 1901 taught us the Welsh formation; and two years later a New Zealand team, which included Gallaher, Tyler, Nicholson, Wallace, McGregor, and Stead of the 1905 combination, visited New South Wales and Queensland, and there on grounds like asphalt they played six matches, and won all, scoring 400 points to 13. We took this to be the success of our system, and subsequent successes over Bedell-Sivright's British team made a future tour in Great Britain a certainty. It may be news to many to know that the system of passing practised to such success by Welsh backs was in vogue a few years back in New Zealand; but so adept in interference did the defending sides become, that it became necessary to introduce variations, until at present it is not considered the right thing to pass across the field to your wings unless you have the odd man in.

By this time our football organisation in New Zealand was very compact, and had outgrown most of its early faults. A New Zealand Union was in existence, duly affiliated to the English Rugby Union, and thus we were part and parcel of the well-defined Rugby world. It became, as suggested, the cherished ambition of New Zealand to send a representative team to the mother country that would prove to it that its time in past years had been well spent, and that it could play a game that at least would not shame the colony in any company. How that consummation was achieved is known to all.

How the enthusiasm and ambition of the individual has been fostered by our system of organisation, which some people regard as almost Utopian, is a story which may best be told in a separate chapter, and it is worthy of such extended relation, since one is forced to the conclusion that only by such methods can anything like the best results be gained from the raw football material of a country, whatever be the conditions, character, and traditions of that country.

THE NEW ZEALAND TEAM IN BRITAIN, 1905

CHAPTER III

ORGANISATION AND EFFICIENCY

Necessity for a complete national organisation—But the simpler the better—The nursing of the player—Local government—The system of decentralisation in New Zealand—Attention to the schoolboys—The Auckland model—The Union for the schools—Towns divided into districts—One club one district—Players' clubs chosen for them—Advantages of the system—The residential qualification—Three fifteens in each club—Competitions for each class—A strong feature—Security of the seconds and thirds—No first players in second teams—The greatest encouragement to young players—Promotion by merit only—Sometimes very quick—A notable example—A system worth copying—Teams not made by money—The system of the common ground—Union takes all the gate money—Ladies always free—The influence of the fair sex—A very important stimulus—Better behaved crowds—Better matches on neutral ground—Fairer tests—Union pays back the funds in kind—Limited incomes of the clubs—And limited expenditure—Automatic insurance of every player—The system of the training halls—A valuable feature—The centre of each club's activity—The country unions—The sole selector—Mistakes seldom made—Arneil's fine record—Tours in the provinces—The Ranfurly Shield—Union must take the initiative—Conservatism a bad fault.

LET the enthusiasm of the individual be what it may, a great national enthusiasm, a united ambition, such as alone will bring about great success in the case of such a sport as ours, cannot be produced or maintained without a very complete national organisation. Individual effort, however healthy or robust, always needs careful fostering, if the best is to be obtained from it. Without constant attention it will wither and die. There is much to be said against the introduction of too much red tape in connection with the playing of our games, and healthy-minded amateurs, one is inclined to think, should always feel averse to too much fancy legislation, and the appointment of Grand

Committees, Boards, and all such like institutions, for the performance of what is unnecessary, or for the purpose of making things and individuals seem very important that are not important at all. Football is a game to be played with a ball, and the less its regulations, permissions, and restrictions are elaborated upon in the councils of those who do not play, the better. But such remarks do not prevent one from realising that wise and healthy government, directed solely towards fostering the game and getting all the football worth out of the youth of a nation that there is in it, is necessary if it aspires to hold its own, or a little more, in competition with its contemporaries. Given two countries with as nearly as possible the same resources, and the same quality of players, one being well governed and organised and the other not, the former must nearly always display a marked superiority over its rival. The work of the head governing body must be active and not passive, and it must realise that while it is necessary to enlist the sympathy of the individual with all its own plans and objects, it is impossible for it to nurse him from headquarters as he ought to be nursed. There should, therefore, be a gradual system of decentralisation, of local government, so that through various agencies the influence of the parent chief authority filters through to the individual player.

In New Zealand we have what has been already intimated to be in our opinion one of the most perfect organisations, and no better indication of its power and its scope can be conveyed than in the simple statement that it makes its influence felt upon the little boys in the public national schools, whom it watches with the eyes of an anxious parent, and has its system so arranged that stage by stage the schoolboy as he grows in years and skill is brought higher and higher until at last the New Zealand Rugby Union gives him his diploma as a master, and perhaps sends him across the sea to wear the fern leaf and uphold the reputation of his homeland.

At the first glance our New Zealand organisation might appear a trifle complicated; but in reality it is not so. There is no unnecessary piece of governmental machinery, and the whole fits together with splendid exactness. The New Zealand Rugby Union being the chief authority, it has immediately below it the various provincial Unions, each province having its own Union in the same way as with English counties, but a province is a very much bigger and more unwieldy thing than the English county, Auckland, for instance, being more than four hundred miles from one end to the other. In each province there are several country Unions, subservient directly to the provincial Union, and through it to the head body. After the provincial and country Unions come the clubs. But the system of decentralisation does not end at this point, for unless some system of graduation of the players were carefully preserved, good men might not so easily or with so much certainty obtain the chance of promotion that they desire. The object of our organisation is to leave as little as possible in this direction to chance. There are the schoolboys below the players in the clubs; and it will be a good plan now to work our way back with more detailed explanation from the minor player in the club to the chief authority.

As a fair specimen of the thoroughness of the local government of the game and the encouragement given to the players, let us consider the state of affairs in Auckland. Here we have the Auckland Rugby Union, which, besides being the chief authority of the province with all the various country Unions in affiliation with it, is also the body for the control of the game in the capital town of Auckland. All the clubs in Auckland are affiliated directly to this Union, and in addition to the clubs there are various minor Unions, each controlling small sections of the game played in the capital. Thus there is a Public Schools' Union with sixteen of the elementary schools affiliated to it, and there is also a Secondary Schools' Union, consisting of five of the grammar schools and colleges that are situated in the capital. The Auckland Union offers cups for competition by these schoolboy teams. In the case of the Secondary Schools' Union, each school club puts two fifteens in the field, and a boy is promoted from one to the other according to the regular system which will be explained. The officials of the higher Union keep a watchful eye on these boys, and, more than the officials, the city clubs to which they may subsequently become attached do so most diligently, as it is to their advantage to do. The boys have the use of the free ground on which to play their matches, and sometimes special facilities are afforded for training, though in the case of these youngsters very little if any training is necessary, as it is in the case of players of older growth. Here at these schools we have the New Zealander footballer in his rawest and most elementary stage; but it commonly happens that before his schooldays are over he is a player of no small parts. He is not allowed to play in proper club football until he is sixteen years of age, and he goes in then as a junior.

Now, in each big town, and in Auckland, which we are particularly considering, there are several clubs called by the names of the respective districts of the town from which they draw their players. Clubs are not organised promiscuously in New Zealand as they are in Britain, or at all events they are not so organised in the large towns, and in the country districts there is not the opportunity of establishing them. The Union decides what clubs there shall be, and supervises their management. In doing so it particularly desires to ensure the thoroughness and effectiveness of the working of each club, the equality of all of them so far as conditions and opportunities are concerned, the maintenance of strict amateurism throughout, the prevention of one club being completely overshadowed by another by reason of superior financial resources, or by any social or other non-financial inducements that it might offer to players to belong to it, and too easy facilities for changing clubs. Cliques and "swell" clubs are often the ruin of a good growth of young footballers, and in New Zealand it has been determined that there shall be no cliques and no inducements to join special clubs. This determination has been carried into effect in a very summary manner. Just as the authority settles on what clubs there shall be, so with the help of a qualification rule it decides who shall play for those clubs. It divides the city into sections, and it apportions one club to each section. The limits of each section are very carefully defined. The Union has its own map of the city, with all the streets marked upon it, and the precise limits of each section are marked by lines, and further defined in the rules by words. Thus the dividing line may, and very often does, go down the middle of a street, so that one side of that street is in one section and the other side is in another. In Auckland there are seven of these district sections, going by the names of Ponsonby, Newton, City, Grafton, Parnell, Suburbs, and North Shore, and the club in each section is called by the same name. A player resident in the city is obliged to play for the club in whose section he resides; and thus it frequently happens that while a player who lives on one side of a street is eligible to play for one club, a man residing directly opposite to him on the other side has to play for another, and that a man on changing his residence has to change his club also, but only then. The residential qualification is strict, and effectually prevents clubs from poaching on the players of their rivals. A player may indeed become eligible to play for another club which for any reason he prefers to that to which he is attached at the time; but the process of change would be a slow one, and the probability would be that by the time it had been brought about the particular occasion for the change would have passed, so that in actual practice it is very rarely done. In order to make such a change, the player would, of course, have to change his residence, and, apart from the cost and inconvenience, and the way in which it might interfere with business interests,— since in these small compact communities it is the object of every man to live as near to his work as possible,—it is often impracticable for other reasons. The young footballer is not commonly a married man with a household of his own. More frequently he lives with his parents, and it is not open to him to make the change of residence that would qualify him for another club.

The residential qualification, as set down by the Auckland Rugby Union, provides that each club shall consist solely of members who have resided within the boundaries of their districts not less than four months prior to the first day of May in each year, and that any player changing his residence on or after the first day of January shall for the remainder of the year play for the district club in which he was residing on that date. Any stranger arriving during the season or within the period of four months prior to the first of May, may be allowed to play for the district in which he is residing, upon satisfying the managing committee of the Union that he intends to become a *bonâ fide* resident; but no application of this nature is considered until the stranger has resided in the district for a month. The officers and men of His Majesty's ships on the New Zealand station are eligible to play for the North Shore district club.

Now, though a man has no choice as to the club to which he may belong, it does not follow that because he is not good enough to play for the first fifteen he may not enter very fully into the competitive club spirit like the senior players. Unless he is a very moderate player indeed, one having no pretensions to playing any kind of a game of Rugby football, he may do so very fully. Each club runs three fifteens, and the same arrangements in every respect are made for the seconds and thirds as for the firsts. The Union offers three Cups for competition by the district clubs on what in Britain is known as the League system, one Cup being allotted to each grade of players in the various clubs.

Thus there is a Cup for competition by the first fifteens, another by the second fifteens, and a third by the third fifteens, and the competition in each case is strictly limited to players of the proper class. The second and third fifteens are not the scratch teams, made up of the discarded or superfluous members of the first team, as is so often found to be the case elsewhere, and which one thinks is a system highly prejudicial to the encouragement of young players. Suppose that in a club's second team there are two or three players only recently promoted to it who are hard-working, intelligent, capable, and generally promising fellows, who are greatly ambitious to go up higher and obtain a place in the first team and then to play for their province, and who yet at the same time, being young and new, are naturally not so secure in this second team as some of the well-tried men who have established their places there and who consider themselves to be on the eve of promotion. Now, if it were the case, as it is in so many other places, that when for one reason or another a man is left out of the first team he should at once be found a berth in the second, partly as a matter of form, partly to keep him in condition, and partly because of the often erroneous assumption that anyhow he must be good enough for the second team—in such a case it would very often happen that the earnest and ambitious second team man would himself be deposed from the place that he had earned and sent back to the third fifteen; and even if he were not, if any system were in force which rendered such a thing possible, it would create a great feeling of uneasiness in the minds of rising players, who would never consider themselves secure, and would in fact be constantly at the mercy of the selectors of the team above, quite regardless of their own form.

This is not the way in which to encourage young talent, and many a promising footballer must have been spoiled in his making through having had to encounter such difficulties in his upward progress. Besides, it is bad also for the senior player. There are many men who would not attach quite so much importance to their place in the first team if they were satisfied that, on temporarily losing it, there was always a place for them in the second; and no doubt there are many more who would even prefer to be one of the giants of a second side, going strongly in its own competition, to merely being one of the ruck in the class above. This unhealthy spirit has also to be stifled, or the standard of the football played must inevitably suffer. There is a third objection to such a system, and it is that when a second or third team may be temporarily strengthened by players from a superior class, in order to effect a much-desired win at an important stage of a competition,—a really unsportsmanlike proceeding, though common enough in some classes of football,—all the interest in such competition is killed, and it is reduced to a mere farce—an excuse for matches.

In New Zealand we have no such bad system, but by a very simple arrangement we satisfy ourselves that at all times we get as much out of both our senior and junior players as it is possible to get according to their natures and abilities, and the matches of the lower grades are scarcely inferior in point of interest, and never in the keen competitive spirit that is introduced into them, to those of the grades above. The rule is that except in the most unusual cases, and then only by special grant of the Union, a player once promoted from one grade to another is recognised for competition purposes as being a player of the latter grade, and thenceforth cannot again play for the lower one from which he was promoted. A player is therefore known and classed as a first grade, a second grade, or a third grade player. The man in the third fifteen is free from the fear that the second fifteen men may be sent down, and that he may lose his place in consequence, and the men in the first and second fifteens know that unless they keep up their form well enough to justify their retention in their respective teams, there is no Cup football for them at all. Such a system also affords the maximum encouragement to young players, who know that, once they have earned their place in a superior class, they are not likely to be deposed without good reason; and another of its merits is that a promotion, once made being more or less irrevocable, the committee having the responsibility of making it does not do so lightly and without the fullest consideration, avoiding rash experiments which may cost a side a man for a long period.

Promotion from one grade to another is, of course, as has been fully indicated, by merit, and the wise committee keeps a constant and most watchful eye upon all junior players, waiting for the time being ripe to send them up higher. Promotion by this system is sometimes very quick, and one of the most remarkable cases of it that have come under our notice was when Ponsonby, one of the Auckland district clubs, won the senior Cup with six men in their team who had only just been promoted not from the second team to the first, but direct from the third fifteen. The thirds had got together a remarkably good side, brimful of enthusiasm and as skilful as anyone need wish them to be, and they were made of the right stuff to take on a very big job and do it well, as they did. When a system like this is in force, and when every young player is made to feel that his future success depends so entirely upon himself, and that great rewards may come quickly when deserved,—that, in fact, he is like the private soldier who carries a field-marshal's baton in his knapsack,—you get the utmost possible out of your young talent, as you cannot when any attempt is made to nurse it according to any other system. From our experience we should have no hesitation in earnestly recommending such a system to any Union or community of players who felt that things were not going so well with their football as they ought to be, and that there was a need for a "waking up" all round.

Another very important feature of our system is that by which we prevent financial considerations from having anything to do with the success or failure of a team. Generally speaking, the New Zealand clubs have neither full nor empty purses; but, arranging their affairs on the true principles of commonwealth, each has according to its needs, the Union, represented by all, making the distribution, as it receives the income of the game. The cardinal feature of this system is the circumstance that the clubs in a city like Auckland have no grounds of their own, and are not permitted to have them. By this arrangement we strike at the root of many evils from which even amateur football suffers elsewhere. We have one large public ground, belonging to the Union, in the centre of the city, and on this ground all the matches and the practice games are played, each club being free to make use of it as its circumstances necessitate, and as suits the convenience of the others, the Union making all arrangements in such matters. The ground is a very large one, and well fitted up with stand and other accommodation, and it is possible for several teams to play on it at the same time; in fact, it is a common thing for three senior games and a dozen junior matches to be going on simultaneously. This being so, and one match succeeding another on the same arena with very little delay, it is possible to get through a very extensive programme in the course of an afternoon. Spectators are charged sixpence for admission to the ground, with extra for stand accommodation, and the whole of the proceeds from the gate are taken, not by the clubs playing on the day, but by the Union, who keeps them. Accredited members of teams not playing on the day are accorded special privileges of admission, and in some cases senior players are more favoured in this respect than juniors.

Everywhere ladies are admitted free to both ground and stands, and, while this is a nice compliment to pay to the sex, it is from the business point of view of the Union very much more than a compliment. It is one of those seemingly trifling details that are really important factors in establishing the success of the football of a country, and one which we may cordially recommend to clubs and governing bodies elsewhere where no such concession is granted. It may not always be realised how powerful is the influence of one's womenkind in a game like this. If the ladies are encouraged to take a keen interest in the game, to understand it thoroughly, and to follow the doings of the clubs and players with enthusiasm, their favourable attitude affects the game in several ways. When a man finds his form and the performances of his club matters of criticism, not only among his own clubfellows, but in his home circle among the ladies belonging to it—and among the ladies in whom he may be interested in other home circles—he obtains a stimulus which in some respects is perhaps more powerful than any other, though he may not admit it, and may even not be aware that such is the case. The situation of such a player is far happier and brighter than that of the man who in his own household finds complete ignorance concerning his chief hobby, in which he is so closely interested, and either silence concerning it or else irritating expressions of indifference or even contempt, with occasional lofty but quite mistaken sermons on the evils attending the waste of one's time. In New Zealand we find that as the result of the free admission and the welcome we always give to the fair sex, they do take a very deep interest in the game, and that this interest reacts on the players in a very salutary manner. The constant presence of a throng of ladies at the ground on match days has another great advantage, in that the crowd is better behaved in every way than it would be if it were comprised almost entirely of the male sex, as is usual when there is no free admission to ladies. In this and other ways their association with the game tends to purify and elevate it. Some people who have not thought the matter out, and who do not know the sex very well, might be inclined to say that if ladies wanted to see a match a paltry sixpence or shilling would not deter them from attendance; but the desire to get everything that is to be got for nothing is much stronger in the lady than in the man; and in this way interest is generated in place of indifference. Besides, many men are mean in small matters, and one of them might often take his sisters and other lady relatives and friends with him to view the afternoon's football, when he would not be inclined to do so if it were not the custom, and if any expense to him were involved in the action.

It has just been said that, as the result of the attendance in large numbers of the fair sex, our crowds are better behaved than they might otherwise be. A further advantage with respect to the crowds is derived from the circumstance of a common ground and not a club's own private one being played upon. The attendance at the matches is a general one, and there may be large numbers witnessing one match who are chiefly concerned in the one that is to follow, while the numbers of supporters of either side are far better balanced than when matches are played on the ground of one or other of the competing clubs. It happens in the latter case that there are large numbers of ticket-holders attached to the club on whose ground the match is played, and the fact that the ground is situated in the district of one of the clubs, and perhaps some distance away from that of its opponents, makes it inevitable that its partisans in attendance should far outnumber those of its rivals. These partisans, when in such a pronounced majority, have a tendency to assert themselves unduly, and as this has a great influence upon the players, the conditions are not equal to both sides. When the match is played on neutral and central ground they are equal.

Again, under the system of clubs playing home-and-home matches on each other's grounds, the team which is playing on its own field has admittedly, in other respects apart from spectators, a considerable advantage over its rivals; and though it may be held that things are balanced in the long run by the return match on the other ground, it is to be said in reply that in neither case is the test a good and fair one, and therefore the double test is unsatisfactory. When there is only a small difference between the merits of two rival teams, it may not be sufficient to enable the stronger one to gain victory on its opponents' ground, and thus we have a weary succession of wins by home clubs, and a tendency towards a general levelling when slight shades of strength have no opportunity of being manifested. When each match is played on neutral ground, it is a more absolute and accurate test of the skill of the contending sides, and two such matches will often mark a difference between clubs when home-and-home engagements would only have left their comparative form in doubt. Of course there are many circumstances in which the principle of the common ground cannot be acted upon, as in the case of country clubs having headquarters at great distances from each other; but, on the other hand, it is always not only possible but easy in large towns, and in conjunction with the other features of our system which are attendant upon it we cannot but think that it must always make for good.

Now it has been pointed out that the Union takes all the proceeds of the gate on these big match days, and that the clubs have nothing from what is in other countries often their main source of revenue. Needless to say, however, the Union has something else to do with these funds than to keep them, and it pays them back in kind to the clubs who are the means of furnishing them. It does so on a wise system, that encourages the serious study and development of the game, and ensures that it shall be played for itself alone, and keeps pure the amateurism of all who have anything to do with it. One must point out, however, that in the nature of things gate receipts in New Zealand cannot be what they are in the populous centres of Britain, and that therefore the aggregate of funds gathered in by the Union from all matches is not by any means so large as might be imagined by one accustomed to hear of gigantic receipts in the homeland of the game. However, in Auckland £100 is often taken at the gates of the common ground on a Saturday afternoon.

With no ground to maintain, the expenses of the clubs are very small, and consist almost entirely of the cost of maintaining proper training quarters. Therefore their very limited incomes are nearly, if not quite, sufficient for their purposes. The members of the clubs only pay very nominal subscriptions, and in addition to the privilege of playing, and the enjoyment of the training quarters and everything else that belongs to the club, each man derives certain other material advantages in return for his payment. For example, when he pays his subscription to his club he becomes simultaneously a member of the Union, and he is automatically, without any further payment, well insured against accident on the football field. The Union insures the whole of its members in a body. When Rugby is properly played according to the code, it is not by any means such a rough game as most people who know little of it might imagine, and it frequently happens that what might appear to be the most dangerous features of it are the least so. Thus, while it may seem that tackling a man below the waist when he is going helter-skelter at full speed for the line is a very dangerous business—for him—experience proves that the accidents brought about in this manner are remarkably few. However, a game in which there was no danger whatever would hardly be worth the playing by a full-blooded Britisher; and therefore, while some accidents are inevitable, it behoves the Union that takes all the money and exercises a careful parental guardianship over every player in the land, to make some wise provision for the benefit of those who may temporarily come to grief while pursuing the game. This we do in New Zealand. A player who is injured on the field so that he is unable to follow his occupation receives a pound a week from the accident fund while he is unable to do so, and is provided with free medical attendance. Each club is allowed to have a certain number of vice-presidents, elected by reason of their personal and active interest in the game, and each one pays a guinea a year to the funds. These are almost the only sources of income of the clubs. They derive a little from letting their training halls for concerts and the like on such evenings as they are not required by the club, and beyond that they have no further receipts.

This training hall is one of the most prominent features of the Union and club system, and is undoubtedly one of the principal means of encouragement to young players, the fostering of the spirit of enthusiasm, and of the perfection of ideas for the better development of the game on its practical side. Each district club in the city has its own training hall—a large shed, well built, fitted up with baths, committee rooms, and all conveniences, and well provided with powerful artificial lighting apparatus. The floors are covered with some soft loose material such as tan, and the interior of the place is so spacious that practice with a ball may be carried out by large numbers of players on a thorough and extensive scale. We find that private practice of this kind in a limited area, with a critical assembly always present to make suggestions and give hints, is more value-able than desultory practice on a playing field, and it has the advantage of being possible and even most popular when the weather is bad and when the evenings are dark. About the kind of training that goes on in these halls there will be something to be said when training systems come to be considered later on in this book. The buildings, and the freeholds of the land, are the property of the clubs that use them, and they were erected in the first place at some self-sacrifice by the clubs concerned, and with assistance from the Unions. While they are paying off their liabilities in connection with the freehold and the structure upon it, the Union gives each club financial assistance to the extent of £25 per annum. Each training hall is the centre of the activity of each club. For the sake of exact exemplification, such details of the system in towns and cities as have been given here are those that are in force in Auckland itself, but they exist for the most part with only slight variations in many other large centres in the colony. In the South Island two or three clubs may share a training hall, as they are not commonly subsidised by the Union. Thus at Invercargill eight clubs have three training halls among them. It shows the interest taken by the populace in the game in this quarter when it is stated that the eight clubs have each about a hundred playing members, and that the population of the town is only 25,000; so that roughly one person in every thirty, the latter figure including all the ineligibles—women, children, and old people—are players. The encouragement given to schoolboys to take up the game in earnest is exceptional in the South Island. Each school team has its coach, and the schools play inter-provincial matches. A strong foundation for the future of the game is thus constantly being laid.

The system that is in force in the capital towns of the province, where naturally there is most and best developed football, is adopted by the country unions, with only such modifications and limitations as are found necessary in view of the way in which clubs are scattered. The common ground system is seldom practicable except where two or three clubs are bunched together in a locality. All the clubs affiliated to a country union (each of which is in turn affiliated to the union of the province) play matches against each other on the Cup or League system, and once a season each union takes stock of its forces, gathers together its strongest team, and pays a visit to the capital, where it plays a match against the combined forces of the district clubs, and in due course the visit may be returned. In this way the capital and the country in each province are kept in close touch with each other, so that when the provinces come to play against each other in matches of one degree more importance, they are able with some confidence to choose their strongest fifteen.

ORGANISATION AND EFFICIENCY

In this connection it may be remarked that it frequently happens that the duty and responsibility of selecting teams for such important engagements are entrusted to one man only. Full confidence is placed in him, and it is found from experience that when he is such a thoroughly trustworthy man, and makes such a complete study of all the players who are eligible for a place in his team, he seldom makes mistakes, and is indeed much more reliable than a committee of persons, who, however fair-minded and above suspicion they may be, have inevitably their own personal predilections and prejudices, which must come to the surface at times, and which often result in the inclusion of a man in a team when there are better men playing in the same position left out. It is a remarkable illustration of the success which sometimes attends the efforts of the individual selector, that J. Arneil was once sole selector for Auckland for seven years, and during that period never once chose a beaten inter-provincial team.

Once in every four years each province goes on tour through both the North and the South Islands, playing all the other provinces, and advantage is usually taken of these journeys to challenge the holder of the Ranfurly Shield for the possession thereof. This is a kind of competition which does not appear to be in force in connection with Rugby football elsewhere, although not at all novel otherwise. It has been found to be exceedingly interesting. It is simply a competition on the principle of the holders retaining the trophy until it is won from them by a challenging team, who are called upon to visit the holders and play on their ground. Thus the holders have a slight advantage at all times, but they may be called upon to play challenging teams more than once in the course of a season, the New Zealand Union seeing to it that they are not overdone with challenges. When a province goes on tour, it gives notice that the match it arranges with the province that holds the Shield at the time shall be the challenge match for the possession thereof, and it ranks accordingly.

This, after all, is only a very slight and inadequate sketch of the management and encouragement of football in the colony; but it may serve to show how the interest of the individual is stimulated. The point one would like to emphasise is that governing bodies must be active and not passive in their government. They exist, or ought to exist, for other purposes than merely to make rules, alter them, consider appeals, and choose representative teams. Individuals and clubs need a guide and help, or on the one hand they will become slack, and on the other there will be little cohesion and sympathy among them such as is necessary for the furtherance of mutual ambition and the success of occasional united effort. The Union must always be ready to take the initiative. Conservatism must be a bad fault in such a body. Our New Zealand Union may not be perfect, but it serves its purpose excellently for the time being, and, in combination with the minor Unions that serve it, it has done everything for the football in the colony.

CHAPTER IV

THE IDEA OF THE GAME

General principles governing the play—Goals and tries—The off-side rule—Limitations in ball propulsion — Elementary methods in olden days — The inevitable advantage of scientific play—The three groups of methods—Combination—Moral and actual advantages—Backing up—Infinite variety of passing movements—Short and sharp work for the individual—An object of strategy—The gain of a man—Slight odds against attackers when forces are equal—Men not gained in tackling—Two men to be drawn to one place—Two attackers and only a back to beat—Individual effort—Opportunism—A difficult and thankless task—Success the only justification—A possible charge of selfishness—"Unofficial and very guarded approval"—The ruse—Neglected possibilities—Ruse must be good—The double edge—Necessity for a side to adapt itself to circumstances—Large stock of variations advisable—The placing of the team—Backs and forwards—A comparison between the British and New Zealand formations—The wing forward and the flying half—The virtues of the five-eighths—Great possibilities for developing an attack—The advantage of the extra line of defence —Capacity to strike in many ways.

BEFORE one can enter seriously into the study of the fine points of this game, one must have some clear idea of what are the general principles governing the play according to the most modern and up-to-date methods—what it is that is required to be done, and what generally are the systems upon which it may be accomplished.

As we all know, there are fifteen players on each side, and the aim of the contending parties is to score tries by crossing the goal line of their opponents and grounding the ball in their private territory as a token of successful invasion. It is further desired to score goals from the tries, the side that has gained the latter advantage having the privilege of an unhampered kick in the direction of the uprights and over the cross bar, such kick being taken from any point in the field of play which is in a straight line from the point where the try was obtained and parallel with the touch lines. When a try, and a goal from the try, have thus been scored, the maximum advantage from a single onslaught has been obtained. Goals may also be secured under certain conditions by direct kicking from the field of play without any previous try. These are the things that it is desired to do, and the fifteen players on each side are permitted to attempt them with very few restrictions as to methods. One of the charms of Rugby is its essential simplicity in this respect, although to those who have only been accustomed to other kinds of football it often appears at the first glance to be an extremely complicated game. It is complicated only in the scientific and purely arbitrary methods which are introduced in order to accomplish the simple objects in view. There are the usual laws and penalties concerning off-side as are common in all ball games where the object is to score goals, and as are necessary for their orderly conduct. The off-side rule is not so complicated as in the case of Association football, and while there is no occasion to make any explanation of it here, since the object of this work is not to explain things for the benefit of the entirely uninitiated, it may be stated that generally the rule is that a player shall not be in front of the ball while it is being played, and that if he is so in front he must be regarded as out of action until such time as the ball is in front of him and he is on-side again. A player may use his hands or his feet for the purpose of working the ball in the direction of his opponents' goal, and he may do so in almost any fashion, provided he does not infringe a law prohibiting him from knocking on the ball, throwing it or passing it forward. Generally speaking, he may impede his opponents in any way except by tripping or hacking them.

These being the objects of the game, and the permissions and restrictions granted to and imposed upon the players in their attempts to achieve them, we come to consider how best

THE IDEA OF THE GAME

and with most certainty the objects may so be achieved by the means at their disposal. Ever since Rugby football came to be considered as a serious scientific game, this has been the problem. As we have seen, in the old days before the game was defined or had rules of its own, somewhat similar objects were attained by the most elementary methods, chiefly consisting of rushing with the ball anyhow down the playing arena, and forcing it in the desired direction by sheer power of numbers and weight. In comparatively early stages of the evolution of the game, it became apparent that a very little science made up for a great deal of weight, and this principle has, in the course of years and decades, been so followed up and elaborated until now, while physical strength is, and always must be, a necessary qualification in those who take part in such an exacting game, it has entirely ceased to be the governing factor. In these days the side which has most fully developed the scientific side of the game, and applies the soundest theories in the most practical manner, is usually hailed victor over an enemy that is inferior to it in these respects. Nowadays the rush of a team in one confused body towards its opponents' goal is, of course, not a practicable form of attack, and for the best reasons it is never attempted.

There are three groups of methods by which points for tries and goals may be scored. They are, firstly, by combination; secondly, by individual effort; and thirdly, by ruse, the last-named usually being supplementary to one of the others. A good team should be well supplied with all these methods in abundant variety, and the greater their variety the more resourceful and dangerous will be the side. Combination in its elementary aspects is well understood. In modern football the men on a side are placed in different specified positions, and each is or should be able to accomplish particular kinds of work just a little better than anyone else on the same side. It is the principle of combination that, when the time comes that the man in possession of the ball finds himself in or approaching difficulty, he should transfer possession to one of those men who are in the position to do the remainder of the work in hand better than he can, and with a brighter prospect of success. This is simply passing, and in the course of a single evolution in attack it may be so frequent and quick as to puzzle the opposition and convert, what a moment previously seemed to be a very difficult position into one which is full of promise. There are moral advantages from combination as apart from actual ones, as, for instance, when a player is making a great and difficult individual effort and is closely attended during this risky period by a trusty colleague ready to take the ball from him at the moment that his own possession of it becomes untenable. While this feature of combination is elementary and obvious, it is one which, to our minds, has not been sufficiently exploited, and we have given it more attention than ever before. It is our constant object always to have a reserve man in attendance on the man with the ball, insuring our position, as it were, against accident. There is an infinite variety of passing movements. The chief of them will be considered in due course when we come to make a short study of tactics, and the only thing that need be said about them here is that there are none too many, and that no side can afford to neglect a single one of them.

There is another thing to be said for the importance of passing movements in combination, which is not always realised as fully as it might be. There is, or should be, always more sting in the effort of a man when it is short and quick. When the task is concentrated into the work of a few seconds, that work is always likely to be more thorough, more determined, and of a higher order of efficiency, than when it is protracted over a comparatively long period. It is simply a case of the new brooms sweeping very clean, and it is these first moments in the effort of a man with the ball that are supreme. The man's keenness is then most tense, and though it may not be apparent or hardly so, it is probable that as time goes on a sense of bewilderment may

THE IDEA OF THE GAME

overtake even the most perfect and cool-headed player if he is being closely pressed. In the strenuousness of a hard match force is very quickly spent, and it is good policy to renew it at the most frequent intervals possible.

Beyond the necessity of passing movements for the sake of relieving pressure upon a man in posssession of the ball, and for the general improvement of the attack in progress, we generally have another object for them, which is one of the fundamental ideas of the game in its most developed state, and that is by combination and strategy so to bring matters about, that at the critical period, when a try is in prospect, there shall be a numerical advantage on the part of the attackers of two men to one, which, being followed up, becomes in the proper course one man to none and a certain score. Supposing that at the beginning of an attacking movement there are—to put the situation simply if crudely—seven men immediately available for the rush forward, and there is a precisely equal number of the opposition in readiness to resist the attack. There is usually a moral and material advantage to the attackers; but, on the other hand, when the attacking and opposing forces are anything like equal, it is always odds against the former being suceessful. If it were not, the scoring would always be much heavier than it is. A score is usually brought about either by the attacking movement being developed to perfection without the slightest hitch, and by some piece of individual brilliance at the climax, or by some failure on the part of the opposition—that is when numerically the forces remain equal to the end. As the movement we have suggested progressed and the goal line was neared, there would not remain seven attackers and seven defenders. Man for man, each side would be depleted until towards the end there were, say, three opposed to three, or two to two. In this respect the chances are still equal. The attackers have retained their moral and material advantage, and they are probably nearer the goal line, but that is all. Their difficulties are still of the most formidable character, particularly when there is a fresh and resourceful back to be dealt with. Well, then, the great scheme of the attack in the first place, and the constant object of those who are engaged upon it the whole way, must be to get rid of this objectionable equality of forces, and to place the attackers in a numerical advantage as soon as possible. The sooner this can be done the better, and the easier will the remainder of the task become, but if it cannot be done earlier it will be quite effectual if it is brought about at the last moment. Now you do not usually gain a man in the ordinary process of tackling and beating, or being tackled, or by any man-to-man engagement of that kind, and it is no good looking upon this as the proper method of achieving such an object. Though the man tackled may have achieved his object before he was overcome, and the ball may have been passed into the safe hands of a waiting colleague who is away with it at top speed, the tackle has cost a man to each side. Both the tackler and the tackled are out of the game for the time being, and one way or another all may be over with the movement by the time they are again in the neigbourhood of the ball.

The desired disparity in forces must then be brought about by strategy. By some feint or cunning, by some delicate placing of the ball in a particular position, or by any means whatever that may suggest themselves at the moment—and there are various means, which will be explained in due course—two men of the opposition must be drawn to one place where one man ready would have served. The action of one man on the attacking side does this, and if the plan has been properly conceived and well carried out, it will usually be found that when two men are thus drawn from their natural sphere to combat an unexpected development, their efforts will be to some extent confused and irregular, and it is more than likely that they will neutralise each other. If this is so and the ball has gone on, the man will have been gained. The attacker who brought

COMBINATION UNDER DIFFICULTY
(NEW ZEALAND SOLDIERS)

it about will be out of the game, but two others of the defenders will be so also, and for the remainder of the rush, if combination is preserved, the attackers will be at a great advantage. Man being taken for man all along the line, it will happen that there are two of the attackers left and only the back to beat. One man takes the back, and the other scores with the ball. This is putting a hypothetical case, as we have stated, in a very simple and crude form for the sake of making clear what has been stated to be a fundamental idea of the game, and when we come to consider tactics at length we will show the cases that do positively arise when a man is to be gained, and how exactly the process may be carried out. When opposing sides are fairly equal in strength, skill, and experience, it is strategy of this kind that must tell best. Fifteen men against fifteen, seven against seven, three against three—everything is equal and nothing is certain. Seven against six, four against three, two against one, and there is a side about to score.

As for the second distinct system of attack—or rather kind of attack, for it can hardy be described properly as systematic—by individual effort, the underlying idea is that great as are the virtues of combination, there are times when a great individual effort offers prospects of success, and when a combined movement is either not at the moment practicable or easy of accomplishment. Generally speaking, the essence of the individual effort is suddenness and unexpectedness. It is opportunism. Individual efforts of a simple or elementary kind are useless; they must be clever and intelligent. There are particular methods of individual play which every man is expected to resort to when the time is ripe for them, and he must put into operation that which seems to be most clearly indicated at the time. The position of the opportunist in these cases is difficult and to some extent thankless. We say that he is expected to do these things on his own account when he sees his chance, and only he can be the judge of the value of that chance. At the same time, in the face of the overwhelming advantages of combination, nine times out of ten one hesitates to lay down individual effort of a protracted character as a cardinal and authenticated feature of the game. The attitude may be unfair, but we judge of individual effort according to its success. Such success is its justification, and its only one. If a single player engages on what is apparently a hazardous enterprise, and he fails, it is naturally declared that his judgment was at fault, that he miscalculated the chances, that he did not play the game, and it is difficult for him to avoid the accusation of selfishness,—the most fatal fault of all in a player. But if he succeeds his glory is great, and we applaud his fine perception. The man who goes in for individualism must take all these risks, and he must make sure that his judgment is at all, or most times, to be relied on. He must succeed, or nearly, oftener than he fails, and he must be ever mindful of the threatening accusation of selfishness. In Britain they appear to have no liking for the player who does not play the orthodox game. We in New Zealand are great sticklers for our orthodox systems of combination, but at the same time we do not prohibit individualism. We have seen too many valuable points scored through it that never could have been scored in any other way, to permit us to do that. Our attitude is one of unofficial and very guarded approval.

As for the ruse, the third general method of gaining advantage over your opponents, little explanation is necessary. In every game deception is a legitimate and recognised form of attack or defence; but its possibilities seem to us to have been less developed in Rugby football than in most other games, though we have found it to be very remunerative. Usually, as we said earlier in this chapter, the ruse is supplementary to combination or individualism. If you can persuade your opponents that you are about to do something different from that which you have determined

THE IDEA OF THE GAME 61

upon, your progress is likely to be much less difficult than it would be otherwise, for a part of the journey at least. But your ruse must be good, and it must be novel or it will be no ruse, and it must have some of the appearance of reality. Ruses invented on the spur of the moment are seldom satisfactory. Each side, and each player on the side, must have their recognised ruses, and if they are little tricks not in use elsewhere and not known to opposing sides, all the better. It follows that a ruse can seldom be tried on more than once in a game, and that a renewal of stock will be frequently required. There will be occasion to deal with these tricks later on, and it need only be said in passing that every ruse has, as it were, a double edge. When you have cut with it one way you can turn it round and cut with it the other. This is to say that, having worked your particular form of deception off on the other side, they look for you to do it again, and you make it appear that in the same situation on a subsequent occasion you are going to do it. They think that this time they know you, and they prepare for the ruse. When they have prepared it is your best plan to do the thing that they thought you were only pretending you would do. You gain by the mystery you create, and nothing has such a demoralising effect on a side as being beaten by these feints. They hurt their pride, and when a man or a side become that way they are not quite so good as before, though they may be more energetic and determined. All this may sound simple and obvious, but it counts for very much in the best game of Rugby football. The New Zealanders in Britain gained many points from the best teams through the exercise of these apparently simple dodges. So we must count deception as one of the fundamental principles or ideas of the game.

In each of these groups of methods there are many variations, and that side is strongest which has perfected itself in most of them. The number of situations that may arise on a football field, in attack and defence, when there are thirty living, moving units as varying factors, is enormous, and yet there are certain ways of dealing with each situation which are better than others. A side should therefore strive to adapt itself to circumstances in the most effectual manner, and to have at its disposal the largest possible number of variations of attack and defence, and should thoroughly understand how and when to apply each of them to the best advantage. It is the multiplicity of its resource that distinguishes the great team from others. Not only are these variations necessary for proper adaptation to particular circumstances, but it is unwise always to play exactly the same kind of game. When this is done one's opponents can always lay themselves out to beat that particular game. It is much better that they should not know beforehand what sort of game they will have to face, and better still if, when they see it, they should find it to be one with which they are not at all familiar.

Having said so much about the features of the game from the broadest point of view, one may step a point further into detail by giving a brief preliminary consideration to the placing of the team on the field of play. This is a question upon which there are many different opinions, and upon which, as will be seen, there has been a very slow evolution of thought. Although we are at a loss to know how to get better value out of our fifteen men than we do by placing them in the positions that we do now and as we did throughout our British tour, we realise that it is not wise to be dogmatic in such a matter, and to assert positively that our formation is the best that can be devised. The history of the changes of formation has seen the upsetting of too many systems that had been well tried and in which a firm belief was held by open-minded and intelligent Unions, to permit of anything of that kind. At the same time we do most earnestly believe that our system possesses very solid advantages over any other, and that it marks another step in the perfection of the theory and practice of the game.

THE IDEA OF THE GAME

Particular systems apart, the general idea of formations in these days is that you shall have something approximating to an equal number of players in the forward and back divisions. To a certain extent these terms, as in common use to describe the different departments, are misnomers, particularly from the soccer point of view. The forwards are not always the most forward players in the movements of a side, and the backs do not constantly remain back as if for defence. The only man who is really a back in this sense is the full back. The three-quarter backs, who nominally constitute the second last line of defence, are actually the most formidable attackers, and those who are most constantly engaged in movements of this character. The forwards, or the pack, or the scrum, as they are variously called, are chiefly useful as a kind of advanced guard to remove obstructions—at all events that has generally been the conception of their purpose, though it is part of our system to find them more work and work that is more serviceable. However, we may take it that the forwards, seven or eight of them as the case may be, are there for scrumming and for general utility purposes. Then there must always be a man immediately behind the forwards to receive the ball as it comes from the scrum,—the scrum half, as he is called,—and to set the attacking movement going. Farther back are variously named backs, who come into operation at such a moment, and thus it most frequently happens that from a soccer point of view they are the real forwards. Behind them is the solitary full back, the last hope of his side in the event of an onslaught by the enemy. In the general scheme of the arrangment of a team, more thought is given to attack than to defence, and, as compared to the Association game, the men generally are much less tied down to positions. There are backs for attack and backs for defence as occasion arises, the fact being that usually the sphere of action changes more slowly and less suddenly than in the game that is played according to the dribbling code.

One may now briefly, and with as little comment, for the time being, as is necessary to explanations, draw attention to the comparative features of the British formation as chiefly in vogue, and of the New Zealand formation as practised in our tour. The two arrangements are clearly indicated in the diagrams that are presented for the purpose in this work. Taking the British system first, there are eight forwards in the pack, arranged when a scrummage is formed in three rows, with three men in the front row, two in the second and three in the back row. There are generally two half backs, one being delegated to attention to the scrum, and the other being by way of a flying half. Then there is a line of four three-quarter backs, the kernel of the team, and finally a full back.

The New Zealand arrangement is a considerable modification on this one. To begin with, there are only seven forwards, in rows of two, three, and two respectively, and we have only three three-quarter backs. The spare forward and the spare three-quarter we put together to make a new line of attack and defence between the halves and the three-quarters. These men we call our five-eighths. For the rest, we have one full back according to recognised custom; a scrum half; and, in place of the other or flying half, we play the wing forward. In principle the wing forward does not differ materially from the flying half, and, as we hope to show later on, any attack which is made on the ethics of the former's functions will apply almost equally to the flying half. Perhaps the former has his duties more clearly defined, and is consequently better prepared to undertake them, and in this clear definition is his merit and his advantage. But there is very little of other difference.

The great virtue of our five-eighths is their adaptability. On paper we see that the English formation has the advantage of an extra man in the three-quarter line; but at times, as when necessary, the New Zealand outside five-eighth would be regarded by a British player as nothing but a

Common British formation of Side.

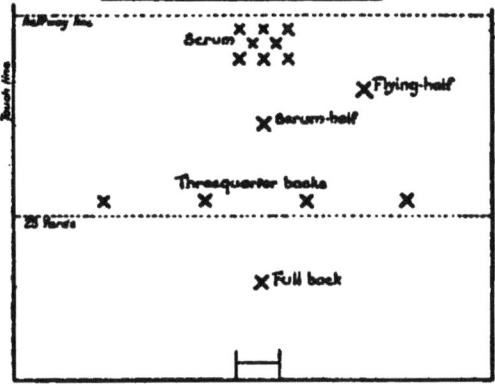

- Scrum × × ×
  × × ×
- × Flying-half
- × Scrum-half
- Threequarter backs
  ×   ×   ×   ×
- × Full back

New Zealand formation of Side.

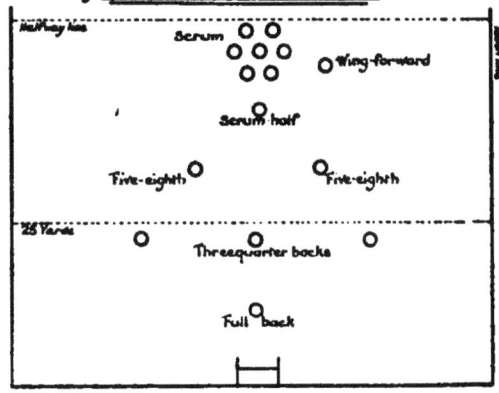

- Scrum ○ ○
  ○ ○ ○
  ○ ○
- ○ Wing-forward
- ○ Scrum half
- Five-eighth ○   ○ Five-eighth
- ○   ○   ○
  Threequarter backs
- Full ○ back

centre three-quarter. On the other hand, according to the development of the game, there are occasions when he has all the appearance of a half back. In defensive movements he is practically the half back pure and simple.

We claim for the New Zealand arrangement that it affords more possibilities for developing an attack than any other, and permits of more of those desirable variations of combination. On the other hand, we are satisfied that the extra line that we have for defence is of great service. We gain these advantages chiefly by taking the man out of the scrum, and instead of weakening the scrum we make it, as we shall endeavour to show, a more compact and scientific machine for the accomplishment of its particular purpose.

This is the standard formation as nurtured and perfected in New Zealand during the last ten years, after frequent opportunities of studying the Welsh system as played in Britain, for the Welsh players were the inventors of the prevailing arrangement. To our minds, this Welsh or British system is lacking in lines of defence, while, on the other hand, it certainly does not provide easy combinations for attack. Many of our tactical plans, which will be described later on, would be impossible with this formation. The capacity to strike in as many ways as can be thought of, and the utmost reserve of defence—that is the object of our arrangement, and we have found it achieve it well.

CHAPTER V

QUALIFICATIONS OF PLAYERS

Need for versatility among backs—Should be able to play in any position but with one speciality—Examples in the New Zealand team—Wealth of variety in attack and defence—Qualifications of the back—A necessity in the wing three-quarter—The advantage of private practice—Punting and fielding—Methods of practice in New Zealand—The donkey man of the team—The work of the half back—The magnificence of Roberts—Methods of the half—His prospects of scoring — His cunning and strategy — Doing the unexpected — More definite qualifications—The five-eighths—Quite indispensable to our system—Attacking movement begun much more expeditiously—An Oxonian's appreciation—Five-eighth must be a quick-witted man—Harmony between the scrum half and the five-eighth—The necessity for a code—The colonial system—The weak spot of the enemy—Some points in tactics—The three-quarters—Forward in attack, back in defence — The centre — Necessity for unselfishness — Fast men wanted — New Zealand's best—The full back—A trying position—Great possibilities—Points of the back—Little of the orthodox—A difference in methods—The forwards—What is wanted in them—Must keep their temper and not talk—Always to be in the pink of condition—Dribbling—And when to dribble—Expensive experiments—The fine footwork of the Irish forwards—Combination among the pack—Need for the exercise of common sense—Speed a requirement.

IN this chapter we shall set forth what we consider to be some of the general and necessary qualifications of players in the different positions, with but little reference to the details or methods which they do or should adopt.

Beginning with the backs, there is little occasion to distinguish between their different varieties, for though we believe in every man being suited to his position, and being happy in it, we are also strongly of opinion that the organisers of a team should demand a large measure of versatility from each and all of their backs (we are using the term generally for the whole division from half to full), and that

QUALIFICATIONS OF PLAYERS

therefore the qualifications of the man who plays in one place are largely those of his colleague in another. One-job men in back play are not the men for emergencies, for the seizing of opportunities, or for relieving a dangerous situation on the one hand, or making an attack from nothing on the other. We want, instead, the handy man who can do everything well, and one or two things exceedingly well. We give him a special commission for doing these one or two things in his own particular line, but at the same time we expect him to lend a hand in the performance of others as occasion demands. When a man can himself play in the position in which some of his colleagues with whom he has to play and combine are placed, he has a better appreciation and knowledge of their methods, and can adapt his own play to them in a much more successful manner, than he could if he were ignorant on these points. So we never consider that a back should be rated as first-class until he is able to play at a moment's notice in various positions in the rearguard with credit to himself and his team. During our British tour, Wallace played in every position except that of scrum half, though he is most brilliant at wing three-quarter and full back. Gillett, a good wing forward, could perform creditably in almost any back position. McGregor, Smith, and Deans would usually play with distinction at wing three-quarter, centre three-quarter, and outside five-eighths. One of the authors of this book (Gallaher) played during the tour at both wing forward and centre forward, although he has played, and is still capable of doing so, in any position on the field. His collaborator (Stead) played in every back position except that of full back. Hunter invariably played at outside five-eighths, and Roberts always at scrum half while in Britain; but each of these men is capable of doing the best work in various other positions. We recommend all players to study the play of as many positions as possible, and to do their utmost to make themselves proficient in the particular methods of the men occupying different posts on the field from those which they themselves habitually undertake. By so doing a wealth of variety in both attack and defence is made possible, as by no other means. The old way of a player moving all his days in the same old groove of a particular position is fatal to ingenuity and initiative.

Now it is absolutely essential in the first place that a back should be able to kick well with both feet, to pass to either side, and to take a ball either when fronting it as it is coming towards him or when running in the same direction. To be able to kick surely and cleanly with one foot only is fatal to the development of a first-class back, as should he be a wing three-quarter he could only play with any certainty at all on one particular wing. A wing three-quarter with such a limitation is only half as good as a wing three-quarter should be, and a committee choosing a side and having a fair number of players from which to make selection, should certainly leave him out in order to include a man who is possibly less brilliant in the one particular position but who is a first-class performer on both sides. It goes without saying that the good back must be a sound tackler and a reliable punt kick. Above all things he should be possessed of really extraordinary speed —it is not enough to say that he must be merely fast. Speed is the good back's most valuable quality, and it is one that he should cultivate at all times to the utmost extent in his power. Half a yard gained in fifty may mean all the difference between a score and an attack cut off at its very inception.

In order to become a tip-top back, much steady patience and perseverance and unlimited practice are absolutely necessary, and it unfortunately happens that it is often very difficult for the average amateur to obtain such practice. A player anxious to keep in form may always obtain a sharp run or a brisk walk a few times during the week, as he may consider advisable, but this will not help his kicking, and it is this for which he most sadly needs opportunities for practice. To those who can snatch a little spare time, even during the midday lunching interval, I would strongly recommend that if possible they should obtain a ball and make an adjournment to the nearest piece of waste ground, and practise punting to a given point with both feet alternately. Let them also practise high mid-air punts and taking the ball therefrom, and they may likewise coach themselves in fielding the ball from the ground when going at top speed. Such work when conscientiously performed need never be dull and uninteresting to the zealous player; and inasmuch as there is a certain gain in increased proficiency,—a far greater gain than many people might imagine, as we have proved over and over again,—surely it is worth the trouble and any little inconvenience that may be involved. In New Zealand, where we are blessed with shorter working hours and a longer twilight than in Britain, it is the commonest thing to see on various empty allotments players in parties of two exchanging punts with one another and also indulging in a round of passing. To the player who has his heart in the game this is a pleasurable form of recreation, as well as something which is of infinite advantage to his development as a back. One may add, in passing, that in the same way you see forwards at work during their leisure hours, and it is this practice as much as anything which has made New Zealand forwards almost as capable as backs in the various features of passing, kicking, and taking the ball. With these observations in general, and such insistence on the virtues of versatility, one may glance briefly at indispensable qualifications for individual positions.

The half back as we know him in New Zealand is the donkey man of the team, the man who in his time has to do a little of everything, and is called upon to do it really well. We look to him to do the hard necessary routine work of watching the scrum and doing the proper thing when the ball comes out on his side, and we also expect him to show flashes of brilliancy on his own account when anything like an opening is presented. Roberts served for the most part as our half during our tour, and he is too good a man, and he performed too brilliantly the whole way through, for it to be in the least necessary for us to sing his praises. It is enough to say that he is one of the best men we have ever seen in the position, and is to be classed with such brilliant exponents of the half back game as Humphries of Taranaki and Braund of Auckland in their palmiest days. One may look upon him as the ideal of what a half should be.

From our point of view, we have, of course, only one half as against the two in Britain, the wing forward having his own special duties to perform. The place for the half is from one to two yards behind the scrum, and when the ball is heeled out to him by the forwards, it is his duty to initiate an attack with all possible speed, keeping a vigilant eye upon the movements of the opposition half, who will direct his attention to him the moment he sees that the ball is going out on his side. Generally speaking, when a half comes into possession of the ball he gives it as quickly as he can to the five-eighth. Everything depends upon his promptness and skill in this respect; the slighest hesitation, the least suspicion of bungling, and the great opportunity will have passed. According to the rapidity with which the movement is executed, so are the chances of a score increased. On some occasions, however, the half may see or make an opening for himself, and get right up to his opponents' three-quarter line before finding it to be necessary to part with the ball. Of course he would be backed up all the time by his five-eighth waiting for him to get into trouble and about to be tackled. There are many occasions in almost every match when the half back has a better chance of scoring than either the five-eighth or a three-quarter, for the simple reason that he is not expected to score and the others are, with the result that when an attacking movement is in progress all the eyes of the opposition are on these others to whom he is expected sooner or later to pass the ball. The half is the man above all others who is called upon to exercise a little cunning and strategy in circumstances of this kind, and to spring the unexpected on the enemy. The chances are nearly always well worth accepting, for, though with a full knowledge of the possibility of this strategy being employed, the opposing side are obliged to concentrate their attention on the five-eighths and the three-quarters, because after all that is the most likely place from which danger will come. It is not their policy to prepare chiefly for the unexpected.

In these few words the chief essential qualities of the half back are already indicated. He must be smart in getting the ball away from the scrum, thereby setting his backs in motion without delay. It is necessary that he should be both a quick and a good punter, and particularly adept at screw punts, so that he can punt over his head into touch without turning round, as on very many occasions he is forced to do from his position at the time, especially when his opponents are on him. He must be a man of quick decision and possessed of considerable ingenuity. Moreover, he must be good at stopping a rush. He may have the whole pack of opposing forwards coming down on top of him, and dash and skill in such an emergency count for everything, if he is to extricate his side from danger. A good half back is a great player. He is the key to the attack, and one of the most indispensable men in the team.

Next in order we come to consider the innovation of the New Zealanders, the five-eighths. As we have already seen, we have two of them, the inside and the outside, and we are not aware that at this time of day any further justification for their existence is necessary than that which has already been presented. To our system of playing they are quite indispensable, and we could no more play a satisfactory game without them—with those two men in other positions and fulfilling other duties than those especially delegated to them—than we could play well without our boots. It is of inestimable advantage thus to have a back closer up to the scrum for both attack and defence than the three-quarter line. In the British system the ball comes away from the scrum half to a three-quarter, and away it travels right across the field. It is a slow business, giving opponents much time to make preparations for what is coming. But when a five-eighth takes the ball the attacking movement is set in operation much more speedily; and there is also a greater range of variety in opening it. In defending, the five-eighth may often stop an attack by opponents before it has become threatening. From every point of view these two mid-way men, these "decimals" as they have been facetiously termed, are quite invaluable, and it has been a matter of some surprise to us that the merits of their position have not been better appreciated in this country. However, an English player who understood the five-eighths when he saw them, and who described them in terms which no New Zealander could improve upon, was R. G. T. Coventry, the Oxford "Blue"; and we should like to quote some of the things he said as being an independent opinion and one with which we fully agree. Mr. Coventry said: "It may have been remarked by those who have closely followed the doings of the New Zealand players, how much of the scoring has been done by the men who occupy the position known as the five-eighth. The reason of this is not far to seek. In a fifteen where individual excellence is so strongly in evidence, the five-eighths have greater chances of scoring than any other members of the team. The flying half of our four three-quarter game has never made use of his exceptional chances for scoring as he ought to have done. He is, in fact, a far less dangerous player than the old style of half back, who used to play close up to the scrum, and had to make his own opportunities. The New Zealanders have not

QUALIFICATIONS OF PLAYERS

been slow to perceive the unlimited possibilities open to the between man, or, as they call him, the five-eighth. And so they have put two men into that position, and those two men their strongest individual players. The five-eighth is in the happiest of positions. He has the ball given him by the scrum-worker, he has three fleet men behind him, and a partner as tricky and determined as himself. He is bound by no stupid convention—such as paralysed the half back game of this country—that he must get rid of the ball as quickly as possible. He can bluff to his heart's content, and use his partner and three-quarters as a blind to his own designs on the goal-line. No one on the other side is quite sure whether he is going to pass or not, with the result that by the time they have made up their minds he is running behind the goal-posts. And he has such an infinite variety of artifice at his command, for he need never do the same thing twice together, and he seldom does."

Herein are already sufficiently indicated the necessary qualities of the capable five-eighth. Taking it for granted that he is a good kick and has all the regular virtues of the good Rugby footballer, he must also be a man of exceptional resource, and above all quick-witted, of the most lightning-like perception, so that the moment a view of the field is sent to his brain through his eye he has it analysed and ticketed, and is already putting into force a scheme based on the results.

It is absolutely essential that there should be the most perfect harmony between the five-eighths and the scrum half, and that they should have the very closest understanding with each other as to the method of their operations. Each is complementary to the other, and any hitch in the combination here is sure to be attended by the most disastrous results. There must not only be the ordinary mutual understanding of the methods of each, but these men must have a code of their own, so that they may communicate to each other freely and nobody but themselves be any the wiser.

Codes, we believe, are common enough among the Welsh teams, and upon this detail of the game it is only necessary to say here that however much the members of a team may understand each other, they cannot—and do not attempt to—play their game properly without spoken instructions and directions from one to the other, and that it is obvious that if these instructions and directions are anything out of the ordinary it is fatal to let the enemy hear them. During very many matches of the British tour, one of the present writers (Stead) played five-eighth to Roberts, and in our case we had a code of Maori words which had the advantage of not being remembered when heard. Letters of the alphabet will serve very well. A may be understood to mean "Pass on the open"; B—"Pass on the blind"; C—"Go on your own"; "D—Short punt." Supposing Jones were wing three-quarters on the blind side, then "B, Jones," as an instruction from the five-eighth to the scrum half, would mean that the latter must pass straight to Jones on receiving the ball from the scrum instead of bringing in the five-eighth as he would in the ordinary course.

It was always an understanding in our play that directly opponents gained possession, Roberts should defend on the opposite side of the scrum from that where our wing forward was located—generally the blind side. Then it was the duty of the five-eighth to glance at the disposition of the opposing backs and determine at once upon what lines the forthcoming movement of attack or defence, as the case might be, should be made on his side. Upon his generalship and his judgment at this moment almost everything depends. He must be able to appreciate the position at a glance, to observe almost instinctively the weak spot in the enemy's defence, and originate quickly the line of attack which is then obvious to him. And then he must have the most excellent powers of dissimulation, and should take every opportunity of deceiving the enemy as to what are his real intentions. Bluff is one of his best weapons.

In playing an attack we do not consider it advisable for an inside five-eighth to try to cut through (meaning "cut" in its technical sense of dodgery), though, of course, it may be done as a bluff occasionally, and sometimes there is a possible opening. Casting one's mind back over the whole series of our games in Britain, one finds that, as a rule, the most successful attacks were those when either the outside five-eighth or the centre three-quarter did the cutting. Therefore we take it that as a general rule the inside five-eighth on receiving the ball from the scrum half should so run as to draw an opponent on to him, and at the critical moment of being collared should pass to his fellow five-eighth, who, if he has not the desired opening in front of him, passes on to the centre. However, in such remarks as these we are moving on towards a consideration of tactics.

Of the three-quarters one finds it difficult to write to much point or to say more than a very little that does not look like mere platitude, for in the men who fill these positions one wants all the virtues of the best Rugby footballer, and the simple enumeration of them is wearisome and flat. Forward in attack, back in defence, and in each case always in the middle of everything, the good three-quarter is most intimately concerned in every phase of the game from its inception to its close. We shall speak frequently of the three-quarter and what is wanted of him when we come to consider tactics.

The centre must be a sterling all-round man, fast, able to kick well with both feet, and a good tackler. He must be absolutely safe in taking the ball and fielding it in the air. The brunt of the defensive work often falls on him. He must pass well so that on receiving the ball from the five-eighth he may feed his wings very accurately and speedily. As no man in the team has more opportunities presented to him of potting at the goal than he has, his necessary qualifications in this respect are obvious. The wing men get many such chances, but he still more. Let him remember that when he does not see an advantage to be gained by passing to one of his colleagues, it is best for him to find touch with the ball or go on until he is collared. But he and the rest of the backs must be the most unselfish men in the team. In New Zealand it is a common thing for a man to be left out of a representative team because of his fault in this respect, even though individually he may be far better than the man who is chosen in preference to him.

Both the centre and the wing three-quarters must be exceedingly fast men, as fast as can be found. It is a prime condition of their appointment. And it must be borne in mind, in the case of the wing three-quarters particularly, that they often have two men to take, and it must always be uppermost in their minds that after them there is only the full back left to deal with the crisis that is presented. Jervis of Auckland, poor Armit of Dunedin (who was killed on the field, having his spine broken), Bayley of Taranaki, and Whiteside of Auckland, have been the finest three-quarters we have bred in New Zealand; and our man, Wallace, has been as good as any of them, and is as fine an exponent of the three-quarter game as has ever been seen.

It is difficult to say whether the position of the full back is the more trying when the game is going against the side or in favour of it. In the former case his duties are of the most responsible character possible, inasmuch as he is the last hope of his side, and on him devolves the task of preventing his opponents from scoring when no one else can do so. In such circumstances he receives thanks and applause when he has saved the situation; but it is not always that the full value of his work is appreciated, whilst there is never any hesitation in attaching the maximum amount of blame to him when the opposition attack has proved successful. On the other hand, when his own side is attacking vigorously he is an idle man, and the dulness of his situation is sometimes pitiable. Thus it happens that the ambitions of a player are seldom in the direction of

QUALIFICATIONS OF PLAYERS

becoming a good full back. This is very unfortunate for many reasons, for after all the post can be invested with much distinction.

As to the qualifications of the player, he must first of all be one of the best kicks in the whole team with either foot, and accuracy in finding the touch line and gaining as much ground as possible are absolutely essential. He must be able to field the ball well in any position, and be a sound, strong tackler, afraid of nothing, as he will commonly be called upon to take his man in very difficult positions. There is less of the orthodox in the play of the back than that of any man, and this remark applies particularly to his methods of collaring an opponent. The one thing that must always be uppermost in his mind is that to prevent a score he must collar him at any cost. On many occasions he is called upon to field the ball from the toes of half a dozen forwards, who are coming down on top of him in a dribbling rush. Perhaps as a last resource he will have to go down at the feet of these men to stop the rush. Iron nerve, cold judgment, and delicate skill are needed at such times. It so often happens that he is called upon to face danger to his side and personal danger to himself, and at the same time that he is acting he must be thinking hard for a solution to the difficulties of the situation, that there must be something Napoleonic in his temperament.

There is one point in regard to the stopping of a rush which we should mention here, which constitutes an important difference between back play in New Zealand and in Britain. Our backs never go down and lie on the ball as they do here—permitted to do so by the referees. The players themselves are not at all to blame in the matter, but only the laxity of the referees, so that this practice has become a system and part of the game. In New Zealand a back is allowed to stop the rush by throwing himself on the ball, but nothing more than stop it, and if he does not get up immediately he is penalised. We find that the lying on the ball, as practised in Britain, slows the game a great deal, particularly when the referee merely gives it a scrum. Besides, this method of procedure is a fruitful cause of accidents.

Now at last we will go to the front and size up the forwards as they should be in a good team. Most of their work is in the scrum, and our New Zealand scrum differing from others, being a unique feature of our game, and being to our minds rather a scientific affair needing careful explanation, we will defer consideration of it to a chapter devoted to nothing else, and similarly the line-out work will be treated in another place. For the present we will treat of the forward in his general aspect.

His task is often a very trying one, and perhaps it makes more demands on a man's complacency and good temper than any other. Football is not a parlour game, and one's first advice to the budding forward would be to keep his passions well under control at all times, and to take in good grace the many hard bumps and knocks that he will inevitably receive in the course of every game. Even when one's opponent does seem to put a little unnecessary vigour into his bumping, it is not to be assumed that it is due to malice. Rather let it be regarded as the result of his exaggerated estimate of the difficulty of disposing of the man against whom he bumps. In a hard scrummage or line-out a man often gets a very nasty knock or kick which is purely accidental, and it is regrettable when such inevitable incidents of the game lead to an exchange of "words." And that reminds one also that the forward particularly, as well as the backs, must at the beginning of their career be warned against talking. They have no business to talk to anyone except in the ordinary way of conveying instructions, and especially they have no business to talk at or to the referee, who, in the execution of his rather thankless duties, has quite enough to occupy his attention without having his every interpretation of the rules questioned or criticised.

QUALIFICATIONS OF PLAYERS

Besides, to the spectators nothing looks more ridiculous than these grown-up men, who should know so much better, talking excitedly and haranguing with each other as if they were a lot of schoolboys. One hastens to add that such an analogy in general is not fair, for schoolboys would not as a rule commit themselves to any serious extent in such matters as these, and we say it with regret that the innate sportsman's feeling is sometimes stronger in the boy than it is in the grown-up man. So, forwards, leave the captain to do what talking needs to be done; in a hard, strenuous game you need all your supplies of mental and physical energy without wasting them on your fellow-players or on the referee. And to these observations, which apply to all, but, as we have said, particularly to the forwards,—partly because so many more opportunities and provocations to be offenders come their way,—we may touch on another hint which likewise applies to all, but particularly to the men of the front rank, and that is that they must take extreme care that they are always in the pink of condition. One has to be careful in conveying such a warning as this, lest it might be imagined that it is not so important that backs should be always in their best condition. One must be paradoxical, and say that while it is more necessary that the forwards should always be fit, it is not less necessary that the backs should be so. The simple fact is that lack of condition will probably tell a worse tale in the case of a forward towards the close of a hard-fought game than it would in the case of any other player.

There are two more big things one demands from the forward. He must be very adept at dribbling the ball with his feet, and he must have the common sense and will-power to play with his feet instead of his hands when the circumstances plainly indicate that the former is the proper thing, as they do generally when the weather is wet. In such an event as the latter the player has far more control over the ball when dribbling it than he would if he were to pick it up and handle it. For one thing there is always a considerable danger of knocking-on when an attempt is made to pick up a wet and greasy ball. But somehow the player constantly finds this temptation to handle instead of dribble quite irresistible. At the most critical moments, and with the remembrance of a hundred exasperating mistakes of the kind in similar circumstances, attended with the most disastrous results, he will yet once again commit the indiscretion of picking up, and will thereby minimise the prospects of a score, although convinced for the moment that he is increasing them. How very often does one see a man unable to resist this temptation when the opponents' goal-line is within measurable distance. Now is the time for his hands, he seems to think. Down they go in a wild, anxious endeavour to field the ball, and—to-o-o-t!—there is the referee's whistle screaming almost instantly for the palpable knock-on. He ought to have known better, that forward then thinks of himself; and he considers that he has been taught a lesson. But he will do the same thing again on the next wet day if he gets the chance. He looks very foolish on these occasions, and he ought to feel it if he doesn't. He is proving a very expensive man to his side, and unless he can display more common sense in the future—it is really a mere matter of common sense—those who are responsible for its selection may feel that they ought to deprive themselves of such a luxury. Common sense, common sense—that is what we want in our forwards. They must have the gumption to realise that you can kick and dribble remarkably well with your feet, and that this item in your physical equipment must not be neglected.

In this connection we would like to say a few words of our appreciation of the footwork of the Irish forwards. There are many fine sights in good Rugby football, but on a calm reflection one is tempted to suggest that there is none finer, none more exhilarating, than that of a pack of Irish forwards sweeping down the field in one combined rush with the ball at their feet and under the most perfect control. To a man who studies and loves the game, this is an object lesson that he will never forget. It will convince him that, oftener than he had imagined, combined footwork among forwards is just as good as combined handling and passing among the back division.

The men of the front division need to understand also that common sense is required of them in regard to matters of combination, and by combination in this case we do not mean mere passing but the fitting of themselves in with the general scheme of the play. There must be the best understanding among the whole fifteen; but it should not be so often necessary to tell the forwards in spoken words what to do in a particular case as it is to tell the backs, because the thing for them to do is more frequently obvious, and also it is more frequently difficult or even impossible to give such instructions. For example, in the case of a line-out a good forward who understands his work should never need to be told to mark his man when his opponents are throwing in from touch. He must have the perception to know which man to mark, and the common sense and the instinct of duty to mark him very completely, or there will be trouble for his side. If his own side is throwing in, and his own goal-line is in danger, he will naturally take the best position for defence by playing close. Every half back and wing forward has known to his chagrin what it has cost to his side when on throwing in he has had to call out or signal to a man to play wide, say, thereby drawing the attention of his opponents to an opening through which a score might very likely have been effected, but the prospects of which are in this way very much minimised.

Again, in the scrummage the work is so varied and changes in its character are so frequent, that it is in the highest degree essential that the forwards should understand it thoroughly, and should never need to be told what to do. And above all things they must be thoroughly unselfish on the field. If we have seemed to labour this necessity among the forwards of exercising common sense and understanding each other, when the same necessity exists for the men in other departments, it may be pointed out that in our system there are seven forwards and in other systems there are eight, and in no other section of the team are there more than half so many players engaged in the same task. Therefore, while the complete mutual understanding is all the more needed, it is, with the complexity of increased numbers, naturally more difficult of attainment, and more pains must therefore be taken to make sure of it.

When we have said that we in New Zealand like to see fast forwards, and are rather disposed to insist on a better turn of speed from them than seems to satisfy so many British clubs, there is not much more to say in a general way. We want special qualifications of a very particular kind in the case of each man, in order that he may fulfil his allotted part to the best advantage in working our own particular scrum formation; but these, and the qualifications and duties of the wing forward, will be dealt with in their proper place. Let it be said only, at the end of this chapter, that we want much more from our forwards than it has been the custom to demand from them in the past. In the days when half the time of the game was occupied in scrumming, there might be something to be said for the big fat forward, who was a good pusher but who did not shine particularly in any other capacity. But those days of eternal, senseless scrumming have gone, and now we want forwards who have brains, and who can do a good many things extremely well that their predecessors did not think of doing. There is still scrum work to do, but even that is a much more refined business than it used to be.

CHAPTER VI

IN POSSESSION OF THE BALL

Science in passing the ball—A man out of action—Compensation wanted—Pass must not be made a moment too soon—Hold to the ball until the last second—Opponent bound to tackle—Passing at the moment of contact—The flick pass in Britain—A pretty thing but rather uncertain—Must be made before the opponent is reached—The New Zealand style—A low swing pass just at the time of collision—No danger of failure—How we receive the ball—Taken with the hands outside and hugged to the body—A very reliable method—The man with the ball—Swerves and cuts—The best swervers born, not made—The time for swerving—Reserve of pace—How it is done—Gliding out of the arms of an opponent—Hunter's corkscrew swerve—How Smith beat Scoular, with Scoular not to blame—A good thing for the wing three-quarter—Cutting is to be acquired—Necessity for constant practice—The point of perfection—As little pace as possible must be lost—Practising starts—A firm foothold wanted—See to the studs—Dodgery—Comes by instinct only—Gwyn Nicholls—A great Welshman—On tackling—Energy wanted—The man must be brought down—Half-hearted tacklers a danger to their side—Tackle low down, just below the hips—Little danger of accident—Watching the man—A battle of wits—When to go for the ball and not the man—Points in place-kicking—The methods of Wallace—Constant practice of all kinds—Drop-kicking and punting.

PERHAPS there is more science in the mere art of passing the ball with the hand from one player to another, or rather, one should say, there is room for the introduction of it to this apparently simple art, than many forwards and backs may think. A player's object in passing the ball is to give possession of it to a colleague who is in a better position for making further headway with it than he is himself. He has had his run, and now he sees that as an opponent is bearing down upon him further progress will be difficult or impossible, while close at hand is a partner who is in attendance for the special purpose of receiving the ball, and who has a clear field in front of him for the time being.

The first consideration is to ensure an absolutely certain and accurate pass to that man—not always quite such a simple matter as it looks. But when this is guaranteed, the question arises as to whether there is nothing else to be gained at the same time. Now the chances are that the man who is about to pass will be put out of action for the time being; or, if not that, he will cease to be the foremost man in the attack, and it is unlikely that he will be expected to take the ball again until there has been a considerable evolution in the movement. Regarding himself as more likely to be done for than not, there are then two points that suggest themselves at once. The first is that he, being a man placed out of action, should exercise his utmost endeavour to secure that a man on the other side is placed out of action at the same time, so that there shall be no comparative loss to his side; and he should also do the best he can to give the utmost advantage to the man to whom he has given possession. The man who is bearing down on the passer is the prime factor in these considerations. If the pass is made a moment too soon, giving the challenging opponent time to swerve in his course and bear down instead on the man who is receiving the ball, the pass may quite likely prove to have been wasted. The passer himself is out of action, but the opponent is going headlong for the other man, and the latter may be obliged to part with the ball in a hurry and not always to an advantage. Now, obviously what the passer should do is to defer his pass until such time as he has certainly placed the opponent out of action, or, at all events, ensured that he shall not molest his colleague. This can only be done by making him come right down on to the man with the ball; and he will only come down on him so long as the passer retains the ball. If the passer does so retain it, the opponent is bound to tackle him. It may be clear to the opponent that as soon as he tackles him, or a little before, the ball will be passed on; but of course, if the man in possession were not tackled, he would continue to go ahead himself.

The psychological moment to pass is evidently the moment of contact between the passer and the challenger, or something very near it—the nearer the better. In the British system the man passes before he reaches his opponent —an appreciable distance before he reaches him. His manner and style of passing necessitate his doing so. We think that this method is imperfect, and that the opponent should be drawn nearer and his cancellation made more certain. Therefore we pass at the moment of contact between the two and never before. This circumstance did not appear to be generally noticed when we were on tour. If we handled the ball in making the pass in the same way that the British players do, we could not pass when the passer was already tackled. Partly for this reason, and partly—chiefly—because it is a better, cleaner, and more reliable way, we have adopted an altogether different method of passing, and it may be added at once, though it does not affect the point under discussion, that the man who receives the ball does so in a different way also.

The British pass is what may be called a flick pass, and is executed with one hand. The player runs with the ball in both hands, and when the time for the transference arrives he poises it in front of him and then flicks it, end on, through the air with one hand, dropping the other hand idly down or using it to fend off an opponent. Now this pass is really a very pretty thing when well done and when it comes off; but it is unreliable, and it is particularly so when the ball is wet. With it there is neither that certainty of direction nor of speed which are essential to give the man who is to receive the ball the utmost advantage, and prevent him having to slacken his speed to any extent whatever. It will be seen that, of course, if the pass were not made before the opponent was reached it would be impossible.

The New Zealand way is entirely different. It is a system that is assiduously practised both by forwards and backs, and it is one which we have brought to a very pretty state of perfection and effectiveness. The player running with the ball waits until he and the opponent who has been bearing down on him are in actual contact, and at that instant he passes. At the moment of coming into contact he gives a slight twist to his body in the direction of the man who will receive the ball. At this time his body and arms have on them a natural swing in the direction of the man who is waiting for the ball, and just when the collision is about to take place he slightly poises the ball (the palms of the hands covering each end of it) so that he can swing it end on, in torpedo fashion, to his colleague. At the moment of contact, with his own body facing his partner, a free passage for the ball, and a good swing, as described, on his body and arms, he swings the ball through the air low down to the man who is waiting for it. The point to be emphasised is that it is a swing pure and simple, and a body swing, and not a throw or jerk. The body movement gives to the ball all the necessary propulsion, and the hands merely balance and guide it as it leaves them. It may be suggested that in passing on this system there is some risk of not getting the ball away. As a matter of fact there is little or none,—at least none that is the fault of the system,—and unless the passer is hampered very few passes go astray. When the movement has been well practised, it will be found that the pass can still be accomplished with ease even when the opponent has his arms round you as you are swinging the ball across.

Neither, as just said, does the New Zealander receive the ball from a pass in the same way as the British player. The latter generally takes the ball chest high with his arms outstretched. This seems simple enough, but it is not by any means so safe as it might be. There is always some danger

THE PROPER TIME TO GIVE A PASS AT THE MOMENT OF BEING TACKLED

HOW THE BALL IS PASSED AND TAKEN

of the ball being knocked on, or even missed altogether. It is easy to muff the pass when the ball is taken in this manner, and the fact that it is not often done in first-class play only indicates what great pains and skill are exhibited by the men who have been trained to the system.

Another one in which such anxious care is not necessary and which minimises the risk of accident is surely better, and we think that our system has these advantages. A man receiving the ball never depends for its security on his hands alone. As the ball comes along low down towards him he extends his hands, and when it is abreast of him he pulls it in towards him, both hands on the far side of the leather, pressing it to the pit of his stomach. It is a safe and easy capture, and it has the additional advantage that it certainly enables the receiver to take it at full speed and with less halting hesitation than if he depended upon his hands. Having received the ball in safety, the man who is running with it at his very earliest convenience works his hands on to the ends so that he has it in control for feint passing, and in readiness for the real pass which in turn he will probably soon be called upon to make. The only time when we do not pass according to the system here described is when there are opponents in the way and the pass low down is out of the question. The lob pass is plainly indicated in such circumstances. The photographs of our passing methods will serve to give a finished idea of the methods we have been discussing.

Now we have to consider such arts and wiles of the man in possession of the ball as swerving, cutting, and general dodgery. There is, of course, a very distinct difference between the swerve and the cut, and the object of each is different, though both are executed to bring about a sudden change in the direction of the player's progress. The swerve, as its name implies, is a graceful curl in the line of progress, usually for the purpose of circumventing some threatened obstruction. The cut is a definite change of route brought about suddenly and at a sharp angle, and most frequently with the object of confounding the enemy by an apparent change of plans, which may, however, have been premeditated.

Really good and effective swerving is not easy. Players to whom it is extremely difficult at first may, by dint of great perseverance and the most strenuous practice, bring themselves to a considerable state of proficiency in it; but the best swervers are those who have it born in them, as some have, and to whom it comes naturally. Thompson, Smith, and Wallace were the most adept swervers we had on our side when in Britain, and the best British swerver we saw was Morgan of Wales—a thoroughly clever man. The technique of the thing is simple enough, and so far as we know it is the same all the world over. A player is going ahead with the ball at apparently top speed. An opponent is bearing down upon him, and in the ordinary course there will be a tackle at a given point. Now, as a matter of fact, when he makes up his mind that he will release himself from the impending difficulties by reverting to the swerving movement, the man with the ball should have a yard or two of pace in hand. Then, almost at the moment of contact with his opponent, he executes his manœuvre. If he intends to swerve to the left he allows himself to list that way as it were, crosses his right foot over the left in the ordinary course of running, and at the same time puts on the extra yard or two of pace that he has in reserve. It is the crossing of the legs when going at full speed which is the difficult thing to do, but which when properly performed is a very pretty thing to see, the swerver making a graceful curl and gliding away at the very last moment from the trap which had been set for him, and to which he had appeared a certain victim. It is a movement in many respects similar to that accomplished by a skater when he crosses his legs and glides in a smooth curve sideways as the result. Over and over again one may witness the accomplished swerver actually glide out of the arms of an opponent. Our man, Hunter, has a peculiar swerve of his own, which came naturally to him, and which might best be described as a corkscrew swerve. He travels at no great pace when he is putting it into operation, but it is wonderfully effective, and is so deceptive that the very best opponents have been beaten by it, and not half so much discredit has attached to them for being so as they may have imagined then and afterwards. In this connection one is reminded of a leading incident in our match against Scotland, and we would like to say that in our opinion, contrary to that of most of the critics, who did not understand perfectly, Scoular was not to be blamed for failing to collar Smith on the occasion when the latter obtained his try. He had no

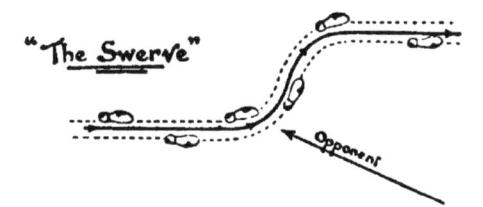

"The Swerve"
Opponent

chance against Smith's swerve. Of course it is a most useful accomplishment for any player, but it is particularly valuable to a wing three-quarter, and every man who plays in such a position should practise it most assiduously. The simple diagram we present shows the curve of the swerve and the crossing of the tracks which effects it.

Cutting is quite a different kind of thing. When a man swerves he keeps on approximately the same route as before; when he cuts he makes a complete change of direction, apparently with a view to an entire change of tactics and in the form of development of the attack, though the idea may have been in his mind for some time, if it was not there when he first came into possession of the ball. Circumstances must be left to suggest the time for cutting, and particular occasions when the movement is desirable, or even necessary, will be indicated when we come to speak of special tactics. There is nothing about it that comes naturally to the player; skill in it is to be acquired, and it can only be brought to a high point by constant practice. It is obviously easy enough to change the direction in which one is running; but it is not such a simple matter to do so and at the same time lose but the smallest fraction of one's pace, and the degree of skill acquired is to be measured by the amount of pace that is lost in making the cut. Of necessity there is a jerk, a halt at the turn. The man who cuts clumsily makes a very awkward corner of it, and there is a very evident lack of precision and certainty in the process, with the result that a valuable portion of a second is wasted. On the other hand, the man who has perfected his cutting wheels himself round, and before anyone has time to realise what has happened—and particularly before his opponents have realised it—he is away many yards on the new tack at top speed, and has already become a serious menace to what is then quite likely an unprepared and embarrassed defence. Nobody we have seen on a football field is more of the past-master in the art of cutting than our redoubtable Welsh opponent, Gwyn Nicholls. Our Deans at centre three-quarter and Mynott are exceedingly clever, and the latter particularly is a wonder at getting up top speed in a couple of paces. When one comes to think of it, it would not be at all an unremunerative form of practice for the benefit of one's cutting, as well as for other things in the game, to practise starts occasionally in the same way as the track athlete does. The success or failure of so many movements in Rugby football depend upon getting quickly off the mark, and the men who can transpose themselves from rest to top speed in the shortest possible space of time are evidently of far greater value in both attack and defence than others who need longer, and would hold a considerable advantage when opposed to them. The old maxim of being slow and sure is of no use in this game of ours. The man must be sure in what he does,—that he is so is taken for granted,—but it is also demanded of him that he shall be quick, and unless he can be quick and sure he must not aspire to honours in the world of Rugby football.

There is just one hint of great importance that may be given to the player in whose playing programme the practice of cutting is likely to form any considerable part, and that is that as it is of the utmost importance that at the time of the cut there should be the firmest possible foothold and complete sense of security in this respect—in the absence of which there will be an obvious danger of slipping—special care must be taken to see that the soles of the boots are well studded, and inasmuch as the sudden stop, which is the indispensable if almost invisible preliminary to the wheel round, is brought about usually by planting one or other of the heels firmly in front, both these heels should be supplied with two studs of the most serviceable order.

In this category of movements in which the player in possession of the ball is taken off the straight line of his course, a place must be given to what can only and simply be described as dodgery, by which we mean the way a man will have of slipping right round an opponent who has come down upon him and who is about to collar him. It is not a swerve, and it is not a cut, but it is simply a feint in a manner that comes natural to a man, and when it is successful he has dodged round the threatened obstruction and is away again on the other side before anyone quite realises the state of things. It is a quite unorthodox movement, and it is impossible to give any directions, for every man who practises it has his own ways which come quite naturally to him, and which he would probably be unable to describe himself, since at the time of each performance he is commonly quite unconscious of them or of any system whatever in what is apparently a wholly unsystematic proceeding. Dodging, in fact, is just what its name implies, and while it may be admitted as an art there is certainly nothing of science about it, and in this case at all events one cannot see that there is even very much to be gained by practice. Either a man can dodge well or he cannot and never will, and there is an end of it. We have occasionally seen Gwyn Nicholls doing some very neat work of this kind—in fact, in all these little subtleties of the game which count for so much in an engagement between two sides who are of the first quality, the great Welshman shows his accomplishment and his great resource. If it be not considered presumption and out of place for the New Zealanders to say such a thing, we would remark that for this player, for his thoroughness and complete efficiency, we have the greatest possible admiration and respect.

Although this chapter is being primarily devoted to the performance of the various special feats of skill that are required of the man in possession of the ball, to the end that he may make the best progress possible with it while he has it, and eventually deliver it to a colleague who will continue the good work, this is a suitable place for considering the reverse situation of the opponent who is doing his utmost to stultify his enterprises, and the moment is appropriate for the few observations we would like to make on collaring and tackling. Now in all cases except one, which we will duly indicate, the prime object of the tackler is to bring down his man. Particularly is this so when the tackler is the full back who, as one cannot say too often for his benefit when mentioning his name, is the last hope of his side in the case of an attack by the opposition which has assumed the most threatening character. He *must* bring down his man, and in his attempt to do so he must infuse all the energy at his command. Never mind what anybody may say about unnecessary vigour at such a time. Tackling is in the game, and it is not and was never meant to be a polite and gentle form of argument with an opponent. A half-hearted tackler is a grave danger to his side.

The proper way to tackle is to throw yourself at your

WALLACE ADJUSTING THE BALL TO SUIT THE CIRCUMSTANCES PREPARATORY TO A PLACE KICK

opponent just below his hips. You should not go any lower if you can help it, because if you do there is a probability that his knees will break the impetus of your tackle and he may escape. At the same time it should be borne in mind that it is better to be too low than too high. Tackling high up is a very uncertain and ineffective form of procedure, and is only to be recommended to those players who are not unjustly suspected of funk, and whose chief desire is to dispose of the task in hand in the lightest manner, regardless of the consequences to their side. When you take a man properly below his centre of gravity, he is bound to be stopped; if you only interfere with the part above, anything may happen. Besides, this low tackling is not by any means so dangerous as some people who do not thoroughly understand the game may think. No matter how small is the tackler or how big is his man, if the former only goes low down there is practically no fear of his being hurt. In such a case the small man seems to throw the big man right over him. One can hardly call to mind a single instance of a little man having been hurt in this way.

Then, just as we have seen how the man with the ball has these various arts and tricks of swerving, cutting, and dodging at his disposal, which he may put into operation as he thinks fit, it behoves the man who challenges him to keep the circumstance in mind, and anticipate them to the fullest extent of his perception. His essential quality for the time being, therefore, is that he should be a good judge of the meaning of the smallest and earliest trifles in the change of attitude of his approaching man. His eyes must be of the very keenest quality, and at this supreme moment he must use and strain them for all they are worth. Let him watch the eyes of his man. He must be something of a thought reader at this stage. The man with the ball dissembles, and it is his object for the time being to hide from his challenger the dark scheme that he has in his mind. According to the completeness which his subtle powers enable him to do so will he judge of the success of his own effort. In the reverse it is the object of the tackler to discover this scheme, and to thwart it accordingly. It is a momentary battle of wits, and if the man with the ball knows his business it has to be confessed that the odds are usually against the challenger in this matter. However, he must arrive at his decision without the waste of a fraction of a second of time, and, having so decided, he must mark the point of his tackle and dive down instantaneously to it.

The special circumstances in which it may be considered unwise to tackle low down—most of which must be left to suggest themselves at the time; they are very rare, and there can be no rules in the matter save this one—include chiefly the case when it is all-important that the *ball* should be stopped. Take the case of a passing rush which has been started from the scrum. It is of the greatest importance here that the ball should be stopped, and it is much less necessary that the man who has it should be floored; while, on the other hand, it is highly desirable that the tackler should remain on his feet to be of assistance to his side in further disposing of this threatening advance. If the orthodox low tackle were made, and the man and not the ball constituted the chief objective, it is just possible that he would be able at the last moment to get in his pass, and in such an event the tackler would be a man lost to his side, with practically no compensation, for the opponent brought down would have done his duty, and the situation would have become more menacing than ever. In such circumstances, therefore, one need have no hesitation in giving the advice to tackle high and tackle for the ball.

In this chapter of the proceedings of the man with the ball, one will naturally say what has to be said about kicking —place-kicking, drop-kicking, and punting.

Beginning with the place-kick, it has to be stated that, as every player who has cultivated this speciality in the game knows very well, skill is only acquired as the result of the

BALL PLACED FOR AN ANGLE PLACE-KICK

BALL PLACED FOR A PLACE-KICK IN FRONT OF THE GOAL

TYLER'S PLACING OF THE BALL IN WET WEATHER

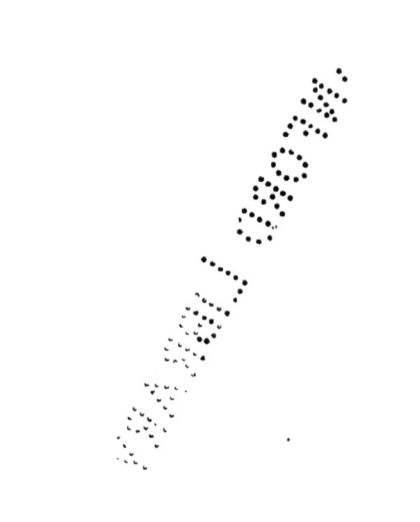

most assiduous practice and close observation. The practice which a player may get on the field in company with his colleagues is not by any means sufficient. The unerring accuracy and deadliness of Wallace's place-kicking, splendidly illustrated in the course of our British tour, have been justly admired; but does anyone suppose that these great qualities were born in him, and that they have needed no cultivation? One might just as well imagine that the man is born who can make a hundred break at billiards without undergoing any course of practice and self-improvement. Wallace indeed has made a complete science in itself of the place-kick, and he is still constantly prosecuting his studies of it. He spends much of his time in kicking to a point from various angles and with different directions and velocities of wind, with the result that he has now come to an exact determination as to what is the best position to place the ball in the conditions of wind and weather that obtain at the time. Too many place-kickers give but a very superficial consideration to these most important matters, and thus their effort, of such vast importance as it is, is often made a very casual kind of affair, from which any good that may come is not by any means devoid of the element of luck. One would like to see more conviction on the part of the place-kicker that he knows exactly what to do, and is assured on the most solid reasoning that he is doing the right thing and the one which is more likely to bring about success than any other.

A player who aspires to honours at place-kicking had better make a long series of experiments for himself, instead of attempting to learn the art from printed instructions; but it may be well, by way of giving a foundation to work upon, to indicate briefly how Wallace places the ball. In the photographs we have the positions for place-kicks under different circumstances. The usual way of placing the ball for an angle kick is lace upwards almost flat upon the turf, as shown in the first of the three photographs. In this case, as in the others also, the kicker is supposed to be standing on the right of the photograph and to make his kick from that direction. When he is running to the ball he keeps his eye fixed very steadily upon it ("keep your eye on the ball" is a maxim that applies to place-kicking in Rugby football with the same force as in different features of other games) and kicks it fairly and squarely in what he considers to be the dead centre as it is presented to him. It will be seen that the position of the ball for this standard angle kick is eminently adapted to getting in a good solid kind of kick that will shoot the ball straight along like a torpedo, and give it just the necessary amount of steady rise. It is always essential that the place-kicker should have a man to place for him who has been trained for the job and has most carefully practised his own special duties. For a kick almost in front Wallace has the ball placed for him as in the second picture—rather tilted up at the end nearer to him. It is evident that in such a case as this, when you are in front of the goal and not any great distance from it, that much driving power is not so essential as a quick rise, and the placing of the ball as in the picture is eminently adapted to attaining this end.

A quite unorthodox way of placing the ball for a kick directly in front is shown in the third of the illustrations. It was introduced by Tyler during our British tour, and it met with wonderful success, for only one goal was missed in eight attempts. As the picture shows, the ball is laid on the ground oblong to the kicker, and the latter really spoons the ball with his instep when he is making his kick. The entire purpose of the double peculiarity of this particular place-kick is to ensure certainty, and it is a method which may be specially recommended when the day is wet and the ball is greasy. One gets a better grip of the ball, and the tendency to skid is reduced to a minimum.

To be constantly successful in the matters of direction and length, drop-kicking also demands the most careful practice. The ball, of course, must be kicked at the precise

THE PROPER WAY OF HOLDING THE BALL PREPARATORY TO PUNTING

THE PROPER WAY TO TAKE THE BALL ON THE FULL

moment of its coming into contact with the turf, and it may be taken as a general rule that it should be dropped gently and smoothly from the hands of the kicker, and in such a way that when it reaches the ground it may be in the same position as in the second of the illustrations for place-kicking.

Punting, when the ball is thrown forward slightly and kicked before it reaches the turf, is the style of kick best adapted for finding touch and for sky-kicks which are meant to be followed up, and are therefore of the variety which give plenty of notice and plenty of time to all concerned. The ball is propelled forward or upward by the application of the instep. By practice and a careful observation of the results of your different kicks, you will find that it is possible to get a spin or curl on the ball something like the swerve which some bowlers can put on the cricket ball.

CHAPTER VII

WORKING THE SCRUM

Seven forwards in the scrum—The British formation—Advantages of the New Zealand system—The Wedge formation—Particular places allotted to each man—Particular qualifications—The hookers—The lock—A heavy man wanted—The side-row men—Two fast men in the back row—How they all push—Pressing towards the centre—One foot behind the other—The resultant of the seven forces — Immense driving power — One of our secrets—Waste of power with the British formation—Facilities for getting the ball out quickly—An open line from the front to the back—Quickness and cleanness—Backs run off their legs—The necessity for the wing forward—The half could not get back in time after putting in—Referees in doubt—Alleged bias on the ball—An absurd suggestion—How the hookers hook—How we screw the scrum—The British system—A comparison—Advantage of the man holding the ball between his knees—When our forwards "heave"—When the back-row men break away—Opponents prefer the scrum to the line-out.

ONE of the chief principles of our New Zealand system of Rugby football, and one in which we found it to differ very materially from the game as played in the mother country, is the seven forward scrum. We believe, and indeed after our recent experiences we are overwhelmingly convinced, that our formation of seven is infinitely better than any formation of eight, and that, given anything like equal skill and strength man for man, the seven will beat the eight every time in the scrum.

By way of preliminary, we will call our readers' attention to the diagram presented of the formations for the scrum according to the New Zealand system, and according to that which was chiefly in vogue during our campaign in England. It will be seen that in the case of the English eight there are three men in the front row, then two men in the second, and

— British Scrum. —

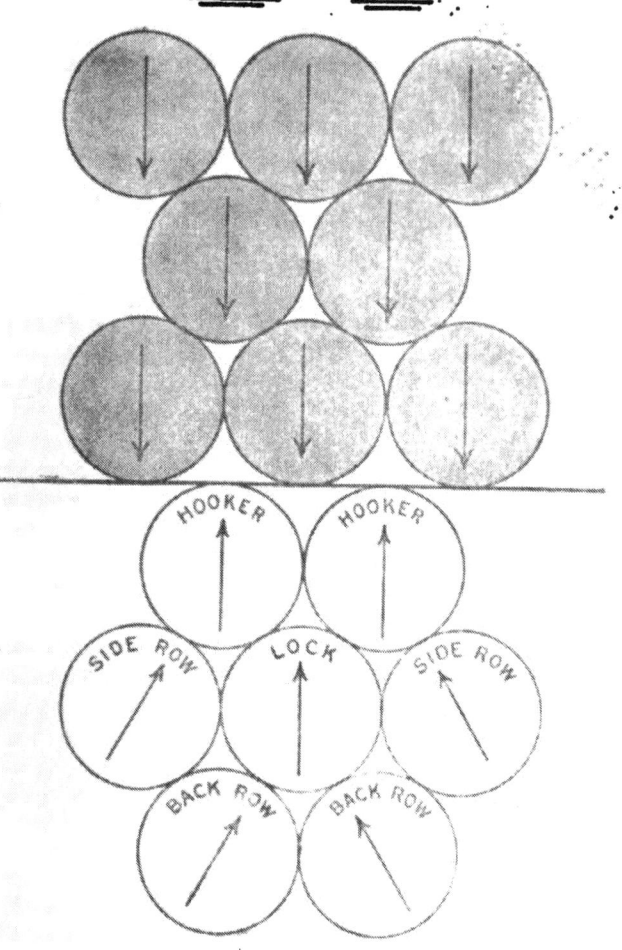

— New Zealand Scrum. —

three more at the back. In our formation there are two men only in the front row, three men in the second, and two at the back. At a casual glance it might appear that the former is the more powerful machine; actually it is far from being so. English footballers may have imagined that their scrums of eight were constructed on scientific lines, and that the strength of the forwards was well applied for the purpose of achieving the object in view. From our present point of view it is a clumsy construction, involving an immense waste of power, with an enormous tendency to become loose and ragged; while in one essential particular it is as if it were specially designed to defeat the chief object of scrummagers —to get the ball out on their own side quickly when the time is ripe.

On the other hand, our formation is made, as we maintain, on the most reliable scientific principles, so that in conjunction with the special method of using it not an ounce of the available strength of our seven is wasted, but every pennyweight is applied to the very best advantage. The evolution of theory and practice in regard to the scrum in the Rugby game has been very slow but sure, and in view of the way in which popular systems have been upset in the past and proved to be fallacious, one has naturally some hesitation in suggesting that perfection has at last been reached, and that there is little more room for development. Yet one is bold enough to believe that we have almost reached the ultimate point in the development of the scrum formation, because theoretically and scientifically it seems so excellent as to admit of no alternative, and because in practice it has proved itself to be immensely superior to any other.

Now let us describe in detail the construction, shape, and the method of working of what we call the Wedge Formation, because it operates as a wedge driving through the opposing mass, and never has such opportunities of doing so as when confronted by the standard British eight formation with three men in each of the front and back rows and two sandwiched in the middle. For the sake of the complete understanding of this important characteristic of our New Zealand game, we will give in full detail the names and the functions of each man of the seven. It should be said that whereas it commonly happens in England that the eight forwards take their places in the scrum more or less haphazard, and as it occurs to them to be convenient at the moment, our seven have each their own particular places allotted to them for the day, and always take those places. A man is chosen for each particular place according to his physical characteristics and the features of his skill, and we hold it as of great importance that particular places should be occupied by men of particular build. We want tall men in one place and short men in another, and it would weaken our system if the men in these places were to be interchanged.

The two men in the front row we call hookers. They are shorter men than the others; but are thickly set, with stiff bodies. They have all the necessary qualifications of a good forward in that they are speedy and of fine stamina, and in addition they are expert at hooking the ball, the very cleverest men we have at getting it out quickly and cleanly from the scrum. They have ways of their own of hooking the ball, of which something will be said shortly. Immediately behind these hookers, in the second row and between them, is he whom we call the lock man, who is likewise an expert for his position. He must be above all things a heavy man, anything from thirteen to fourteen stones, and he must be as strong and muscular as he is heavy. His duty is to hold or lock the two hookers compactly together with an arm round each, and he must be able to screw or wheel the scrum. In Cunningham and Newton we had two really fine lock men during our tour, Cunningham having rather the advantage in experience. While it has been suggested that each man in the scrum keeps to his posi-

HOW THE HOOKERS (ON THE LEFT) PLACE THEMSELVES IN THE SCRUM

SHOWING THE HOOKERS IN THE ACT OF HOOKING OUT THE BALL

tion for the match, some of the men may change their places from day to day; but we regard the offices of hookers and lock as being so essentially those for experts only, that we never change the men occupying them except in case of accident, as in our match against Cardiff, when, one of our hookers having his collar-bone broken, the captain relinquished his duties as wing forward in order to take his place. He did so because he had had much experience as a hooker at home. The men on each side of the lock man we call the side-row men, and the qualifications that we demand from them are that they shall be tall men, good strong scrummagers, and above all that they shall be fast—considerably faster than the hookers or the lock—and able to break away smartly. In the back row of the scrum we put two of the fastest forwards and two of the best collarers that we can find. We call them our two "deadly tacklers." Those are the seven.

Now, if the diagram is examined closely, and particular attention is paid to the direction in which each man pushes, the true significance of the Wedge Formation will soon become apparent. Each man pushes so as to get the maximum of his power applied to the blunt point of the wedge as represented by the shoulders of the hookers. In the English system the eight men push forward, with the result that there is inevitably a considerable amount of waste, as we shall show. In our system only the hookers and the lock man exert their strength in a line direct ahead; the others press in from the sides so that every ounce of their force shall be driven home to the centre point and concentrated there. They stand, not with their feet level with each other, as one usually sees the men do in the case of other formations, but with one foot behind the other. The right-hand man of the side-row pair applies his left shoulder to the right-hand hooker in front of him, and when he does so he throws his left foot forward and the right foot behind it. He is thus in the most advantageous position possible for pressing his hooker up with every ounce of strength that is in him. In the same way the left-hand side-row man applies his right shoulder to the hooker in front, throws his right foot forward and the other behind, and he also is then able to press towards the point to the best effect and with no waste.

Now take note of what is happening at the same time in the back row. The back-row men may touch their side-row colleagues, but they do not apply any pressure to them. Their whole strength is applied to the lock man in precisely the same way that the side-row men apply theirs to the hookers, that is to say, the right back-row man puts his left shoulder to the lock man, and while he throws his left foot forward he puts the other one behind it, and the left back-row man presses the lock with his right shoulder and gets his right foot in front of the left. Thus we have the hookers pressing forward and the lock with them, the side-row men press on the hookers, and the back-row men push against the lock, and it could be demonstrated conclusively by dynamics that the resultant of all these forces is one force almost equivalent in magnitude to the full extent of the combined seven, being directed in a straight line through the middle of the wedge to the hookers, who thus, and with their narrow width, press forward when necessary with immense driving power, which is certain to be too much for the loose formation of three front men as practised on English sides.

Now in these words we have told for the first time the secret of the success of our Wedge Formation—a secret which baffled all who played against us, and which every man in the team was sworn to preserve until we had played our last match. Those who saw the formation, and realised its effects, were still unable to understand it or how those effects were achieved, and when the more enterprising of our opponents flattered us by trying it for themselves they got no good from it. They could see the arrangement of the seven men; but what they could not see, and what we would not tell them, was how and where each of these seven, but

HOW THE SIDE ROW MEN IN THE SCRUM PACK THEMSELVES AND APPLY THEIR POWER
IN DRIVING. IT IS THE RIGHT-HAND SIDE ROW MAN WHO IS SHOWN IN ACTION. NOTE THE POSITION OF THE FEET

particularly the side-row and the back-row men, applied their force towards one common centre. Gwyn Nicholls could not understand it. He told us one night after we had finished with Wales, that they had practised our formation but could get nothing from it, and then we gave the secret away to him and Winfield, who was with him, and they saw it at once. Of course English and Welsh sides who tried this formation without the full knowledge naturally pushed straight ahead, as their instinct and experience told them to do. The result in such cases is that the side-row men are rendered next to useless, for while their own force when applied straight forward on the hookers is much less than it ought to be, the back-row men also pushing straight in front are pushing the side 'men out, so that the latter almost entirely lose their hold on the hookers. With our Wedge Formation the push straight ahead is an absurdity which can lead to nothing but quick disaster, and we are not surprised that our opponents who copied us were more mystified than ever after doing so. But even with the formation of eight that we had against us the push straight in front is surely a mistake. There is nothing in the nature of a common centre—only several straggling, uncontrolled forces, with a great waste of power through the side men in the front row being pushed out by the middle row. We believe, and think all others believe when they understand it, that our scrum formation has no equal for driving power, and that with seven men, equal to eight on the English system, it cannot be improved upon.

There are, however, other substantial advantages derived from our system. One of the foremost of them is the splendid facilities that are afforded for getting the ball quickly out of the scrum as soon as the opportunity is presented. Now just compare the English formation with ours, and see how much easier it must be for the ball to be sent cleanly through after it has come into the possession of the front-row men. In the case of the English formation there is no clear passage through the middle of the scrummagers, and the ball has to find its way in a haphazard sort of fashion through an entangled collection of legs. With our formation, however, there is a clear and open line from the front of the scrum to the back, with the result that the ball may be shot out with lightning-like rapidity once the hookers have gained possession of it. Behind them is the lock man with his legs wide apart, and the back-row men are on each side, so that there is absolutely nothing between the hookers' feet and the half who is waiting in the rear for the coming of the ball. Quickness and cleanness in getting the ball out of the scrum are absolutely ensured by this system. We believe in this quickness and cleanness as an essential feature of our game, because we have fast backs who would be wasted in standing about. We desire to get every ounce of ability out of them, and this can only be done in the way we have indicated. As it is, on two occasions during our tour our backs were run clean off their legs, so smart was the work in the scrum. At such times we are constantly attacking, and on several occasions when playing British teams we were attacking in our own line. In New Zealand we would never think of doing such a thing, because, as we have forwards and backs of equal calibre who play the same game, it would be altogether too risky, and likely to lead to very different results from those that attended our efforts in England.[1]

This formation and the working of it make it impossible for the ordinary half to be utilised satisfactorily for the purpose of putting the ball into the scrum, and so this duty is delegated to the much-discussed wing forward, whose office was undertaken by one of the present writers in our tour, and about which we shall say something later. Such is the lightning-like rapidity with which the ball is heeled from the scrum and sent out clear at the back, that on a majority of occasions the half who put in the ball would certainly not have time to get behind to receive it; whereas in the slow and, as one cannot help saying, clumsy English system the half has time to saunter round and make himself comfortable before the ball comes out. We think that this simple circumstance of the ball coming out so quickly, so very different from the manner in which it comes out from the English scrum, has been the cause of exciting suspicion in the minds of referees as to whether there may not be some illegal practice somewhere, with the result that they have come to a determination in many cases that the ball must be thrown into the scrum unfairly. The first time when a British referee officiates in a match in which we take part, he cannot understand it. In the English scrum the ball winds about, and sometimes does not come out at all; with us it is shot out like a bullet. But after refereeing in our matches two or three times, the official mind is brought to realise the situation fairly, and after such experience referees have admitted to us that they then understood the whole thing perfectly, and that any suspicion which they might have entertained at the outset had been removed. Mr. Percy Coles for one, and Mr. Gil Evans for another, admitted to us that they came to understand and fully appreciate our methods. It has usually been suggested that the particular form which our unfairness[1] takes is through some wonderful bias being put on the ball, which curls it round to the feet of our own men. How this idea originated one cannot say. Someone was searching for an explanation, and invented this one as there was no other forthcoming, and such very original ideas have a way of spreading. One must confess that in a whole career one has never heard anything so ridiculous, so palpably absurd, as this suggestion that the ball is given unfairly to our men by bias being put on it when it is thrown into the scrum, because one holds it to be quite impossible to do anything of the kind with a Rugby football. Some marvellously dexterous person might possibly be able to put screw on the ball by holding it shoulder high and throwing it straight down on

[1] My "unfairness," I should say, since I am the wing forward who put the ball into the scrum.—D. G.

its end, so that if everything went off properly it would bounce in the desired direction on reaching the ground, but we have never seen it done, and we have certainly never attempted it ourselves. If we had done, of course we should have been penalised immediately, as such a fault would have been so glaring as to preclude even the argumentative discussion that has taken place over this question of the alleged bias.

There is another feature of the work of our forwards in the scrum that calls for explanation, and to which must be attributed much of the quickness with which they heel out the ball when they have obtained it. In Britain it is the custom to hook the ball in the scrum with the outside feet crossing over those on the inside. We, on the other hand, always do our hooking with the inside feet, and to our mind there cannot be any question as to which method is the more advantageous. When the ball is hooked from the outside, a very insecure hold of it is obtained, and it is most difficult to direct it with any precision, so that it goes wobbling about everywhere. When you hook with the inside foot you get the first hook, and with our formation the hooker gets it with his heel or by the buttons, and it goes straight away. This method is now universal in New Zealand. C. Brady of Auckland initiated it, and he taught it to Tyler, one of the expert hookers of our recent tour. Our hookers get their bodies low down and practically horizontal, with their legs stretching well out behind them (see the photograph of the method), because in this position they find that they can give a very much longer sweep with their legs when hooking the ball out than when they take a more erect position. This largely accounts for the speed with which the ball is shot out.

Our method of screwing the scrum differs from that which is practised in the home of the game, and we have always found that our way has been warmly approved by those who have been made to understand it. When we

THE SCRUM
(NEW ZEALAND v. MIDDLESEX)

WORKING THE SCRUM

decide to screw the scrum instead of letting the ball go clean out of it, the lock man gives the word. At the same time he dips down and picks the ball up between his knees, and he retains it there until the screwing movement has been completed and he is clear of the scrum, when all he has to do is to let the ball drop and go ahead with a rush, the side-row men following him up and all combining to the best advantage. As soon as the word is given to screw, the back-row men bring their feet together to prevent the exit of the ball, and the lock man, who has the ball between his knees, throws his arms clear of the hookers and grasps the side-row men. This is done in order to facilitate the movement, for the lock man in his endeavours is then helped by the two front men, who pull their opponents' scrum round in the opposite direction to that in which they (the screwers) desire to go, while at the same time the two side-row men push and pull him until he is clear and away with the ball. The scrum formation on the attacking side breaks down the middle, and the back part goes off with the ball in the usual manner.

In the British system the ball is usually got into the back rank, and while keeping command of it on the ground the three back rankers gradually work round until they are clear of the scrummage, and start a loose forward rush with the other forwards following in the rear. In such a case the opposing wing forward, if there was one, would naturally come round to that side where the screw was being attempted, and would try to hamper his opponents, which he would often succeed in doing, since the movement is so slow. In Britain our backs were always told what was going on, and got ready for it; even our forwards were able to do the same. On the other hand, our screwing movement is so quick that the other side has no time to do anything to upset the scheme, and we certainly think it is the best known way of screwing and keeping command of the ball at the same time. There is, we admit, much to be said for the British style, but its most fatal defect, apart from its slowness, is that it is so easy to lose command of the ball. The scrummers so seldom know exactly where it is, when it is all-important that they should know. In our case, when a particular man has always the ball between his knees, there is obviously never any doubt as to where it is, and the four other men who break away with the lock from the scrum can complete all their arrangements for the immediate future because they are quite safe in this knowledge. When the ball is on the ground one can never be certain.

As a rule we only resort to this screwing when the day is wet and we are on the defence. It is then a safer game than the other. It came off very well for us in the second spell of our match against Surrey, which was played on a very dirty day. Still it is good for a change, and is generally a safe form of defence.

There are one or two other points in connection with our scrumming on which one must lay some emphasis. It was said by some of our critics that we never seemed to be pushing very much. That is on account of the way in which we go into the scrum; and partly because, with our formation much movement would be difficult and is not wanted. As a matter of fact our front-row men, who have a very hard time with this formation, rarely do much pushing. The only time when they really do so is when they lose the ball altogether, and then you will hear the word given to "Heave!" and the whole seven at once try to heave themselves over the top of the ball. There is certainly pushing then. On many occasions our scrum, with its immense driving power due to the Wedge Formation, has pushed itself clean over. Pushing is all very well in its way when it is necessary, but it seems to us that there are some things in connection with scrumming that are more important than this, and we cannot help thinking that the English eight scrum, when it is doing its best in pushing, is very much inclined to lose command of the ball.

WORKING THE SCRUM

Another point of tactics in connection with our formation, is that in the case of possession and an attack by our opponents the two back-row men at once break away to whichever side the attack is coming from, and help the backs in collaring. They never need to be told to do so; they do it mechanically, and it is a feature of their play which is of immense importance.

Many English clubs against whom we were pitted preferred having the scrum to the line-out. We don't know whether they did this with the mistaken idea that we ourselves have a preference for the line-out. We certainly have not, as we are usually satisfied with our prospects in scrumming, but we believe in giving our forwards a little breathing space sometimes when there is an opportunity, and the line-out comes in very conveniently in this way. We particularly noticed that when Bedell-Sivright's team came out to us they took the scrum every time in preference to the line-out, for the simple reason that they never attacked from the line-out. These tactics particularly suited the New Zealanders, for we had a very strong set of scrummagers in who practically pumped their forwards out. We don't know whether one ought to say it, but our forwards always seem to me to be more eager, to follow up better, and to do a far greater amount of work—back work as it might be called—than the majority of those we encountered on our British tour. In England it seems to be considered unorthodox for a forward to take part in a passing movement or initiate an attack from a line-out, but we believe in our forwards being as quick as the back division in taking the ball; in fact we drop behind three or four forwards for a kick off to take the ball and help the backs in many respects. We hold it as a principle that the forward should be nearly as good a kick as a back, and that he should be able to take part in a passing rush if called upon to do so at any stage of the game. In our play when a back is not there to take the ball from the man who wants to pass it, it is given to a forward, and anyone who cared to look at the number of tries that were scored by forwards in our tour must be convinced of the soundness of the system. At the same time it is an unwritten law in our Rugby code that if a forward is dribbling the ball along, and he sees that a back has a better chance of getting through, he must immediately pick it up and send it out to him, a course of procedure from which a score is the direct result on many occasions.

CHAPTER VIII

THE WING FORWARD

His duties—A thankless task—An unprepared public—British teams must try him—A surprise—Our usual game—The origin of the wing forward—Arneil and Mackenzie—An earnest pupil—Variations in different parts of the colony—The spare man—A matter of names—Inevitable errors—A necessity to a system—The commission given to the winger—What the half back tries to do—Too late—Qualities necessary in a good wing forward—He should be tall and fast—Keen eyes—Good at reckoning up a situation—When the ball comes out at the side of the scrum—Ready to receive it—As to obstruction by the winger—No basis for argument—An addition to the science of the game—The winger makes the game faster and not slower.

A CARDINAL feature of our game, one which is practised to the uttermost in every match in our country, and one which we do not hesitate to say is to a very fair extent responsible for our success over fifteens that do not practise our methods, is the commission given to one player to act in the capacity of what we call a wing forward. His duties involve the utmost responsibility, for his side looks to him to nip in the bud an attack by the opposition when the ball has come out on their side of the scrum; but for a variety of reasons his task is a very thankless one, and it was never more thankless, or really unpleasant, than in the case of our tour through Great Britain. This chapter on the wing forward is a very personal matter with one of us, because, as has already been said, the captain was the man to whom the duties were delegated during this tour, and he fulfilled them throughout, and, as we think, with some fair measure of success.

In the course of our tour it very soon became evident

that the British Rugby football public, never having practised the system themselves, and inevitably suffering considerably from its practice by opponents, were very far from being prepared for such an innovation, and would require much educating to it. At the conclusion of the tour they were not so educated; but despite all that they have to urge against the system at the present time, we have a very complete measure of confidence that if any of the "All Blacks" have the happiness to pay another visit to Britain in a few years' time, they will find that the much criticised winger will by then be a permanent institution. Some British teams are sure to try him forthwith unless there is special legislation with a view to his extinction, and it is quite certain that those teams will reap an immediate and direct advantage, with the natural result that their opponents will be obliged to adopt the same tactics.

We will explain where the wing forward came from, what are his special qualifications and functions, and we will justify him according to the rules of the game as they exist at the present time. Despite the fact that the British knew little or nothing about this idea, the great hostility that was shown to the winger came as some surprise to us, and one cannot help thinking that it was unfair to suggest that we gained our success in this manner through the adoption of tactics which were contrary to the spirit and the rules of the game, that in fact we came out for blood and were going to have it at any price, with the result that in this particular we deliberately sailed as close to the wind as we dared, and often much closer than we were to be permitted to do. Most decidedly we had never any idea of hoodwinking the referee, as was freely stated. We played the game that we play every day at home, and which every other New Zealand team plays and has played ever since one can remember. The only difference is that we played one winger only, whereas in many cases in New Zealand two are commonly played.

The wing forward is simply a detail of the natural

THE WING FORWARD

development of the New Zealand game in the direction and with the object of the greatest possible economy of speed and power in the team, and for the purpose of exercising the full measure of its resources in every contingency. We have already shown how in the scrum we have, as the result of years of thought and practice, arrived at a formation and a working of it which result in a great economy of power, and the maximum application of our resources. We have given the same study to every other department of the game with good results, and cannot admit that in the case of the English, Welsh, Scotch, or Irish game there is not at the present time a great deal of waste.

In a previous chapter we mentioned that Mr. W. W. Robinson relates how, when captaining a team of Auckland against Canterbury so far back as 1876, he played two wing forwards, and even then the idea was far from new to him, for he says that he noticed in his school-days that wing forwards were very useful in a fast team when it was not desired to keep the ball close. From that time the wing forward became part of the system of the game, and a few years later it was developed to a very fine point of perfection by J. Arneil of Auckland and W. Mackenzie of Wellington. They were much the best exponents of it, and the captain of the "All Blacks" learned his own game by studying their methods and watching them closely at every opportunity, though he never had the luck to play against Arneil. In the North Island of New Zealand we play two wing forwards, and have only one five-eighth, but in the South Island we have one wing forward only and two five-eighths, playing on the same system as we did in our tour. In some of the provinces the functions of the winger vary slightly. For example, in Otago he is employed as a pusher in the back row, breaking away when his time comes.

The wing forward comes as the natural result of the formation of seven in the scrum. In comparison with the

British scrum formation, there is a forward to spare, and one supposes the question would arise as to what was the best thing to do with him. We answer the question by converting him into a back, as he really is, though we give him this other name, and we cannot help believing that, if when we first came over we had relinquished this name, which is strange on this side, and simply called our winger a half back, there would have been little or no objection to him. As we called him a wing forward, it was taken for granted that he was part of the scrum, and this mistaken idea was never eradicated. He is not part of the scrum; to all intents and purposes he is a half back. The Welsh, English, Scotch, or Irish half is a wing forward every day he plays. We can say without fear of contradiction that these men have been offside or overrun the ball when playing against us just as often as our winger did, not with any idea of wilfully breaking the rules, but simply because of their ignorance of the precise situation at the moment. With the best and fairest of intentions, and the utmost desire to adhere strictly to the letter of the law, it must happen that the winger and the half back must err through ignorance in this manner, and when they do so they accept the inevitable penalty with a cheerful heart.

The wing forward, playing just the game as he played in Britain, is an absolute necessity to our system; without him our scrum formation with all its admitted advantages would be largely wasted. In this country it is the rule for the half back to put the ball into the scrum and then go behind to his proper place in readiness for its coming out. He has plenty of time to do so. But if a half back, playing the ordinary stereotyped British game, were to attempt to do so when his scrum was working with our formation, he would find that he would never be behind in time. With our scrum the ball comes out so quickly after being put in that it is absolutely necessary that the man should be waiting behind to receive it at the very instant that the scrum is set in action.

Therefore we keep our half ready, and we give a special commission to the other half, whom we call the winger. We appoint him to put the ball into the scrum, and thereafter we charge him with the special duty of giving the closest attention to the opposing half with the object of pouncing down upon him instantly and frustrating his plans in the event of the ball coming out on that side.

Taking their legal status for granted, as we have no other option, the advantage of these tactics must be apparent at once when compared to the system in operation on this side. What our winger does the English, Welsh, Scotch, and Irish half back has to try to do. If the ball is going out on the other side he has to try to get there to prevent an attack; but he is so circumstanced that he starts on this endeavour with a heavy handicap and very rarely succeeds. For one thing, he is bent down and cannot see what is going on, and very often the ball is out on the other side before he knows anything about it—or at least it would certainly be so if his opponents were playing with our two-three-two scrum formation and the hookers knew their business. Moreover, even if he were given any notice of the impending turn of events in this direction, he has to wheel round the scrum, and arrives on the other side in a state of semi-bewilderment at a time when every quarter of a second sees an important development in the situation. He is too late; time and a man have been wasted, and the penalty has to be paid. He may be equal to the emergency, and the system may be wholly satisfactory in the case of the tedious three-two-three scrum formation, but he is hopeless with the other. The fact of our winger having always been accustomed to playing against our own scrum formation, as well as with it, is sufficient explanation for his constant anxiety always to be up and on the opposing half at the first sign of danger, and with the eight forward formation in the scrum this anxiety may often have been needless, and have led to his overrunning the ball and unwittingly breaking the offside rule. But our opponents' halves sometimes make the same mistake, as they are bound to do.

The qualities necessary in a good wing forward are that he should be a tall fellow with a fleet pair of legs, and generally alert and nimble. A short and thickly set player would be at a disadvantage in many obvious respects. Moreover, he must have a very keen eye, and should be a good judge of reckoning up the probabilities of a situation in a scrum. Unless he is such a judge, and is agile enough to act upon the instant that he sees his anticipations are being fulfilled, he stands a fair chance of being beaten when two front-row hookers have sent the ball clean through.

The wing forward is also the man indicated to deal with another emergency, as when the ball happens to come out at the side of the scrum. He is then ready to receive it, and having done so he is in a position either to dribble it away, and initiate a forward attack if the circumstances are inviting, or to pass it to his half or to the three-quarters. Here again his speed and alertness are the essence of his position, and unless he uses them to the full advantage he will be a disappointment as a winger.

Apart from the other phase of the objections which have been lodged against him in this country, there has been some controversy in the English press upon the legality of his situation from the point of view of obstruction. We do not think that this objection has any better basis than its brother, for we contend that if a wing forward has one foot behind the ball he is on-side, and no argument against him in such a position can possibly hold.

When he is a good man in himself, and the game is being played on the New Zealand system, the value of the work of the wing forward cannot be exaggerated. When we finished our tour we feared that the British crowds and players had still but a very imperfect idea of the possibilities, and even the necessities, of the position. The latter could never be completely demonstrated unless our opponents were

THE WING FORWARD

playing the same game as we were. Moreover, we think the winger adds considerably to the science and the general interest of the game. And instead of retarding its progress in any way, as suggested by some critics, that is to say by making the game less open, we are still of the opinion that with the opportunities afforded him in his particular position, everything must point to the exactly opposite view being held by anyone who has thoroughly studied all the phases of wing-forward play.

CHAPTER IX

PLAY FROM THE LINE-OUT

Possibilities not realised—What we did with the line-out in Britain—Too limited idea of the possibilities of forward play—Two situations when we do not attack from the line-out—In our own twenty-five and when the weather is wet—A simple and effective method of procedure—Mistake of putting the scrum half to throw in—One of the short hookers is the man to employ—The unmarked man—Not difficult to obtain in practice—Attackers do not need to mark men—Everything in their favour—The unmarked man knows he will receive the ball—Others in ignorance—How the men are disposed—The gap between the thrower-in and the other players—Attackers make the gap to their own size—The scrum half and the unmarked man—The unmarked man may go off with the ball if permitted—The usual course of procedure—A pass to the scrum half—Something that referees do not always understand—An attack upon stereotyped lines—Tries scored with backs standing still—Where the attackers lead others must follow—A lively form of attack—The Gap movement—Pure bluff—How it is worked—The open space—The wing three-quarter who is ready to rush in—Others in ignorance—The ball thrown short—A fast sprint—A good example by an over-eager three-quarter—A limit to tactics of this kind—A puzzled opposition—Defence on the line-out—Tactics for the time—The loose ruck—Heeling out the ball—A man to the good.

IT has been borne very strongly upon us that the possibilities of well-organised and most effective attack from the line-out are by no means properly realised in Britain. To us, indeed, the attacking movement from the line-out has become a well-developed and favourite system, and as we have brought it to some state of perfection we have profited immensely by it. In England it seems to be the rarest thing to have a passing movement properly and intentionally begun from this point; the usual course of procedure is a forward rush from which anything may or may not happen, the whole situation being dealt with in a very haphazard

PLAY FROM THE LINE-OUT

sort of fashion. On the other hand, one need only mention that in our tour we scored no fewer than thirty-three tries directly from this definite passing attack from the line-out. It appeared that British teams came to realise how formidable were our manœuvres in this respect; and we could not help noticing, as we have already said, how they took the scrum in preference to the line-out time after time, presumably on account of some apprehension as to what might happen if they had chosen the other alternative. And yet they never tried attacking on these lines for themselves. It becomes particularly clear to us in this connection that British players have a too limited idea of the possibilities of their forwards. They allow it to stick in their minds that forwards are there only to scrum and to dribble, and as long as they go on with this understanding they will continue to throw away numerous golden opportunities.

There are practically only two kinds of situation in which we do not attack from the line-out in this manner. One is when we are in our own twenty-five, and the opposition are therefore within striking distance of our goal line. On such occasions we make the line-out a purely defensive movement, as it is obvious that anything else would be altogether too risky. Such a defensive movement will be considered presently. The other case is when the weather is wet, and the ball as a consequence is slippery and difficult to hold. As a necessary preliminary to such an attacking movement as we shall speak of, is that the ball shall be thrown some distance out and then passed by hand, it is evidently a rather risky proceeding when it is difficult to hold. On such occasions, therefore, we play a quite different game, make the line-out very close, and play pretty much the same game as would be played by a British side in the same circumstances.

But when the day is fine and our own goal line is safe, our method of procedure is quite different and is as simple as it is effective. Two players are usually the chief factors in the inception of the movement—an unmarked man and the scrum half. They begin things, and the rest follows in due course. In England the scrum half is usually delegated to do the throwing in. This is a mistake. Nobody is or should be better able to institute an attack of any kind than this individual, and it is a waste of his valuable time and services to put him to the task of throwing in. Our plan is to give the ball to one of our short hookers as some kind of a short rest for him from his very arduous labours in the front row of the scrum.

For very good and obvious reasons the unmarked man is for preference a tall man—he can reach the ball so much more easily than others—and even if he becomes so surrounded that he cannot obtain possession he may still pass it back to one of his colleagues. But, it may be urged, you must first get your unmarked man, and it may be suggested that in the majority of cases this will be an extremely difficult thing to do, and is certainly not a performance that is to be relied on as something approximating to a certainty. In actual practice it will be found that it is to be depended upon, and when the situation is studied an explanation for this being so is not difficult to discover. It may be taken for granted that the side that throws in, having such an advantage to begin with, is the side that is going to do the attacking, and the opponents will accept this as the natural and proper state of affairs. Well, then, this side wants an unmarked man, and there are various members of the team who are more or less stealthily contriving to become that man. It naturally follows that the opposition, when they have a knowledge of the kind of game that is being pursued, do their utmost to see that no man is left uncovered; but at this game of hide-and-seek there is an enormous advantage in favour of the hiders, and it is almost an impossibility unless the men are clumsy to prevent one of them being successful. As they are the attackers, they have no object in marking the men on the other side. It does not matter in the least to them if the whole team is left uncovered; the ball will not go to them. It would indeed be much better if many of these opponents were left unattended, since in that state they could not be pressing their attentions on members of the aggressive side. The attackers have, therefore, no need to watch the other men, and their entire attention may be taken up in watching the hooker, who has the ball in his hands and is about to throw it in. A man in doing this can tell intuitively when he is being shadowed by an opponent. Without taking his eye off the man with the ball, he always knows when an enemy has crept up to him. In the same way, through the corner of his eye, he can always see where there is an open space which is very likely an ideal situation for him, and it is the easiest thing for him to become the occupant of that space while still keeping his watch on the man with the ball. Despite the manner in which we have declared its methodical certainty, it may still appear to those who have not attempted this procedure, that there must be something extremely doubtful and speculative about the obtaining of this unmarked man, and one can only leave a trial to bring the conviction that words may fail to do. It must be remembered that the shadower has to—or feels that he must—watch the ball and the man too, and in the double attempt he becomes more or less bewildered, while at the supreme moment, when the thrower-in is about to do his work, instinct prompts him to give his undivided attention to the ball.

A man having by the exercise of his manœuvres become so entirely unmarked has some considerable confidence that the ball will come to him. Throwers-in realise the situation as well as anybody, and when they are men who know their business they never miss opportunities. The unmarked man sees the thrower-in look at him,—only they know that the glance was interchanged between them,—and the next moment the ball has passed from one to the other. Even in this process there is a great advantage to the attackers. The unmarked man knows that the ball is coming to him, and that he has only to stay where he is in order to receive it; but he is the only man who knows exactly where that ball will drop when it is first seen leaving the hands of the man on the touch-line. In the first moment of its flight through the air it is impossible for any man without definite information from the sender—as the unmarked man obtained—to say where it will come, and by the time it has gone so far that some exact idea on this point can really be formed it is too late to do anything in the way of molesting the man for whom it is then plainly intended. It was meant for him, he has it, and there is now as a rule nothing to prevent him from putting the attacking machinery into motion in the usual manner. Everything is ready, and one should take a glance now at the disposition of the attackers.

The unmarked man is probably from fifteen to twenty yards out from the touch-line, and between the thrower-in and the nearest of the other players there is a considerable gap. It will be realised that the attackers have the option of making this gap as large or as small as they please, since where they lead the opponents, having to mark their men, must follow. From the point where the gap ends, and from the unmarked man, the whole forward line extends right out to mid-field, and the backs are in order. In immediate proximity to the unmarked man who has obtained the ball is the scrum half, who now becomes the foremost man in the calculation of the movement. As a matter of fact the ball has really been meant for the scrum half all along, but it would never do to make a practice of giving it to him, inasmuch as it would quickly be seen through, and the half would then naturally have the greatest possible difficulty in getting himself unmarked. The task would indeed be impracticable. Instead the scrum half makes it his business in this preliminary manœuvring to watch for the man who does become unmarked, and who is evidently the one designed for the ball. When his expectation seems about

LINE-OUT PLAY
(NEW ZEALAND v. DEVON)

MOBY I.A

PLAY FROM THE LINE-OUT

to be realised, he gets himself in attendance on the tall man, and he is invariably in close proximity and ready for action when the ball comes along. Now, if when the ball reaches his hands the tall man finds that he is still unhampered and has a clear way in front of him, he may very possibly and not at all improperly be tempted to make off with it himself and do the best he can, being assured of complete support from the whole of the attacking line. But it will usually happen that opportunities of this kind are not very excellent, and so he ends his duty for the time being by receiving the ball and passing it to the scrum half. Without looking about him he knows that the latter is at hand and waiting, and, turning about, he passes the ball on to him without delay. Often it happens that at the moment of the ball coming to him he is threatened with being pressed, and this is one of the cases where his tallness is an advantage. Reaching high up he does not attempt to seize the ball, but simply knocks it back with his hand to the scrum half,—a proceeding, by the way, which, not being used to it, referees in this country are often disposed quite wrongfully and illegally to penalise. We have had some very promising movements stopped at the beginning in this most aggravating manner.

The preliminaries having been arranged in this careful manner, the rest is easy, and is to be explained in a very few words. The scrum half is in possession, and the remainder of the back division are in readiness for attack in the usual way. It then proceeds upon stereotyped lines. So simple and easy is the business, that we have constantly seen the ball passed from the half to the five-eighth, from him to the centre three-quarter, and then to the wing three-quarter, while all these men have been standing quite motionless, and the attack has been wound up with an easy score. The basis of the whole business is that where the attackers—the side having the throw-in—lead others must follow, and the movement is all the easier when the opposing side have not had much experience in combating it. After a time they may be able to mark their men more effectually, but there is always an advantage to the attackers, and this is one reason why we so regularly choose the line-out in preference to the scrum, another being that it is a much livelier form of attack and serves to keep the game fast and open.

There is a variation of it which calls for mention, which not only is effective in itself, but serves to make even the standard method of play just described more certain through adding to the confusion and doubts of the opposition at the time that the throw-in is being made. It is what we call the Gap, and is a bluff movement pure and simple, and one which has been astonishingly effective. The preliminaries are exactly the same as in the other case; indeed, it is a condition of success that they should be. The attacking forwards and backs line out in exactly the same manner, and though care must be taken that it is not done at all ostentatiously, every effort should be exercised to make the gap between the touch-line and the first men as wide as usual, and if possible a little wider. There is the usual shuffling and marking of men, and everything points to the ball going right out to one in the line in the usual manner, and as a matter of fact the attackers out there are themselves unconscious that any other movement is in contemplation.

Now the Gap movement consists in a realisation that there are opportunities for utilising this blank, unprotected space between the touch-line and the bunch of players. Is there no means of getting a man into that nice open place all by himself, and thus giving him a fair start with the ball? It is clear that this is not practicable with any of the men who are forming part of the line that goes out to mid-field. If any of them attempted to come in closer, he would, of course, at once be attended by one of the opposition, and the only result would be to embarrass the whole situation. A little stealth on the part of a wing three-quarter does all that is necessary in the circumstances. This winger comes up

ANOTHER GOOD EXAMPLE OF PLAY FROM THE LINE OUT

PLAY FROM THE LINE-OUT

quietly fairly close to the touch-line, but some yards in the rear of the spot from where the throw-in is to take place. In this situation he is either unnoticed, or, if he is noticed, no dark designs on his part are at all suspected, since he is apparently quite out of it for the time being so far as receiving the ball from the thrower-in is concerned. It will very likely happen that even the men on the attacking side are fully expecting the ball to come out to them, and to be received by an unmarked man according to the system already set forth, so that it is no wonder that in such circumstances the delusion is very complete and effective.

What happens then is very simple. There is probably an exchange of glances at one moment or another between the thrower-in and the three-quarter. It may appear to be very casual and commonplace, and there would be nothing whatever in it to excite the slightest suspicion, and nothing would ever be farther from the minds of the opposition in these circumstances than that this momentary look backwards down the field could have any meaning in it. It will have been arranged, however, between the man with the ball and the three-quarter that the glance, or some particular and quite unobtrusive signal, or both, shall indicate that the Gap movement is going to be attempted. Then the three-quarter takes stock of the situation, gathers his wits about him, and prepares for a fast sprint. The man with the ball throws it in. Even until it is on its way the men on the line-out are ignorant of the ruse that has been employed, and before they fully realise the state of affairs the Gap has succeeded or the plan has failed. The thrower-in, instead of sending the ball right out, simply throws it short into the open space, and at the psychological moment the three-quarter whips in, takes the ball and dashes through with it, the opposition not having time to get up and interfere even if they discovered the dodge earlier than they usually do.

The diagram will show very explicitly what the Gap movement is, and advantage is taken to present an actual case, and the further progress of the three-quarter is indicated. This case occurred in the International match against Ireland, and the three-quarter who came into the Gap and took the ball with him was Smith. It was a most remarkable run, and would have resulted in a score that counted instead of the obtaining of only a "moral" try, if it had not been for the over-anxiety of the workman to make his work quite perfect. Smith was in the Gap and past the line of his own and the opposition forwards before they knew what had happened, and then, being threatened by the Irish three-quarter bearing down on his right, he swerved off to the left and raced past him at top speed in close proximity to the touch-line. It might have been dangerous in the circumstances to have attempted to veer round towards the goal posts very much before crossing the line, as there was the full back to fear, and so Smith crossed the line not far from the corner flag. Being then unattended and going at headlong speed, he retained the ball and swung himself round with the idea of planting it behind the goal, which he actually did; but the pace he had on him and the sharp twist that was necessary resulted in his just stepping over the dead-ball line in coming round, and so no try was scored, much to the discomfiture of our adventurous three-quarter. Although there was no try, it was the most admirable example of the successful working of the Gap movement.

Now there is obviously a severe limit to the number of times that tricks of this kind can be worked in a match. A side must be satisfied with one performance if its opponents were previously aware of its nature, and even if they were not, twice in one match should be considered an excellent day's working for the Gap. After that the enemy know too much, and the wing three-quarter may have no passage through. But apart from the advantage that may be obtained directly through the regular Gap movement as described, it will have an influence beneficial to the attackers on the occasion of every line-out through the whole of the

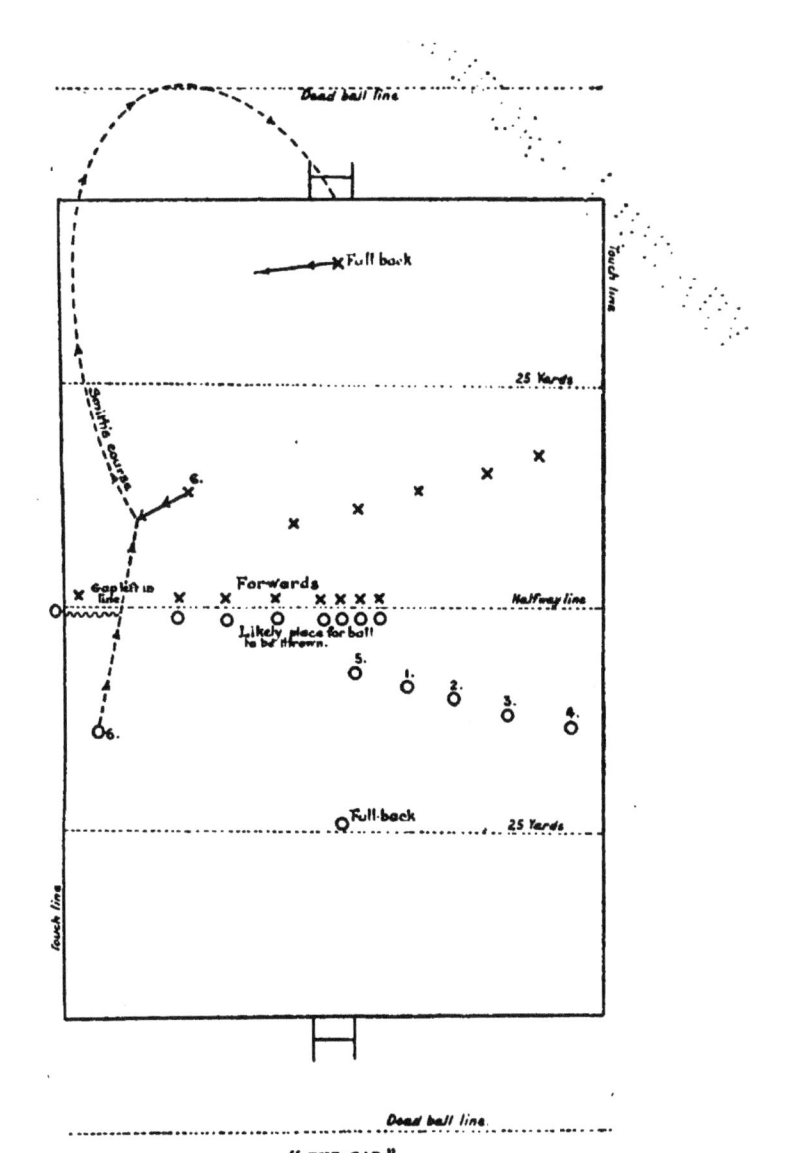

"THE GAP."

match, and this influence at times is so strong that scores may result from it. The point is that a successful ruse of this kind has a most demoralising effect upon a beaten enemy, and they are prone to be nervous and uncomfortable every time that a line-out comes to be played. In the first place they were beaten through the ball being obtained by an unmarked man and an orthodox passing movement among the backs being instituted. Now they find that their search for unmarked men is time and trouble thrown away. Next time they don't quite know whether they shall continue to look for unmarked men or close up the Gap. Probably they will decide on a half course, with the result that more men are left unmarked than the attackers have any need for. Thus, whether it is Gap or no Gap, the introduction of this most doubtful element into the situation has made the task of the defenders an exceedingly difficult one, and the result is the scoring of some very soft tries by the attackers. It was in this way that Johnston in our match against Cornwall brought about a try which was too absurd for anything. He simply received the ball and walked with it right between the goal posts. Tries were never meant to be scored in that fashion.

The case has to be considered where the line-out takes place within the twenty-five of the side having the throw-in. The situation here is evidently critical, and the object must be to prevent the opposition from taking possession of the ball and opening out the game. On the part of the side with the throw-in the movement then should be purely one of defence. We have not seen other sides adopt the same tactics as we do in these circumstances. We have found them very successful. Our forwards play closer to the line than when we are attacking from the line-out, and they arrange matters so that they get one or two of their own tall men in front of them. The others stand directly behind. One of the tall men receives the ball, and as soon as he does so it is either put down and they try to rush it through, or, in the event of his holding it, they push him through in front of them with the object of crashing right through the defence. In such circumstances a man with the ball always has an advantage, and by this method the hopes of the other side are most effectually frustrated.

What we call a loose ruck, generally in front of the touch-line, must be spoken of. It represents the disordered state of things occurring, for example, when an opponent, a back, has slipped and stopped the play when trying to block a forward rush. One man is down, and all his other colleagues in the back division are induced to come up to his assistance. In such a case it has been our policy to enter this ruck with the particular object of heeling out the ball. Our backs are all ready to strike if we can do so, and when the ball is duly heeled out the scrum half sets them going and they are off, not the least important considerations in this situation being that we are a man to the good numerically—one of the others being down—and that all the other backs are out of place.

CHAPTER X

ON TACTICS IN GENERAL

Nothing like good tactics—Mere combination is not tactics—A refinement—The need for study—Hall or class-room is a good place for the purpose—Dummy players—Tactics not rules—The need for novelty—No finality to the study—Good to study the old tactics and adapt them—Trifling changes afford complete alternatives—Great variety of tactics wanted—Special methods for special occasions—Forwards must be good—Tactics spoiled when front rank is weak—On pulling a match out of the fire—Everything to be sacrificed to attack—Playing a gambling game—All possible play wanted out of the ball—Every forward must become a back—Course of procedure when points up—Every man is a defender when time is approaching—The high kick up the field—How the taker may be hustled—On a wet day—Backing up—Insuring against accident—Extra confidence given to the man with the ball—A little drudgery, but it pays—On clinching an attack—All possible energy and resource wanted at the last moment—Full back who goes to the three-quarter line—When the wing three-quarter is jammed on the touch-line—Man in attendance an absolute necessity.

IT almost goes without saying that tactics are as the soul of Rugby football. Nothing in the world pays a team so well as the accurate performance of sound and sensible tactics. Individual brilliance is a beautiful thing to see, but it never wins a match on its own account. You may have a team of stars, but if they have no tactics among them, they may, and very likely will, be beaten by a fifteen who could at best only be described as a good average lot but who are the happy possessors of a bookful of carefully studied tactics. And in this connection nobody must imagine that mere combination is tactics, as is so often done. The combination is assumed; and the tactics are a refinement of it. By tactics, as has been suggested, a team which man for man is far below the strength of its opponents, may accomplish a fairly easy victory. By tactics, fourteen men, having had a colleague injured, may overcome the full fifteen of their opponents ; and by tactics again a side that has been playing a losing game, and is in a bad plight towards the end of the second spell, may still pull that game out of the fire. When it is once understood that there is a severe limit to what is possible by individual effort, or to combination in its elementary forms, there will surely be more attention given to this most valuable study of tactics.

One would, therefore, earnestly recommend every club to insist upon every member of its team giving the closest attention to this study, and it is essential that to be of any use they should be studied in each other's company. And, mind, the field of play is not the only or the best place for this study. There is nothing like a class-room or hall, or any private apartment, where in close company, in comfort, and in cooler blood and a more thoughtful mood than are usually associated with the opportunity for chasing a ball, the problems of attack and defence may be carefully considered. A team that wished to make the best of itself would have one night set apart for meeting in every week, when it would consider the possibilities of a game from every point of view. On such occasions it would be found that dummy players of some kind would come in very useful for the clear elucidation of the various problems and movements. Black and white skittles placed on the floor, or men on a chess-board, serve the purpose well; and there should be a blackboard and chalk at hand to drive home more quickly and plainly the meaning of any movement.

While in this chapter and the two that immediately follow it, we shall endeavour to point out what are the main features in our own system of tactics, it must always be remembered that tactics are not rules, and that they depend for their value, and even for their very existence, on their novelty. When your systems have been in long use, and your opponents know them so thoroughly that they can safely anticipate them, there are no tactics at all in the matter, but merely certain forms of combination, or perhaps not even that. Therefore there can be no finality whatever to the study of tactics, and the methods which are to-day regarded as the most brilliant, and which are the most constantly successful, may be obsolete in a few years' time. One must always be searching for some new construction, some new movement, the very ingenuity of which will flabbergast the enemy; and the side which has most of these will be the strongest. At the same time, one must take account of past experience in this matter, and there is no such way of inventing new tactics as by the close study of old ones. If any wise footballer at the beginning of his first-class career were to make a practice of committing to paper after every match a record of some kind of the best and most successful movements that were introduced into it, with explanatory diagrams, and kept this up until his football days were no more, this reference book by that time would be the most valuable thing that any club could be possessed of, that is if the said club were intelligent enough to place it to proper account. Study the tactics of the old masters, and then adapt them to modern conditions; make some trifling alteration that will have the effect of completely transforming the appearance of the whole method without interfering with its effectiveness, and you have new tactics which will be outside the calculations of your opponents.

It is wonderful what a trifling change will do in the way of furnishing a most complete alternative to an existing system of play. In many cases — some of which shall be explained in due course—the missing out of one man in the passing movement, and the passing of the ball to the man next but one to the passer, will throw the whole of the defensive machinery of the opposition out of gear, while making no perceptible difference in the working of the attack. It is such little subtleties as this—things that seem almost too trifling to set down and carefully explain in print—that count for everything in the gaining of the upper hand in a hard-fought match; indeed, it must always be remembered that tactics do not mean complications, but that rather are the simpler tactics the better. But though the simpler the better, it is not a case of the fewer the better also. The greater variety that a side possesses in its recognised movements, the greater are its chances of springing surprises on its opponents. It may play one set of tactics on one day and another on the next, and it may reserve a few peculiar movements for use only very occasionally. Such a side will be a constant embarrassment to all others that have to meet it. And, of course, it will have special tactics for special occasions. One kind of game will be played when a very powerful enemy is feared, and another one when it is realised that the opposition are only strong in a certain department; while a different kind of game will be played on a wet day from that which is played when it is fine. Every variety of circumstance must be carefully considered by the team in concert, and an almost equal variety of tactics should be stocked for use as opportunity suggests.

In laying down a few general principles as a preliminary to the explanation of a number of tactical movements which may be taken as models, one would like to say at the outset, with reference to the constitution of the team, that while tactics serve to get the very last ounce of ability out of a side, and will often enable a team to triumph over another which on paper is its superior, we consider it highly essential that the forwards should be more of a real fighting pack than they are generally required to be. In far too many cases we have noticed shocking neglect in the choice and cultivation of the men of the front rank. The prevailing idea seems to be that anything is good enough for a forward, and that you put in this department all those men who are not thoroughly capable for any other task. Our principle is that every forward should be a potential back, and in the team that toured through Britain there was not a man in the pack who could not have fulfilled the duties of a back, if emergency had demanded that he should, with credit to himself and to his side. What we particularly wish to emphasise is that you cannot be tactically successful when you are faced with the knowledge that you have a pack of forwards who have some good shoving power in them, but who beyond that are worth very little. The best backs in the world are absolutely helpless in such cases, and their degree of helplessness is in direct ratio to the inferiority of the forward division. No tactics will make up for such weakness, and we would rather not consider the case in which a team with such a poor pack wants to win its match against a side that is strong in this department.

Whenever you begin to teach a man anything about tactics, or to impress him with their importance, he is sure at the very first opportunity to put the blunt and elementary question, "How can we pull a match out of the fire?" By this he generally means that he wants a prescription for winning a match which in its closing stages shows a debit balance to his side. They are points down, and there is not much time to go. If there were a reliable panacea for this all too-frequent malady, the game of Rugby football would be a very queer business. Still, such a crisis is essentially the time for tactics; but one can only express some more or less obvious truths. For example, the first thing for the side to make up its mind upon is that things could not be worse than they are at the time—that is, if they are really several points down and there are but a very few minutes left for play. To all intents and purposes that side is then well beaten, and yet it is wonderful how stubbornly some sides decline to accept this as the state of affairs, or how, on the other hand, they seem helpless in it. Mind, not for one moment would one ever recommend a team to give up a match as lost; hope must ever be the part of the Rugby footballer, and the side that ever loses all of it until the whistle has blown for its defeat is a poor thing at its best. But what the side must realise is that its present methods are beaten, and that nothing but an enormous upheaval of its own game can be of any use in the circumstances. When the men realise this, and make up their minds that things could not be worse, and that absolutely everything must be sacrificed to attack, something may be expected. A gambling game must be played.

If you are ten points down and there are only five minutes to play, what is the use of hesitating to put a bold plan into operation because it may fail at the start, let in the other side, and result in the addition of another three or five points to that adverse balance? That consideration is not of the slightest importance, in view of the fact that the scheme may come off and would then result in a gain of the three or five. Practically you are no worse off fifteen points down than you were when you were ten; but you are very much better off only five points down than you were when ten. You are then within a single successful effort of making a draw of it, and you will have effected a considerable moral gain as well. Therefore, one would say that in proportion as you are down take more risks and bigger ones. Sacrifice everything to the last chance in attack.

In such difficulties as these it must be remembered that you want to get all the play out of the ball that is possible. Time is all-important, even though it has been the case that the longer the game has gone on the more points you have lost. You cannot be winning while the ball is out of play or in the middle of a scrum. Therefore, do everything possible to keep the game open, and avoid scrums as much as you can. Forward play of the ordinary sort must be practically done away with, and every forward must become a back. Let every individual in the team be given an opportunity to score.

The course of procedure in the opposite case—where a side is a point or two ahead shortly before the termination of the game—is plainly indicated. The enemy will be attacking with the very open game which we have just been advising, and that will have to be combated by every means in the power of the side that is points up. Every man will become a defender. The ball should never be thrown in far from the line-out. The forwards must be got to bunch up close from the line-out with a couple of the tallest men in front to take the ball, and the others closing round to rush it ahead and prevent at any cost the other side from gaining possession. The backs will play nothing but a defensive game. When they get the ball, if they see that they have nothing, or practically nothing, to gain by running with it or passing, they will gain touch by kicking it as far as they can down the line.

One of the points to remember about attacking is that when a kick has to be made up the field it is best that it should be a high kick. At the first glance it might appear that the high kick gives a better chance to the opposing defence; but a careful consideration of all the pros and cons of the case will make it plain that the advantage is with the attacking side. When the kick has been made, the whole team go rushing up, and in such circumstances there is a considerable chance of the taker being so hustled or hurried that he may misfield the ball. Also, the taker may wait for the ball to bounce,—generally a very bad thing for him to do, but a practice which is quite common in Britain,—and in that case the attacking side may get possession instead. Never play any tricks with the ball. Make sure of it while you have the chance, particularly if the situation is at all critical. A moral on this point was written very largely in our match against Cardiff. Especially may attackers be recommended to kick high and follow up quickly on a wet day, for then the chances of the taker misfielding are very much greater than usual on account of the greasy state of the ball. It is obvious that for all this kind of thing the side that has poor forwards is at a great disadvantage.

As one of the last of these preliminary words of generalisation, but not by any means the least important, let every side put in the forefront of its system of tactics the rule that every man engaged on an important movement to which the least degree of risk attaches, shall be backed up by a colleague to whom he may appeal for assistance in taking the ball from him whenever it should become necessary for him to part with it. We never played a match in which our players were not thus guarded, and our gain from the precaution must have been something too enormous for calculation. It is perhaps not too much to say that fifty per cent. of the attacks that fail could be made successful by a backing-up man in attendance to the player who lost the ball. All kinds of accidents happen on the field even to the cleverest and most careful of players, and these should always be insured against by backing up. It is not only that when a mistake is made there is someone at hand to retrieve the position, but that the very knowledge that he is being backed up gives the man with the ball an enormous amount of confidence in which he would otherwise be lacking, and when a man has such complete confidence his play is twice as good and has twice as much good, solid devil in it as it has when he is unattended and unsupported. Even on the simplest occasions this backing up should take place. When a back is taking the ball from a long kick up the field, there is every reason for having another man almost at his elbow. One is obliged to say that backing up of any kind is very poorly done in Britain, and that the English people particularly must learn that it is no good inventing fine tactics if you are not going to take reasonable and proper precautions that they shall not come to grief through neglect of this sort. If it were a business enterprise, and it was one to which you attached so much importance as you do comparatively to a well-meant and carefully thought-out attack on the football field, you would "make sure." Well, then, make sure on the football field. It may mean a little trouble and drudgery for different members of the team from time to time, but it pays.

ON TACTICS IN GENERAL

Many attacks which are well meant and well developed in their early stages fizzle out in the most disappointing manner at the last moment, through a seeming inability of the side to grasp adequately the needs of the situation and to press home their advantage with all their energy and all their resource, to clinch it when the time is ripe. This is to say that the importance of an unusually big effort all along the attacking line at the last second is too often not realised. It is part of our New Zealand system that the attack shall be at its strongest just when it is about to be completed, and that in its ultimate stage there shall be less left to chance than in its early period. With too many sides it is all chance at the finish. To illustrate our meaning, we may say that it is a point with us that, unless the risk is too great, the full back generally goes forward to the three-quarter line and makes a fourth three-quarter of himself, when it is seen that with a little extra effort there is a likelihood of the attacking movement proving successful. Either on the outside or inside of the wing—but generally the former—he is invaluable as a last man to take the ball in a passing rush. In this way Wallace has scored tries for us on many occasions. Of course it is a risk, and it is one which we might not be disposed to take so often in our own country as elsewhere; but it frequently pays. In this and other ways the British back play, as we have seen it, seems to lack initiative and a proper appreciation of its scope for usefulness. The importance of the finishing touch is not realised.

Take another point. How often do you see what looked like a promising attack fail miserably when the ball reaches the wing three-quarter after travelling all along the line, because he is jammed on the touch line and is in a helpless state, with the alternatives of kicking the ball out of bounds or being collared with it? What is a crying necessity in the situation is a man close up to whom he can then pass back, and who in turn will pass along the line again and so keep the attack swinging along. It will constantly happen that when the three-quarter finds himself in this predicament there is only the back in front of him to beat, and if he had another man of his own side in attendance on him the scoring of a try would become an exceedingly probable event. But the man being absent, the whole movement is quashed. In our system the man is always there, and as the result fewer chances are squandered. In our suggestion of neglect in this matter we make an exception of the Welsh teams, who decidedly give far less away in this matter than any others we saw in Britain.

CHAPTER XI

TACTICS—COMBINED ATTACK ON THE OPEN SIDE

The standard form—Diagram explained—The need to gain a man—The functions of the inside five-eighth—Takes stock of the situation—Scrum half instructed by code word—How the scrum half receives the ball—Ball taken at top speed—Attitude of the defence—Probabilities of the situation—The opening for the attackers—The next pass—The importance of not passing too soon—An alternative in defence—Adaptation of the attack—The man gained—The advantage to the attackers—Setting a trap for the defence—Useless passing without gain of ground—When the five-eighth cuts in toward the scrum—An adventurous movement—When unnecessary it can only be justified by success—The other backs mere spectators—No rule against it—Prospects of success—A tight corner—Possible help from the wing three-quarter—A lob pass under difficulties—When he opposition know too much—Leaving the five-eighth out of the movement—A dash round by the scrum half—Better on the blind side—An alternative—A pass direct from the scrum half to the outside five-eighth.

BEGINNING the study of back tactics in attack, the first thing to consider is what may be called the standard and correct form of a combined attack on the open side of the scrum and initiated from it. To make our meaning quite clear on the various points, we will refer the reader right away to the diagram "Standard Form of Combined Attack on the Open Side." Here you have a scrum formed near the middle of the field, and the chief human factors in the situation as they affect our argument are indicated by O's for the attacking side and by X's on the other. To each man, for the sake of further lucidity, we have given a distinctive number, and to tax the memory of the reader as little as possible, and to make it all the easier for him to follow these diagrammatic explanations, we shall adhere to the same lettering and numbering throughout the series. Therefore we may state at the outset that in these diagrams O_1 and X_1 stand for the opposing inside five-eighths, O_2 and X_2 for the outside five-eighths, O_3 and X_3 for the centre three-quarters, O_4 and X_4 for the wing three-quarters on the one wing, O_5 and X_5 for the two scrum halves, and O_6 and X_6 for the two other wing three-quarters.

It does not happen that the forwards or the full backs constantly enter so particularly into the calculations of these movements as to necessitate their being distinguished by a number. By the time the full back is reached, if everything has worked out properly, the attack has been virtually completed—as, for example, when two of the attacking side have the ball between them and only the back to beat. And here at the outset let it be said that it is the chief aim and object all through these various movements that we shall describe to secure the advantage of a man in this manner, as we suggested in the early chapter on the idea of the game. When by skill and strategy this advantage in numbers can be gained, the question of further progress is reduced to a certainty; but while there is no advantage to it in this way, a side is either dependent on the mistakes of its opponents or on the individual skill of one of its own men—both very uncertain quantities at any time. Well, now, we will see how we may gain our man in the simplest and most general form of attack from the scrum—a form which is practically devoid of ruse.

It is assumed, of course, that the ball is heeled out of the scrum on the O or attacking side, and it is received at once by O_5, the scrum half who is lying up close to the scrum, and is there, as his name denotes, for the specific purpose of acting as intermediary between the forwards and the backs, who are ready to strike. At this moment O_1, the inside five-eighth, who, in the ordinary course is the next man to come into the attack, finally takes stock of the situation and particularly the disposition of the opposing backs,

"Pass" shown thus ⌇⌇⌇⌇

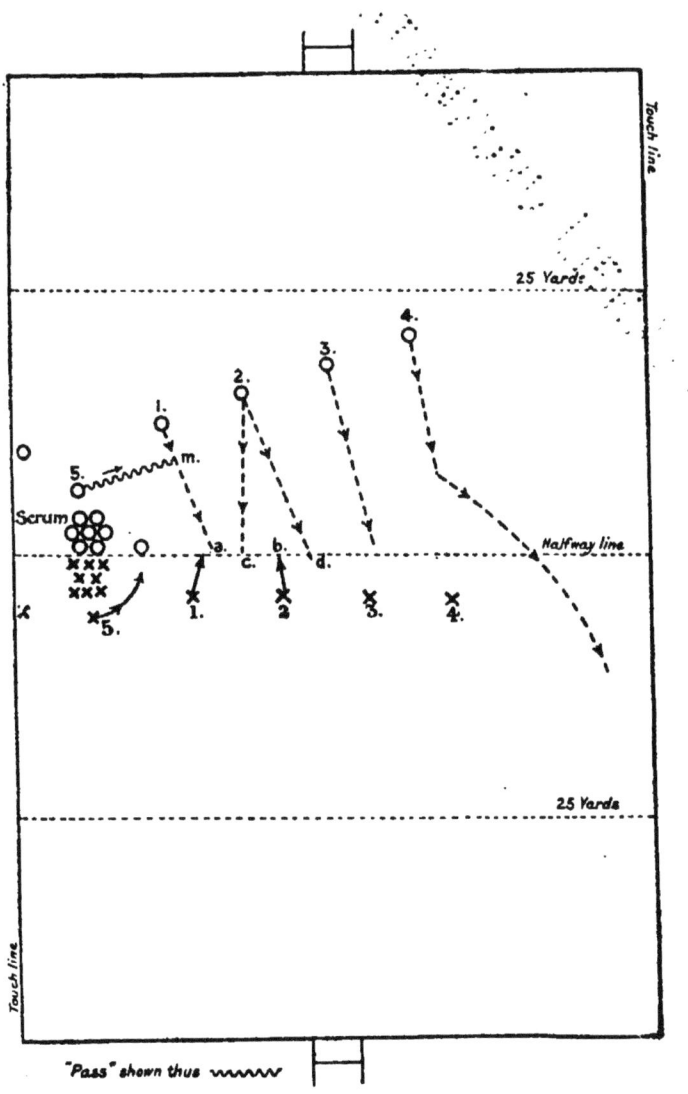

STANDARD FORM OF COMBINED ATTACK ON THE OPEN SIDE.

COMBINED ATTACK ON THE OPEN SIDE 149

and by code word passes on to the scrum half any instructions that may be necessary in the circumstances. Generally both sets of backs at this time will be disposed very much in the order set forth in the diagram, and, in the absence of any special instructions, the ball is transferred from the hands of the scrum half to those of O_1, the inside five-eighth. But in the meantime, in anticipation of the pass, O_1 has put himself in motion, and when he receives the ball is going at top speed in a direction rather off the straight line, to the left. Time being of the essence of a smart attack, it is quite essential that O_1 should thus have set himself off as soon as he sees the ball reach the hands of the scrum half, and the latter, when making the pass, has to make allowances for the fact. Therefore he does not pass right back to what was the original position of O_1, but to some yards in front of it on the line that he knows he will take—so much in front that O_1, racing up, takes the ball at full speed at the point m, without any break whatever in his pace. This also is essential.

The defender who now regards O_1, the man in possession, as his objective, is naturally X_1, who faces him, and it is inevitable that O_1 must draw X_1 on to him. In the ordinary course their point of meeting will be somewhere about a, and while this is being brought about O_2 has been making his preparations for the next phase of the attack, in which he will be the chief performer. His own particular enemy is X_2. The probability is that X_2 will make for a point about b, and is already doing so, so that he should be there by the time that the collision takes place at a. In such an event the obvious opening for the attackers is at the point c, and accordingly O_2 dashes for this point at top speed. At the moment of the collision at a O_1 passes the ball to his colleague.

It has already been emphasised that these passes must not be made until the passer is actually in the preliminary stages of being tackled, as we have regularly observed them to be made in Britain. The importance of this advice is made more manifest from an examination of the attacking situation which is now unfolding itself. If O_1 is in too much of a hurry to get rid of the ball, and passes before X_1 is actually on him, the defender, if he is a smart man, can change his course in the last instant and bear down on the point c, with the most disastrous results to the attack. So far from the attackers having gained an advantage of a man, they will have virtually lost one, for O_1, having made his effort, will be out of it for the moment, while O_2 is being threatened in two places. But when O_1 has deferred his pass until X_1 has come down on him, he has made certain that his opponent has been put out of action. Man has been lost for man, while the attacking movement has advanced a step and O_2 has at any rate no other dangers to face than he expected to have.

What may happen afterwards can best be explained by setting up the alternative—practically the only possible one—to this opening of attack by the pass from the scrum half to the five-eighth. The challenge direct from X_1 is certain, but it is not so certain as to what course will be taken by X_2 in the exercise of his judgment. In the first case we supposed him to make for b, and if he had done so and O_2 had received the ball in safety, the latter would have had a fair chance of whipping past him, with the other backs following him up in full cry. But what if X_2 had instead been tempted by O_1 to make for the point c, as it is quite possible he may have been? In that case O_2 changes his course, and instead of making for c swings round to d, where he waits for the pass and confidently expects to receive it in the same way. The pass may be rendered more difficult through the interception of X_2; but it is generally quite practicable, and when it comes off a great gain has already been effected, for both X_1 and X_2 will now be virtually out of action, and O_2, O_3, and O_4 will then be left with opposition only, so far as the three-quarter line is concerned, from X_3 and X_4. Thus a man has been gained, and though a little smart work

COMBINED ATTACK ON THE OPEN SIDE 151

may be necessary to solidify the advantage, it is undoubtedly there, and in the proper working out of the remainder of the attack a try should be scored. Of course, in reckoning the outcome of paper tactics in this manner, one assumes a machine-like working such as is the ideal of every combination, but which is seldom absolutely obtained, and it is not the place of such theory to take account of human errors and weaknesses which constantly go to the upsetting of the plans and the prevention of the tries which, as in this case, we say should be easy. A theory of this kind which made allowances for flesh and blood, to say nothing of temporary stupidity on the part of some one or other, would not be worth the enunciation.

Now, what was accomplished when the two defending five-eighths were drawn on to the one attacker and still failed to stop the pass, must be done at some other point in the attacking line in the event of X_2 proceeding in the direction we originally marked out for him to b; and, without going into the long list of possibilities and probabilities, it is sufficient to say that the chances are strongly in favour of these two men being drawn to one if the passes are properly done and the backs know their business, if only because there is always the great advantage to the attackers of possession of the ball, which counts for everything. Sooner or later in their desperation their opponents will be driven to this double assault, or will fall into a trap carefully set for them by one of the O's, having for its specific object the attraction of two X's to one place. The easiest trap of this kind for an O to set, and one that he sets constantly, is to dash along a line which may leave a couple of X's in doubt as to which of them is by way of being challenged, and it usually happens in such circumstances that the defender puts it to himself that he should be "on the safe side"—and they both go. In any event, as each of the O's is threatened, he passes on to the one farther on his left, and all the time ground is being gained, and the opponent's goal-line being neared, so that the prospects of success for an individual effort are momentarily increasing. It is the passing at the last second, just when the opponent thinks he has made sure of you, that is bound to tell sooner or later, and which results all the time in gain of ground. When the pass is made earlier, the ball goes from one man to another and on to the next without any such gain having been made, and the result is that when the ball gets to the end of the line things are no better, or very little, than they were at the commencement. It is no use passing the ball right along the line parallel to the goal-line.

Now, there is a variation of this back attack on the open side which calls for mention at this point, although one is not quite happy in describing it as a variation at all. It is something done by O_1 when he receives the ball from the scrum half which puts the game into his own hands, and it may either be done because of a reckless determination on the one hand, or because there had been a slight hitch in the earlier part of the proceedings which would make it considerably difficult for him to go on with the orthodox passing movement. The case is when O_1, having received the ball at m, instead of going straight on with it as he was shown to do in the first diagram, executes a cutting movement and works in again towards the scrum. O_1 does this cutting either because he is possessed at the time of a very large belief in his own individual ability and wants adventure, or because the movement is forced upon him through the pass from the scrum half having been rather late, with the result that he had to slacken speed to take it, and found himself in imminent danger of being surrounded. In the latter event, of course, he is doing everything for the best; but when he voluntarily embarks on this expedition in search of glory, it is impossible to defend his action in any other way than by the plea that after all it is a variation, and variation is nearly always good. But when O_1 cuts away to his right in this way and faces all manner of dangers, he utterly destroys

"Pass" shown thus ⁓⁓⁓⁓

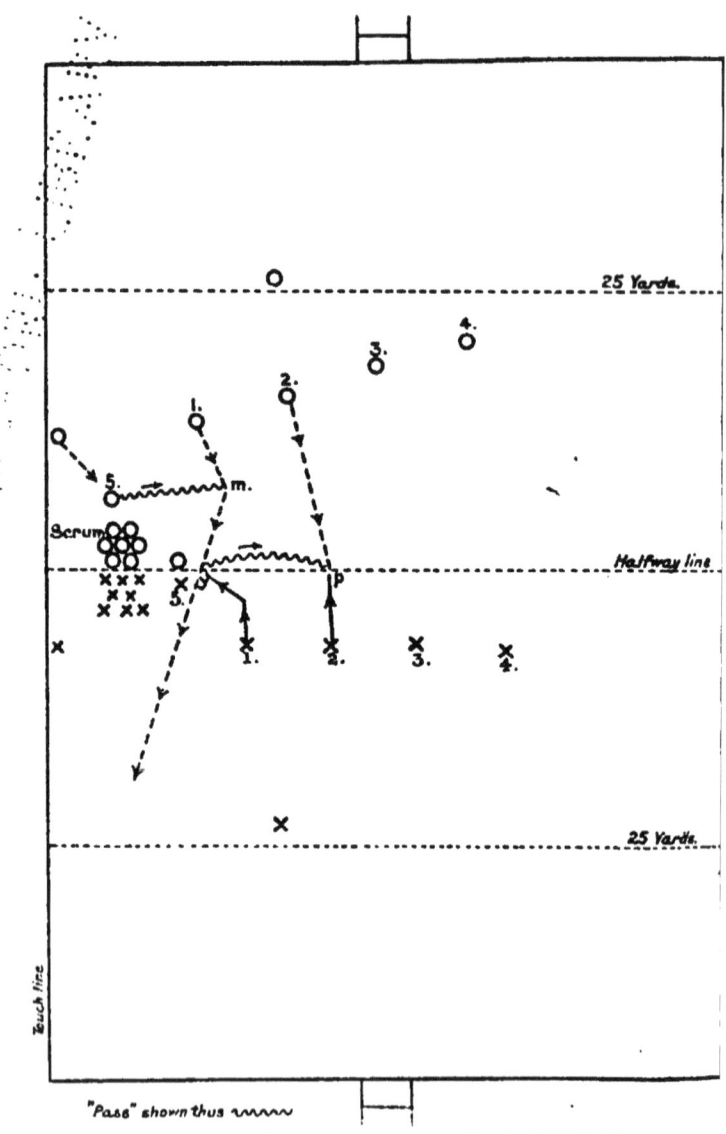

FIVE-EIGHTH'S VARIATION OF ATTACK BY CUTTING-IN.

COMBINED ATTACK ON THE OPEN SIDE

every possibility of combination. The other backs find themselves mere spectators for the time being. Consequently one must lay it down that, while accepting with reservation the plea that it is a variation and passing the matter over in silence if it succeeds, the only possible justification of this movement is success. The man who makes it must take the responsibility for it, but one would not lay it down as a rule that it is so improper that it must not be undertaken, because such a rule would kill that initiative and individuality which are so valuable to a team. But anyhow players may be warned in the strongest terms that they must not attempt it too often, for in the best of circumstances chances are against them.

O_1, when he makes his cut, goes straight in to the point y (Diagram — " Five-Eighth's Variation of Attack by Cutting-in "). By the time he gets there it is pretty certain he will find himself in difficulties. The opposing scrum half will have come round to wait for him, it is likely that a couple of forwards will be in readiness, and it is quite possible that X_1 will have come up also. Thus he will be faced by four members of the opposition, and unless he is a wonderfully smart man he will find himself one of a regular jumble. If his speed, dodges, and swerves enable him to get past, well and good. But he has to be left to work out his own ends, for it is a matter of impossibility for his colleagues to give him assistance. The only hope he may entertain in this respect is that the wing three-quarter on the blind side may have come up at the last moment to help him, and that there may be succour from the wing forward. Failing this, and it being impossible to get through, there is only one other practicable way of retrieving a very desperate position. He may try a risky lob pass to O_2 at p—risky because in these circumstances X_2 has just as much chance of receiving the ball as O_2. It is exhilarating to see a man really get through and make a success of his cut, and it is the kind of thing that comes in for unlimited applause from the stands and from the newspapers, when O1 is held up as the hero of an electric run; but it is a very sad spectacle at other times, and the backs who feel that their colleague has fooled them have some righteous cause of complaint.

It frequently happens that when opponents thoroughly understand the system of attack from the scrum on the open side on the lines laid down, they set themselves very energetically to nipping such attacks in the bud, and according to their skill and their degree of realisation of the tactics of their opponents they are varyingly successful. Their objective is generally the five-eighth, and it is either their five-eighth (X1) or their scrum half who endeavours to get started a little earlier than usual and to be down on the O1 before he has time to do his work.

When these efforts have been showing a tendency to become successful, it devolves on the attacking side to make some new departure which in itself may be successful, and which, if not, will at any rate have the effect of putting a stop to these too close attentions. A remedy of this sort is not easy to discover; but there are two possible changes of tactics which may be exercised, and both of which have served well on occasion. One is individual and the other is by combination, and both of them are very well worth practising. In each case the five-eighth (O1) is left out of the movement altogether, and if the other side made precipitous haste to reach him in anticipation of the usual manœuvres, so much the better. They will know better next time, and this next time he may go back to the standard methods.

The individual effort is risky, and consists simply in the scrum half himself for once in a way endeavouring to get round the scrum with the ball. O1 must be the director of the operation, and it must be left for him to call for it by the proper code word when he sees that something of the kind is necessary. The scrum half will take directions from him, and according to the information that is given he will make his dash on either the blind or the open side of the scrum;

COMBINED ATTACK ON THE OPEN SIDE 157

but it will readily be understood that in the great majority of cases the blind side is the only one possible for it to be attempted on. If the five-eighth saw danger to himself on that side, there is obviously at least equal danger to the scrum half if he were to try to get round, whereas if X's five-eighth and scrum half were both directing their hasty attention to that side, there would evidently be a fair prospect of a tolerably clear passage on the blind, and O_6, the wing three-quarter, might be of some service in backing up. When O_1 has given the word for this movement, he must endeavour to facilitate it by every means in his power, and particularly by way of bluffing the other side into the certainty that the ball is coming to him, and that he is about to start the usual attack. It is almost a condition also that the scrum must be very near to the opponents' goal-line, for this piece of individual play does not stand much chance of success when the scrum half has very far to go. What he is able to accomplish is a short, quick dash, which for the moment takes all the X men by surprise, so that he may be over the line before they have been able to bring into action any defensive remedy.

The alternative and more reliable and satisfactory process of leaving out the inside five-eighth, and a process which is often attended by the best results, and is therefore a valuable alternative, is for the scrum half on receiving the ball from the scrum to pass direct to O_2, the outside five-eighth. Here again it is left to O_1 to give the direction, and upon doing it at the instant that he sees the ball coming out from the scrum he leaves his mark—a little earlier than usual—with the intention of making certain of drawing X_1 to himself before that player realises what is on foot. When the pass is given to O_2 the ball goes behind O_1, who at that moment will be slightly in front of the point m on the first of these diagrams of tactics, and thenceforth the attack proceeds in the usual manner. To further satisfy himself upon the situation, the reader may be referred generally to this diagram, which can be made to indicate quite clearly what is meant.

CHAPTER XII

TACTICS—ATTACKING ON THE BLIND SIDE, AND OTHER VARIATIONS

Two methods—Defence turned into attack—A commission to the wing three-quarter—Only serious difficulty the full back—The five-eighth on the blind side—Bluff is wanted—May be left with an open field—The pass-in—The rule in Britain—An excellent variation—A splendid chance given on the pass back—The advantage of surprise—Another movement which is all surprise—A punt over the heads of the opposition—The duty of the second five-eighth—He knows beforehand—Successful ventures when on tour—A useful manœuvre when the defence is good—A complete novelty in attack—The Taipu movement—The second five-eighth cuts in to the right—The ball transferred behind his back—Opposition taken off their guard—Opening an attack from opponent's drop-out—Object is to bustle the taker—A dash into the open—Two courses open to the taker when pressed—He may pass or take a line kick at a good angle—Another advantage—Opposition will take precautions—An adventurous alternative—Pure bluff in tactics—The man without the ball—A daring but sometimes successful manœuvre—Demoralisation of the opposition—A cross punt forward and a chance to the outside three-quarter—Tactics in defence—Advantage of numbers—Assistance from the back-row men in the scrum.

THERE are two methods of working an attack on the blind side of the scrum, according as to whether the opponents are on the attack or the defence.

The first case is an example of defence turned into attack, and calls for dashing play on the part of the wing three-quarter; but is nevertheless a movement which, when chosen at the right time, is frequently most beneficial. It is practised almost exclusively when we are in our own twenty-five, and consists of giving a pass direct to this wing three-quarter, O6, and a commission to him to sprint off and do the best he can in the almost clear field that is usually in front

ATTACKING ON THE BLIND SIDE

of him. It generally happens in such cases that all the opposition are lined out for attack on the open side, and a reference to the diagram ("Wing Three-Quarter's Attack on the Blind Side") will make the situation clear. The value of this movement, like so many others, lies in its surprise. The chief dangers that the wing three-quarter will have to face will be the opposition scrum half and the three-

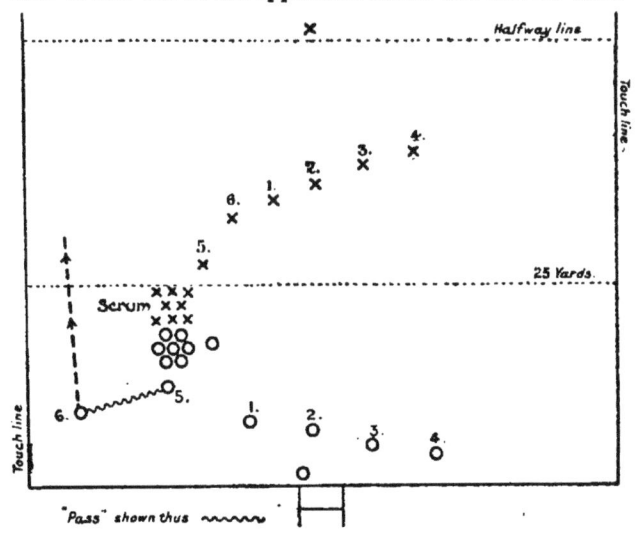

WING THREE-QUARTER'S ATTACK ON THE BLIND SIDE.

quarter X6. If he is smart he may very likely beat the scrum half, but X6 may be anywhere, and we fancy that in our own case, if we were playing a side that had all these tactics in its repertory, we should take care that he was posted at some point where he would be very useful in emergencies of this kind; but the fact remains that in our matches in Britain we constantly found him somewhere about the point where he is marked on the diagram, with the result that O6's only serious difficulty was with regard to the full back. To indicate the effectiveness of this method of tactics, we may say that we worked it twice with the most complete success, in our match against Munster and once against the Hartlepools. If O6 finds himself hampered, his best plan is to make ground by a line kick.

The other form of attack on the blind side is made when we, the O's, are attacking, and when it is usually the case that X6 is standing opposite O6. In such an event some kind of combination is called for, and the movement now suggested is a very pretty thing when well done, and it was this one alone which resulted in McGregor scoring no fewer than four tries in very simple fashion in our International match against England, despite the fact that England were then playing five three-quarter backs. As before, O1 is the general manager, and, having made up his mind as to what is best to be done in the situation, he gives the code word to the scrum half to make the pass on the blind side. But the ball is not intended for O6, who makes no effort to come up at this juncture. O1 is going on to the blind side himself to receive the ball, and he has no sooner given the code word, and has seen the ball being hooked out, than he dashes off at top speed to receive it at the point m in the diagram ("Five-Eighth's Attack on the Blind Side"), where the scrum half, in accordance with his reading of the code, will expect him to be. Before he has thus shown his hand, and while still in his normal position, he will naturally have appeared to make all the usual preparations for an attack on the open side, so that the deception of the enemy may be complete. In all these cases the minor methods of bluff are called for. Thus the opposing backs will be in a safe place on the open side, and the probability is that when O1 comes into possession on the blind there will be nothing in front of him at the time except X6, while O6 will now, of course, race up to give his support, and will be in readiness for the pass when it is necessary to give it. The scrum half may come round, and if he is dangerous

ATTACKING ON THE BLIND SIDE 161

O6 must have the ball; but there is an equal chance that both the half and X6 may be drawn on to the same point, and in that case the pass would very likely leave O6 with an open field. Being so far up in opponents' territory, and the full back in all probability only beginning to make his way from somewhere about the middle of the field, there are very distinct possibilities of a try being effected in such circum-

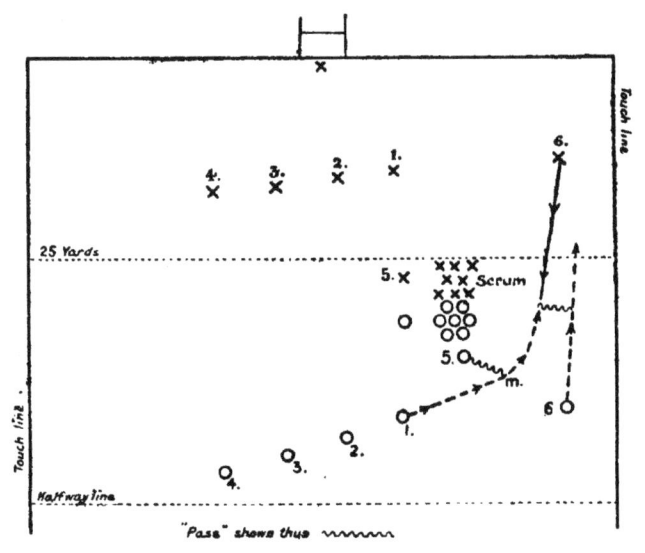

FIVE-EIGHTH'S ATTACK ON THE BLIND SIDE.

stances. We commend this movement as a most excellent variation upon the standard form of attack on the open side, but it will not generally be found practicable and successful four times in a match, as it was in our case at the Crystal Palace.

Another variation of the usual open attack is the pass-in, and two or three times in a match this may be exceedingly useful. Welshmen alone in this country seem to appreciate its possibilities, and they employed it against us with some effect in the Cardiff match. In several of our own engagements we scored handsomely by it. Thus in the Bedford match there was some very pretty and effective passing-in between Hunter and Mynott and between Hunter and Roberts.

The pass-in is simply what its name denotes. Generally speaking, it is the rule in Britain that when the passing movement begins from the scrum, the ball shall go along the line from one to the other until it gets to the wing three-quarter, and that he on receiving it, if he does not see a chance for an open run down, of swerving round his opponents, or of gaining a try on his own account in any other manner, shall either cross punt, drop at goal, or pass-in. This seems to be a hard-and-fast rule, and we have seen it set down very decisively in text-books of the game. Thus it is orthodox for the wing three-quarter to pass-in, but apparently for no one else. But we hold that passing-in long before the ball gets to the end of the line makes a most excellent variation. Such passing-in between the centre and the five-eighth is good, and so it is even between a back and a forward if the inside man is in a better position than any-one following up on the outside. Supposing one of the middle men, as we may term them in this connection, gives a pass on being only partially tackled, and then gets well away again clear of all obstruction. If the man who has taken the ball then gives it back to him, it will usually be found that this original possessor now has a splendid chance, and in any case it is not to be forgotten that ground has been gained and that a back or two have been saved. Besides, it is another way of breaking up a monotonous regularity; and inasmuch as it will usually come upon the others in the nature of a surprise, it has always this to recommend it as an additional advantage.

And as we have so frequently mentioned its surprise as one of the good features of different forms of attack, let us now mention one which is surprise and nothing else. The

ATTACKING ON THE BLIND SIDE

first five-eighth receives the ball from the scrum half in the usual manner. Now, instead of passing it on in regular style or running with it himself, he makes a short punt over the head of the second five-eighth on the opposite side. It must be a low kick, and the object now is for the second five-eighth on the attacking side, who is the man who would have received a pass in the ordinary course, to race through and get possession. It must be borne in mind that he has all the advantage of knowing beforehand what is going to be done, and can time his movements accordingly, while his *vis-à-vis* is taken completely by surprise and has to double back. Three times on our tour when we tried this movement the outside five-eighth was able to race through and secure the ball on the fly. It comes in particularly useful when the opposing backs are showing good defence.

A complete novelty in attack, and one that is a very good one, is what we call the Taipu, after the code word that we used to signify to those whom it concerned that it was about to be put in operation. It is so much of a novelty that it has not yet been tried even in New Zealand. We invented it ourselves for our tour, and on the various occasions on which we tried it it worked very well indeed.

The ball comes from the scrum to O_1, the first five-eighth, who transfers it to O_2, the second five-eighth, in the orthodox manner. O_2 proceeds with the ball along his usual course in these circumstances, but after he has gone a little way he suddenly cuts to the right in the direction of O_1's line of movement, and eventually he crosses that line just in front of O_1 going at top speed. This movement has the effect of drawing X_2 in the same direction, and it is highly probable that X_1 and X_2 will come together at about or below the point a in the first of the diagrams. But O_2 in rushing past gives the ball behind his back to O_1, who then, bearing to the left, has an open field in front of him. The two outside backs are rushing up to his assistance, and these three men have only X_3 and X_4 in front of them before reaching the full back. Thus the man has been gained. X_1 and X_2 have no time to recover themselves and be in action when they see what has taken place.

There is a very valuable form of attack to be opened from a drop-out by your opponents, which we have practised a great deal and with much profit, but which we have not seen done systematically in this country. We have mentioned the custom when dropping out so to kick the ball—high—that your forwards may bustle the taker and prevent him from taking it. To do this successfully, it follows that your forwards and backs must be so disposed on that side of the field as to be within easy reach of the point to which the ball has been kicked. At the same time the backs invariably line up to receive a possible return on that touch-line.

Now look at the diagram ("Attack Opened from a Drop-out by Opponents"), and study a typical case which is presented, and the form of attack that we would open in the circumstances. The ball has been kicked by the X player to the point m, which is just too far to be effective,—that is, it is too far for the men on his own side to get up in time to bustle the man and stop the return. Nevertheless, it has the effect of drawing several men up towards O, the receiver, with others scattered down the touch-line. This kick, fatal to the X side's chances of attack, has opened out great possibilities for O. Too many sides might be disposed to return the kick down the touch-line, which would be a proceeding from which they could not possibly hope to gain much benefit on account of the straight angle with which they would be confronted. The better course is the one we will indicate. The taker of the ball, who is not necessarily a back, though it is better for the success of the movement if he is, suddenly makes off with it at top speed, his probable course being from m in the direction of n, in which case he will have three of his side backing him up, as is evident from what is the natural disposition of forces at the time.

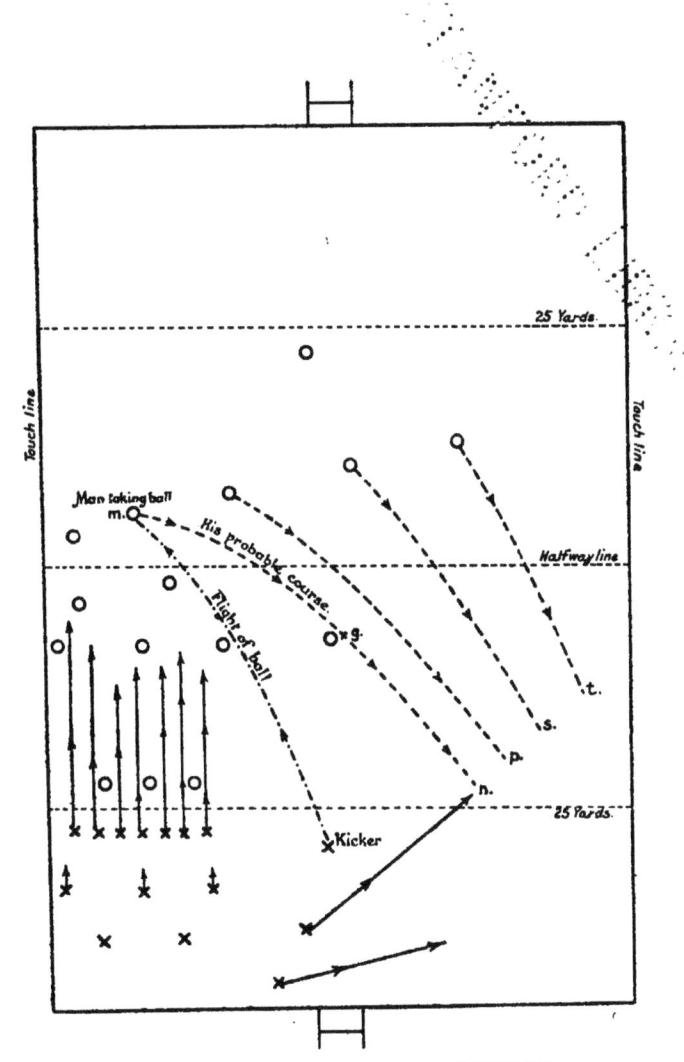

ATTACK OPENED FROM A DROP-OUT BY OPPONENTS.

ATTACKING ON THE BLIND SIDE

Now the possibilities of the situation, even if he does not reach the point *n*, are obvious. If X forwards cut across and he finds himself hampered by them at about the point *g*, he has two courses open to him, either of which is likely to prove advantageous. In the first place, he will have three men coming up on his left flank to his assistance, to whom he may give a pass at any moment, and in the second he may take a line kick and may now do it at a good angle. If the former course should be taken, and any of these men on the flank to whom the pass was given should find himself in difficulties at, say, *p*, *s*, or *t*, he would still have a splendid opportunity for a cross punt to the forwards, who would be in the middle of the field. And even if this variation in attack,—perhaps a little unorthodox,—should not prove successful in the obtaining of a try, its introduction will have had a considerable moral effect upon the other side, which will be apparent in what takes place subsequently. It will almost certainly have the effect of altering the disposition of the X team at the next drop-out. The X team will not have been slow to realise what were the possibilities of the movement, and they will perceive the necessity of guarding against any such future tactics. Yet whatever they do they must to some extent play into the hands of the O team, because if, for example, they send the ball straighter up the field on the drop-out, they will thus give to O a much better chance of getting in a good line kick from a better angle than was presented on the other occasion.

It is not to be overlooked that the man who received the ball from the drop-out in the original case had open to him the other alternative of trying to thread his way down the field; but such a proceeding would belong to the category of adventurous individualism, for which it would be impossible to give any rules. It is evident that the risks would be most serious, but a great player might occasionally surmount them. The prospects of success are greatest with the flank attack. Quick decision and great speed are necessary to the move ment, and when it is engineered with these advantages it will very often yield a try.

The possibilities of pure bluff in tactics are endless, and as no rules can be laid down for procedure on such a basis, it must be left to suggest itself or be suggested by the ready ingenuity of the inside five-eighth or of the man in possession of the ball. As an example of the most impudent and merciless bluff by the means of which we have gained advantages on more occasions than we should like to confess, one may mention the case of the ball coming out of the scrum, and of the five-eighth, X_1, thereupon making off at top speed as if he had become possessed of it in the usual manner, and as he is always expected to be. But he has not got the ball at all! The scrum half has given it to the second five-eighth, who has been conveniently placed on the blind side of the scrum, and this individual has now a very good opening. His opponents took it for granted, of course, that X_1 had the ball, and he drew them to him before they discovered their mistake. Once in three matches is quite often enough to try a little dodge of this kind, for if it is done more frequently it will be talked about and will be watched for. If you are going in for bluffing, as you must do, you must have many different bluffs and must ring the changes on them as often as you can. To make anything approaching a system of any particular one is fatal, and besides it would tend to spoil the game. Its skill in ingenious but straightforward attack is what a team must depend upon to win its matches, but all these artifices must be adopted in turn if only for the sake of change and to bring about the demoralisation of the opposition, so as to make the standard attack easier and more certain. Successful bluffs have an enormous moral effect upon the enemy, who hate to feel that they have been "had" in this way. Their tendency, then, is to wonder so much what will come next, that eventually they fall a prey to the simplest stratagem.

ATTACKING ON THE BLIND SIDE

There is the very exasperating case to be considered of the side that thinks it has discovered the nature of all the leading items in your list of tactics, and, being convinced that it is not good enough to beat them and win, goes in for playing a very deliberate spoiling game—merely plays to ruin every movement without making any attempt to attack itself. Such methods as these on the part of an inferior side will often upset the game of the best one. When this kind of thing is going on, it is very difficult to continue with the original programme, and the best thing to do is to change the whole style of play, and try to spring something on these spoilers which they really do not know. For example, the scrum half, instead of feeding the five-eighth cross punts into the open over the heads of the outside three-quarter, which gives a chance to his own outsides to be on the ball before the other side can turn and recover the position.

The five-eighth is the man who decides when this course of procedure shall be followed. When he so decides he gives the proper code word to his scrum half, and the latter at the same time gives a known signal to the outside three-quarter, who thereupon moves up at top speed in anticipation, and, on the half cross punting according to arrangement, he is able to be up and to secure the ball before the opposing three-quarter has time to turn. We have tried this manœuvre many times, and it came off successfully five times during our tour. It must be borne in mind that the kick must be long and low in order to get the ball quickly to its destination, and so prevent the full back from getting up and taking it on the fly, and also that it will fail if it does not place the ball behind the three-quarter. Simple as it may appear, it is a kick that requires much practice.

In the nature of things it is impossible for there to be any such tactics in defence as there is in attack. There can be no initiative, inasmuch as there is no possession of the ball, and everything depends on the course of procedure adopted by the side that is attacking. But there is one feature of our play when we are thrown on the defensive which may be worth mentioning. In the case of defence, numbers are valuable. For the accomplishment of a sound and successful attack many men are not as a rule necessary—too many will only result in the clogging of each other's movements. But when a side is defending, spare men are often of the greatest advantage, and it is therefore our practice to strengthen our back division at the earliest opportunity with two of our forwards whenever we have failed to secure the ball from the scrum.

The two extra men we utilise for this purpose are the two back-row men, and their action may most easily be comprehended by a reference to another diagram ("Strengthening the Defence from the Scrum"). In this case the O's have lost the ball in the scrum, and the result is that the X side have at once put a strong attacking movement to work in the usual manner. As soon as they realise that this is the case, the two back-row men, F and G, break away with all speed from the scrum, and race off to a point well behind the three-quarter line, and away over on the opposite wing, where they are an extra line of defence, intermediate between the three-quarters and the backs at a point where the attacking movement is likely to have reached its most dangerous state. Needless to say, the back-row men have to be very smart in doing this job, and they should have some kind of understanding with the full back and with each other as to their exact course of procedure.

"Pass" shown thus ⌇⌇⌇⌇

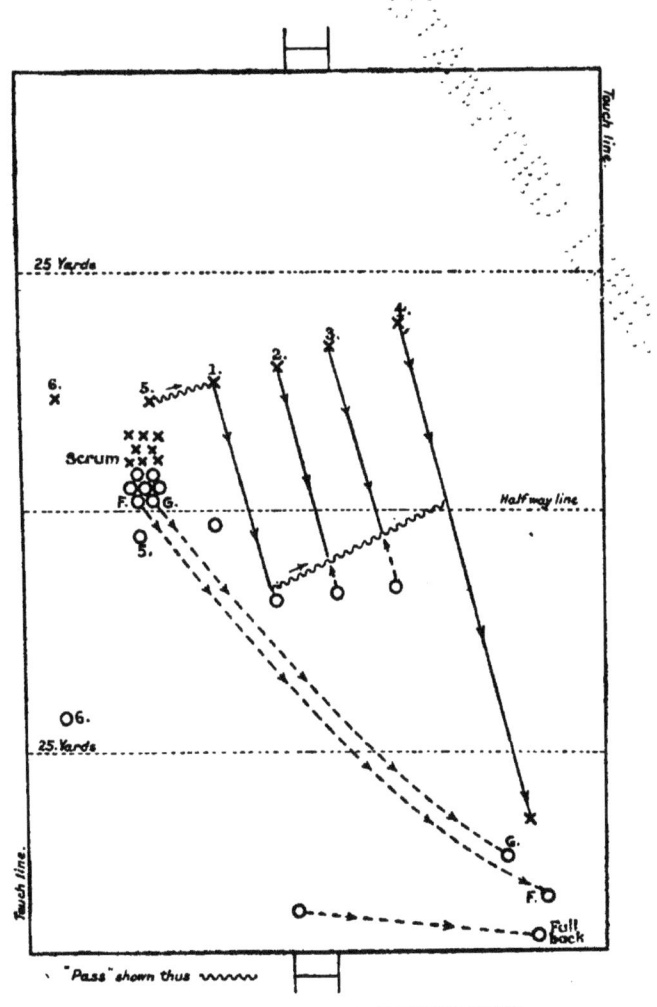

STRENGTHENING THE DEFENCE FROM THE SCRUM.

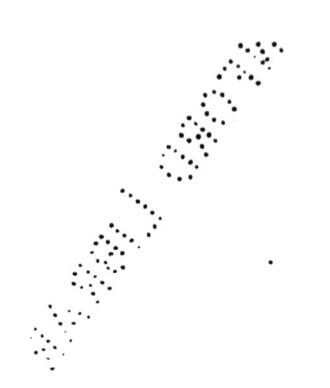

CHAPTER XIII

ON EQUIPMENT AND TRAINING

A first-class constitution wanted—Visit the doctor—Good digestion and good eyesight—Unfit men should stand down—Must feel well to play well—Good jerseys—A strange delusion—Knickers, stockings, and shin guards—Another delusion—Gloves for the back division—Players with too heavy boots—The shape of the buttons—How to make them bite—The care of the boots—The importance of training—Irksome and unpleasant methods—An undesirable reaction—A system in which we do not believe—Differences of opinion—No training, no play—Men who are always in condition—The polishing process—The system of the training halls—A busy centre—Men in large cities and towns—A sharp run before breakfast—A strict rule—An evening walk—The advantage of companionship—Backs' cultivation of their speed—The question of diet—The rival schools of thought—No belief in special diets—Eat what you like—Advice of a great surgeon—When on tour—Smoking and drinking—The day of the match—A midday meal—Beauty sleep—The danger of being overtrained—Recipe for a rubbing oil—The common-sense life—No such thing as special training.

THE most important item in the equipment of a Rugby football player is a first-class constitution, without a flaw in it anywhere. A man who has the least doubt about himself, and to whom a doctor will not give an absolutely clean certificate, should cease playing the game at once. Rugby football is a fine, healthy game for those who can stand it, but it is not one of those games that a man may play for the sake of improving his health. The health must be there to begin with. It would be a good thing if every youngster when he first becomes enthusiastic about the game were to pay a special visit to a reliable medical man, tell him of his doings, and, if necessary, explain precisely what he has to go through in the course of his two spells in every match. Even though all were apparently going well with him, it would not be an unwise thing if a player were to repeat this visit every three or four years, particularly if he were one who has to spend most of his time in a sedentary occupation in a large city, in which circumstances dangerous ailments breed more frequently and more insidiously than when a man leads a healthy outdoor life in an invigorating atmosphere. Heart trouble, so often unsuspected, is what is most dangerous, and the man who would play hard football for two thirty-fives or two forty-fives, as the case may be—we play forty-fives in New Zealand—must have none of that. A bad digestion is also rather against a Rugby player, though rather because it will prevent him from playing his best than that any ill effects will accrue from his playing. He must have first-class eyesight, or he will never be much good on the field, and it goes without saying that he must not have a particle of nervousness in his composition, but must be able to face what is sometimes real danger without any other thought than that of doing the best possible thing for his side in the emergency. We always think that a man who is not feeling fit on the day of an important match in which he is selected to take part, ought in justice to himself and his team to stand down. It is a mistake to begin a game when feeling below par, in the hope that when it is a little way advanced you will be a little more chirpy, and able to produce your customary flashes of brilliance when they are wanted. No man can play his best in this game unless he feels thoroughly well and in buoyant spirits, and the effect of a few mistakes at the beginning would be to reduce him to a terrible state of nervousness, when he would be a constant danger to his side, who long before the finish would wish that he had stayed at home by the fireside.

In New Zealand we all believe in wearing good strong jerseys—much stronger than those which it is customary to wear here. Our jerseys are, indeed, altogether different from those that the players of the mother country wear. We have a canvas yoke sewn over the upper part, covering the chest and the back of the shoulders, and the edge round the neck is bound with chamois leather. As this jersey would not stretch for the head to be put through it, and would not fit properly if it could be stretched, it is laced down the front. The great advantage of this jersey is that it will not tear. You will find that most jerseys that are torn on the field during play are so torn down the middle. We would strongly recommend English clubs and players to try these simple devices. Interruptions of the game, such as are permitted in this country, through players' jerseys being rent asunder, and time being given to change them, are exasperating to all concerned. A curious idea got abroad when these unusual garments of ours were first seen in Britain. It was declared that we were playing with eel-skin coverings round our shoulders, so that opponents who tried to collar us would be unable to obtain a fair hold, their hands slipping on the smooth surface, and in consequence giving us an unfair advantage over our opponents. Of course this was a very absurd suggestion. This sort of jersey is in general use in our colony, where an attempt is always made to collar a man by the legs in preference to the shoulders. Not the least of the advantages of this class of field clothing is that it effects a very considerable reduction in the club expenditure under this head in the course of a season.

We do not think that the knickers should go below the knee, as they so often do. When they are too long they are a nuisance and a constant irritation. Stockings may be thick, and it is customary with many of our men to wear elastic knee bandages as a protection against kicking. In matters of this kind prevention is much better than cure. Always wear shin guards. There is no shame in doing so as some people seem to imagine, as if such a precaution were a sign of timidity. The risks of the game are plentiful enough in all conscience, and it is wise of a player to seek to minimise them as much as is possible beforehand, so long as he does not handicap himself on the field. Generally, the New

Zealander wears his guard underneath his stocking—for the look of the thing—and during our tour the captain was about the only one who wore them on the outside, as he found that in the case of a kick in proximity to the buckle the latter was apt to be rather a nuisance when next to the bare skin. The British public, however, put another interpretation on the circumstance. It concluded that he was the only one of the New Zealanders who played with guards at all, and that they were necessary in his case on account of his more doubtful tactics and the trouble that they brought on him! We have never known a public that thinks so hard and so ingeniously as that which gives its attention to Rugby football in the old country. It is never beaten at finding an explanation, but we could wish that it were not always so adverse to the opponents of its favourites.

One forward at least, the lock man, should wear ear guards to protect himself during the scrum, when his ears would otherwise come in for some very bad mauling as a rule. Some players do not like the look of them, but neglect to wear them often results in a lifelong disfigurement.

On a wet day we think that the backs should always wear cotton or woollen gloves. We always do, but it is very seldom one sees a British player doing so. The advantage of wearing them when the weather is wet is that the player is enabled to take the ball much better and with greater accuracy. A back will often pick up a ball when he is gloved when he would have failed to do so with his bare hands, and he has less of a tendency to knock it on. The gloves we wear have open ends to the fingers, allowing an inch or two of the latter to come out. They are really about half-way between mittens and gloves.

Generally speaking, British players wear boots that are much too heavy for the best work. In New Zealand we believe in wearing the lightest boots possible consistent with strength. Others who have examined our footgear have declared that it is far too light, and have curiously

ON EQUIPMENT AND TRAINING 177

enough been disposed to complain about it on that ground. It is certainly heavy enough. You cannot expect the fastest work from a man when he is handicapped down below, and wherever else the boots have weight they should be light on the sole. Hand-sewn boots should be given the preference always, and we think that a little more thought might usefully be given to the shape of the five buttons on the sole. British players have these buttons with perpendicular sides, so that the apex is as wide as the base. We recommend them to have them slightly longer than is customary and with tapered sides, so that the apex is much narrower than the base. By this means the buttons bite better and a very much firmer hold is gained. A player should take great care of his boots. When they have had their turn for the day they should be dried thoroughly and then rubbed with a very little neat's-foot oil. Too much of it will clog the leather and have an effect opposite from that intended. On a wet day we find it a very good thing to polish the soles with black lead before going out to play. This has the effect of preventing the mud from sticking to them and caking in the spaces between the buttons.

No words of ours can ever express too emphatically what we consider to be the extreme importance to the player of Rugby football who aspires to skill and honour, of regular and constant training on a sound and sensible system. It almost seems that we in New Zealand and the players of Great Britain view this question of training from entirely different standpoints. In New Zealand we consider it to be part of the season's regular work, and as necessary to the man who plays the game as the eating of his meals; but it would almost appear that in some parts of England the man who does any regular training feels that he is doing something of a self-sacrificial character, and that he has a right to expect his colleagues to be grateful to him accordingly. Moreover, it seems that training in these cases is very frequently of a spasmodic character, and that a man will do a week of it, or a fortnight as the case may be, when a match of unusual importance is pending, and thereafter relapse into his usual mode of life, and perhaps neglect. This, at all events, is apparently the system on which the professional Association teams sometimes do their special training, and they are frequently held up in these matters as patterns to other players of the game. Training of this kind is generally irksome and unpleasant, it involves a number of rules and restrictions that tend to make life less enjoyable for the time being, and we believe it constantly happens, as the result, that when the big match is over there is a reaction of an undesirable character. Frankly, we do not believe in this kind of training at all. Training should be constant and regular, and special preparations should never be necessary. We do not think it is ever needful for men to be sent away to the seaside or lonely country places as the Association professionals are, provided that in their ordinary course of life they keep the necessities of their game in view. Of course some players of Rugby football—not in New Zealand —declare that they are amateurs, and that they cannot be expected to make such a business of the game as to do all this training; that they play simply for the sake of having a good game, and that the game must take them as it finds them. Differences of opinion arising from varying dispositions in temperament are involved in this matter, and we have only to say that our point of view is embraced in the old maxim that if a thing is worth doing at all it is worth doing well, and that we think it our duty to train as much as we can consistently with a full measure of attention to all the other occupations of the life of a man who has to work for his living. What is more, in New Zealand it is an inexorable law that the man who does not train shall not play, or at least shall not play in the class of football in which he would like to do, and in which he is entitled to by his known abilities, record, and even present form.

In an earlier chapter we gave some indication of the

PASSING PRACTICE.
(DEANS AND GILLETT)

ON EQUIPMENT AND TRAINING 179

splendid system which we have for teaching the game, and for training the men who play it. We think that our training system approximates very nearly to the ideal. The man who does not train is not allowed to play, because we lay it down as an axiom and a binding principle that he is not fit to go through a hard game of football. The games between our club teams are desperately hard, and we know that no man can last through one of them unless he is thoroughly trained. Now the majority of men who play football in New Zealand are men engaged in some form of manual labour in the day-time. Leaving all questions of means and social position on one side, it follows that in a young country in the making, like ours, where there is so much more to be done and so much less of reckoning up of what has been done, there is a much smaller percentage of men engaged in clerical and other indoor occupations than in an old country like the mother land. Therefore most of our men are, so to speak, being automatically trained all the time when they are at work, and in such cases all that is necessary is that in their spare time in the evenings they should be polished up to suit the special needs of the game. Thus it is this special polishing process which we call training and which we insist upon. It is carried on every night of the week in those large gymnasiums and training halls, several of which exist in each large town, and which are, as we have already explained, subsidised when necessary by the provincial Rugby Union of at least one large centre, namely Auckland. Every player in a club team is required by his committee to turn up at his training hall on at least two nights in each week, and unless he does so he expects to be left out of the team, and his committee see that his expectation is fulfilled. Such a happening is always regarded with great sorrow by the neglectful player, who properly regards it as something of a disgrace upon him.

The training hall is usually about 120 feet long and 40 feet wide, and has either tan or sawdust on the floor. It is lit up brilliantly by large electric incandescent lights, all of which are well protected, and there are no windows to break. Here the different teams of the club may go through courses of dumb-bells, or, as they do more frequently, play a small game of football. They regularly go through different exercises in scrum work, and the backs take part in passing rushes up and down the hall. Most important, considerable study is made at these meetings of the theoretical side of the game. If a man has a new idea for a new movement, he talks about it and it is discussed, and if it is felt that there is anything in it it is given a practical trial on the spot. Not only the members of the senior teams but the youngsters also participate in the evening's work, and while the juniors are at practice their elders coach them. In this way the training hall of the district club of each town is a busy centre of eager and ambitious athletic manhood every evening from seven o'clock until half-past ten.

As we have said, we in New Zealand have in our opinion come very near to the ideal in the matter of keeping ourselves in the most perfect condition and training for the hardest kind of Rugby football; but we realise that amateur players who live in large cities and towns in the mother country have not, and in the nature of things cannot have, the same advantages that we possess, and in their absence they must devise some scheme of their own for doing the best for themselves in this respect. Now, in a general way, we do not think that there is anything in the world that is better for keeping a man in good condition for the practice of such a game as ours than good walking and running exercise, of which we think it would be difficult for him to get too much, so long as there is no likelihood of him getting overtrained. If a man is engaged in business for the best part of the day, and his opportunities even for walking and running are limited, our suggestion to him would be that he should turn out early in the morning and take a sharp run at a fair pace for about a quarter of an hour or twenty minutes. This ought not to be done immediately after breakfast; but, on the other hand, it should not be done on an entirely empty stomach. This will bring all his limbs into action when they are best prepared for it; and even if the man is of a somewhat lazy disposition and is rather inclined to shirk the task at the beginning, he will soon find that it will become more and more agreeable as time goes on, and that in the end it will be a positive enjoyment, resulting in a fine feeling of exhilaration each time. The essence of such very gentle training as is comprised in such morning running is that it should be throughly regular and systematic. Occasional runs would be almost useless. It should be a principle of the player that his matutinal run is the most binding engagement of the day, only to be broken in the case of really genuine indisposition on his own part or the sudden death of a near relative. This will satisfy his training needs for the best part of the day, and then, when evening comes and his business duties are over for the time being, he should, with the same system and regularity, take a brisk walk, lasting about from half to three-quarters of an hour. If this is done every day,—not four or five times a week, but absolutely every day, omitting only the evening walk on playing days,—there is little need for any more training in the way of special exercise.

In cities and towns where the members of the same team often live at considerable distances from each other, it may happen that there is considerable difficulty in arranging for such training spins to be done in company, but when such an arrangement is possible it is very advisable, for not only does it considerably lessen what some men might regard as the monotony of the proceeding, but also tends towards thoroughness and regularity. A man alone might be disposed to funk a wet or dirty morning, but would not like to admit that he did so when there was a moral obligation upon him to turn out to meet another. Moreover, such a daily meeting would be useful for the discussion and comparison of ideas, and we can conceive of nothing that is more stimulating to the ambition of a player than such constant intercourse. Here the Englishman might have the best substitute for our nightly gatherings in our training sheds in New Zealand, for we think that these regular assemblies, and the talk that takes place at them, have an enormous effect in screwing up the determination of our men, and in this sense even mere conversation may be said to constitute an important part of the training curriculum. We do not care how enthusiastic a man may be, or how conscientious he may be in the matter of training and keeping himself fit, it is still very difficult if not impossible for him to retain that keen edge on his ambition which is absolutely necessary if he is to excel in the game if he has only opportunities of association with his colleagues on one or at the most two days of the week. You cannot play great football when a "Let-me-see-where-did-we-leave-off?" feeling is in possession of the player at noon on the day of his weekly match. Reverting to the morning sprint, if we were official trainers of a team, we would insist that all our men should take this special exercise, but in our own minds we should regard an occasional defalcation on the part of a forward as of less importance than on the part of a member of the back division. Speed is one of the prime qualifications of the back, and it is not to be kept up at its best unless it is constantly practised, and therefore in the case of the back men we should be inclined to lengthen their morning run out to half an hour, and to tack a sprint of ten minutes or so on to their evening programme. We need hardly say that field practice with several other members of the team once or twice a week is extremely advisable, but it is often impracticable, and therefore it would be useless to lay down any rules on the subject when they could not in all cases be observed.

Now, there is that grandmotherly old question of diet. Half a dozen players of experience, or half a dozen professional trainers, would no doubt among them be able to supply at least three "best" systems. Once upon a time a man was not considered to be training at all unless he was doing something with his stomach that under no circumstances did he do at any other time of his life; and, generally speaking, he was supposed to be training best who departed farthest from the usual routine of his table, and who made matters the most uncomfortable for himself. When a man confided to another that he was training, the latter would ask, "Oh, and what are you eating?" Any thoughtful person ought to have entertained his suspicions about the value of these old systems from the mere fact that they varied so much and were so constantly contradictory. One man would be a strong advocate of plenty of well-cooked meat with a tendency to cinder about it; another would like a little steak carefully weighed with ounce weights and as red as when it came from the butcher's shop. All kinds of views were entertained about vegetables generally, and particular vegetables. There were rival schools of thought about eggs and cheese. Even bread had its enemies. Liquids had to be measured with a measuring glass, and the general impression that a stranger might gather from watching the process of this regimen was that the unhappy man who was training was in the last state of physical decay, and that only by extremely gentle fanning was the spark of life being kept aglow. We have said that this used to be the state of affairs; but there are many good men who believe in such systems in only a modified form to-day, and even at this stage of our experience there are books written in which tables of diets are carefully set forth.

Let us say bluntly, then, that we believe in none of these things, nor does any member of the team that we had the honour to lead while in Britain. Special diets are to our minds rubbishy fads. If there is such a man anywhere—and we do not believe there is—who needs special food when he is training for a football match, that is to say different food from that to which he is daily accustomed (always assuming that the latter is substantial and wise and healthy), we think that that man ought not to be playing football at all. Our principles in this matter are the principles of Nature. We believe in a man eating just whatever he fancies, provided there is no obvious and indisputable objection to his taste of the moment. Let him eat plenty of good wholesome food, and we cannot see that there is any harm in drinking alcoholic beverages in strict moderation. Nature is the best of prompters in these matters. We cannot bring ourselves to believe that it is all mere personal whim and caprice when a man comes to think that for his forthcoming meal he would like a little of this or a taste of that. Nature knows her own business very well, and we believe in supporting Nature every time. We have been told—and feel happy in the knowledge—that one of the greatest British doctors, one who has attended constantly upon the King himself, has expressed absolutely the same sentiments in relation to the curriculum of ordinary daily life; that is to say, he has emphatically expressed himself against all diets and such like nonsense, and in so many words has prescribed the convenient system of eating and drinking just what the man fancies—provided his instinctive common sense does not tell him it is unwise—as being the best for health, and the one that is most likely to be productive of happiness and physical fitness. We have never dieted ourselves in our lives, and we trust we never shall. We do not think that any members of our team have ever done so. Certainly they never did while we were on our big tour through Britain. We know that there was a very general impression, at the beginning at all events, that we did diet ourselves in some extraordinary fashion, this being supposed to be part and parcel of some weird and quite ususual system of training, never before invented, that was directly responsible for our scoring more tries and kicking more goals than our various opponents. We simply partook of the ordinary hotel fare all through the tour, and if a man wanted anything special as the result of a sudden fancy, he had it for the asking, with no objections raised from any quarter. All our tastes were of the very simplest character. After the first six or seven matches, we did no special training of any kind whatever, our two matches every week being quite enough for us.

If a man is a smoker we do not think there is the slightest objection to his continuing smoking to the full extent of his desires during the whole period when he is in what he would call "strict training." The majority of our men are fairly heavy smokers, and when we were on tour we know that there was a general disposition on the part of the spectators and opponents to view us with wonderment—which would have been sympathy but for our success—when the majority of the fifteen were to be seen pulling away at their pipes with great vigour in the dressing-room just before going out on to the field of play. Suppose that for the sake of argument smoking does very slightly impair one's powers of wind and digestion, we are sure that any advantage to be derived in this respect from abstention would be more than counterbalanced by a lowering of spirits and irritation at the abstention. Pipe smoking is the best. We do not think cigarettes are so harmless, and one of us at all events is certainly very strongly against the habit of inhaling them. There is no doubt whatever in his mind of the great injury that this practice does to the constitution of a man; he has seen too many cases of the evil to have any hesitation in condemning it. In the same way, while we think that beer and wines in moderation can do no healthy athletic man any harm, we are not inclined to give the same free certificate to spirits.

So far as the day of the match is concerned, we have only one suggestion to make, and that is that the midday meal should be taken not less and hardly earlier than two hours before the beginning of play, so that it may be given a fair time to digest, while on the other hand the engine may not have begun to make a demand for more fuel. It was our regular plan while we were on tour in Britain to have a rattling good meal at twelve o'clock on the day of every match.

There is no occasion for us to enunciate such axioms as that late hours are not good for the constitution, and that the man who is earliest to bed and—within reason—earliest out of it—is likely to feel a few points better than the two o'clock to ten o'clock man who never knows the delights and the invigorating properties of a beauty sleep.

There will be many occasions, as when he feels stiff or sore or bruised, or fears that he may feel so, when it may be desirable for the player to be rubbed down well with a good rubbing mixture; and we offer to our readers the special recipe for that mixture which our team used exclusively when on tour. It is as follows:—

Eucalyptus	60 parts
Whisky	30 ,,
Hartshorn	10 ,,

Our whole bodies were rubbed down with this training oil both before and after every match, and we can confidently recommend all other players to adopt the same system.

We have one thing to say very emphatically at the close of this chapter on training, and that is, avoid overtraining as you would your greatest enemy. Only once in the life of the captain of the "All Blacks" did he overtrain, and he is quite certain that never did he feel worse. The man who is in this state is at a hopeless discount, and if we had to make a choice for a vacant place in a team between a man who was thus overtrained and another who was not trained at all, we should have not the slightest hesitation in taking the untrained person into the fifteen. A man is always better ten pounds overweight than half an ounce under it. He is in a dangerous state when he is strung up to concert pitch, and he has no reserve force. He must have that reserve force for a hard football match.

Our readers will have perceived that this little gospel of

ON EQUIPMENT AND TRAINING 187

training is merely the gospel of the ordinary common-sense life. It is that precisely. If a man plays Rugby football, his captain or committee should be able to call upon him unexpectedly at three o'clock on any day and find him as fit for playing then at a minute's notice as if he had been in strict training for a month with the match of that day in view. This is just to say again, finally, and by way of summary, that in the season at all events there should be no such thing as special training, but that there should always be training. That is our system in New Zealand, faithfully followed by the great majority, and it has never failed us, nor has any possibility of improvement upon it ever been made manifest.

CHAPTER XIV

ON CAPTAINCY

A hard man to find—A list of necessary virtues—His relations with the team—A crude team but fine material—The captain's duty—Must see that his men are in agreement—Knowledge of the rules—New ideas—The omniscient captain—A human compendium of football law—The peculiarities of the fifteen—Little differences—The proper pegs in the proper holes—The place for the captain on the field—Wing forward or five-eighth—What to do in emergencies—Possible changes in the arrangement of the side—Advantage of knowing his men—Filling sudden vacancies with the smallest loss—The weakness of the one-position man—Practise men in different positions—Studying the other side—A valuable mental file for reference—The captain's tactics—On listening to the advice of others—On resource—Hope to be sustained—Some points in tactics—When the toss has been won—Fatherly superintendence over the team—A priceless man—Good captaincy worth more than good play—The pride of the old general—The greatest honour that a footballer can ever gain.

IT is one of the most difficult things in the world to find a really good Rugby football captain, and the man who is ideal for the post has not yet been identified, and probably never will be. The qualities that go to the making of the good captain are so numerous and so varied as to be in some cases almost contradictory. His must indeed be a rare blend of virtues. A good captain is born—he is a born leader of men. He must know all that there is to be known about the game in theory and practice, must be a master tactician, must be possessed of the most acute perception, must be a keen judge of human nature, must know every peculiarity of each one of the men under his command and as many of those of his enemies as is possible, must be able to effect the most tactful combination of the *fortiter in re* with the *suaviter in modo*, must be cool in success and hopeful when things look black, and his resource must be infinite. You may readily believe that the man about whom all these things may be justly said is not to be found on every playing arena.

Consider first the relations of the captain with the members of his team. In New Zealand a captain has never anything to do with the choosing of the team. This office is usually performed by a small selection committee of three, and then the team is placed in his hands for him to make the most of it. At such a preliminary stage as this the value of a good captain to a crude team is very great. When we speak of crudeness we do not mean it individually, but as regards the combination of the team. You may have a team composed of fifteen star performers; but if they have all been used to different kinds of games, have different ideas about tactics, and even place different interpretations on rules, they would be but a very crude team to begin with, and their efforts would be likely to be futile. Such a team in its first essays would probably go under to one which in individual excellence was not to be compared to it. Yet here is the material for an invincible combination, and it is the captain's part to see that it is properly cultivated.

Thus one of the first duties of the captain at the beginning of a season, or when circumstances necessitate any drastic changes in the constitution of his side—as they often do, especially in times of adversity—is to see that all his men are in general agreement on main points. Let him see, to begin with, that every one has the most thorough understanding of every rule of the game, and that they all place exactly the same interpretation upon each one of them. Such a precaution as this is by no means so unnecessary as it might appear at the first glance, and a little lecture on the subject by the captain from time to time might be very advantageous. It would be especially so when he had any reason to believe that a difference of opinion which did not exist among the players originally had grown up since they came to play together. Such things will happen while men continue to think and to play their game conscientiously. Just as the game generally is undergoing a slow process of evolution, so this evolution owes itself to the subtler changes of thought and feeling that are going on in the minds of individual players, and which inevitably will make their existence felt in the style of the man when on the field. The wise captain will take note of these changes of attitude of his men towards the recognised rules and systems, and, while never discouraging originality to any extent whatever, will try to arrange things so that the latest ideas of the thinker, with as little damage to his self-respect as possible, may be made to harmonise completely with the general system of the team. A possible contingency, of course, is that one of the ideas of this man may be of an unusually valuable character, and that it may be worth while to lead the other fourteen round to it without delay, instead of attaching the one to the fourteen. For the good captain always walks about in the world of football with his eyes very wide open. He admits that there is no finality in method, and that, given a fair amount of equality in other respects, success will be to that side that avails itself first of the newest and most effective methods of attack and defence. The moral effect upon opponents of the introduction of such methods is always worth a try or two.

There should be no point in the rules upon which the captain is not able, without any reference to book or person, to give the completest possible explanation. In his mind there must be a complete compendium of football law past and present, and it will be all the more valuable if it is supplemented by a comprehensive list of leading cases. A school knowledge of this football law is not sufficient. The law itself and the interpretations put upon it are subject to constant change, and the captain must at all times be a close and observant student of these changes. Nothing could be more humiliating to a captain, or more calculated to weaken his position with his men, than, when an appeal is made to him to settle a controversy on some particular point, to be obliged to confess that he has not sufficient knowledge of it to be able to decide it off-hand. Here have his men been looking up to their leader as a wise and omniscient chief, and there is an inevitable little revulsion of feeling—it may be very slight, but it would be much bigger a second time—and they wonder whether they have not been setting too high an estimate on this leader of theirs.

He must know to the final detail the peculiar qualities, the little faults, and the various idiosyncrasies of each man who is under his command. Here there is for him a most fruitful field for study and research, and all the knowledge that he acquires will serve him in good stead in every match in which his side takes part. No two players are alike in their capacity and their characteristics. They may be so much so that they are regarded as twins, and are used to duplicate each other whenever occasion demands, such a process being carried out without in the least degree disturbing the other arrangements and methods of the team. But there are inevitably subtle differences, and a proper appreciation of these differences will enable the captain to effect a slight advantage or avert a threatened loss sometimes when it is exceedingly valuable to do so. At every available opportunity he should study as closely as it is possible to study every movement of each man, and should even make every possible effort to get at his thoughts, by direct inquiry whenever it is necessary to do so. Let him watch his footwork, the way he uses his hands, his body movements, his swerve, his dodgery, the peculiar features of his kicking, and so forth; and he must have a retentive memory, and have filed in his mind the most complete statement of the characteristics of each man. If he does all this he will never be guilty of putting the round peg into the square hole, of calling upon a man to do something of which he is incapable, when there is a master of the process looking idly on, and of helplessly witnessing the discomfiture of his side as a consequence, having all the time the humiliating conviction that somehow or other—but he had forgotten exactly how—it was possible to have averted the disaster.

If the captain must study all this constantly, and many other things that must be studied while the game is in progress and that will be considered presently, the preliminary question arises as to where he should be placed on the field. In our formation we regard the best position for him as that of either wing forward or five-eighth, and those were the respective positions occupied by the authors of this work as captain and vice-captain during the British tour, partly because of this desirability, and partly because they were the positions that they occupied when playing in their own teams at home. It is clear that in such positions they are within easy seeing and speaking distance of both departments of their side, forward and rearguard, and also that they are in the best possible position for conveniently studying the tactics of the other side. In the case of other formations, a near approach to the advantages occupied by these positions will at once suggest itself. It is clear that on no account should the captain be one of the scrum. In such a position he would be capable of observing next to nothing, and his captaincy would at all times be merely nominal.

One of the matters upon which he must have come to a complete understanding with himself beforehand, is as to possible alternations in the arrangement of his side as may suddenly be necessitated in the course of play. A man may be injured, or he may fail utterly through some other unexpected cause, and the captain in such an awkward emergency must not need much time to think about what is best to be done, and when he puts his remedy into effect he must have no doubt whatever that he is doing the very best thing possible in the circumstances, and must leave it to work with no other chopping and changing about such as would inevitably bring about a speedy demoralisation in the team. If he knows to a nicety all the varying characteristics of each of his men, as we have said he must do, it will not then be a difficult matter to come to an exact determination as to what are the best things to be done in this way as occasion arises; but in the course of his private studies of the game and his men, when away from the field, he should have thought out all these many problems in their aspect towards each of his fifteen. He must have decided that if perchance A should go wrong K is the man to take his place, A in his inferior state being best adapted to filling up the gap left by K; or, on the other hand, that he will put K in A's place, and that the best thing then to be done will be to send A to C's and put C into K's. Likewise if D is reduced to the position of a non-combatant, or practically so, he must be prepared with the knowledge that the best way out of the difficulty will be to put X to do his work, and make the best use, if any is possible, of the services of D. It will be evident that the number of possible permutations of this kind is enormous, and, as we have said, he must be armed with the knowledge as to which are the pick of the batch, and which must be chosen to suit each individual case. Such knowledge is not to be acquired without much thought and calculation; and it is of great value when it is acquired. The captain who wonders what on earth he shall do when he is faced by such difficulties as have herein been suggested, is a very wretched individual.

The case of a man being injured, or otherwise being incapable of playing his usual game, is not the only one in which a change of places becomes desirable or even necessary. An unexpected situation may bring about the necessity for a drastic change in methods and tactics, and to effect this in the proper manner a new disposition of forces may be called for. This emergency also he must have contemplated down to its final detail, and it will usually be one not to be met by the change of one man for another, but by a much more extensive variation in the constitution of the team.

In this connection it will be realised how great is the

advisability, not to say necessity, of each man in the side being able to play what is to all intents and purposes a perfect game in more positions than one, as in an earlier chapter we strongly urged that he should be. The player who is a one-position man only is a serious handicap to a resourceful captain, and it is not to be wondered at that the influence of such a captain will always be against the continued inclusion of that man in the team, however great may be his merit when playing in the place to which he has exclusively given himself up. It is good to specialise, but it is better still to be versatile, and one cannot be quite certain that the old warning about being Jack of all trades and master of none has quite such a thorough application to Rugby football as it may have to some other things. We would like our man to be Jack of all trades and master of at least two or three, and that should not be beyond the scope of any individual of average intelligence and industry. In order to keep his men tuned up to the play in the different positions which they are capable of filling, the captain should give them frequent opportunity of practising in them. A match in which no serious opposition is expected will afford a good opportunity of making some of these alternations, and when for a short period the side is not doing quite so well in its matches as is expected of it, some of them may be put into force on a more permanent basis. We rather believe in these changes. We do not think that it is a good thing to stick always to exactly the same arrangement. It is not good for the team. A man will get tired of always playing exactly the same kind of game, and in a new position with new duties he is likely to be intensely interested and to put an amount of thoroughness and enthusiasm into his play as will have a most beneficial effect on the strength of the side. The old proverb that change of work is as good as play has its application to our game as to everything else. That in this respect we practise to the fullest possible extent what we preach is amply proved by the records of our British tour, when such changes were effected in almost every match, with the almost invariable result of gain and the postponement of the staleness that was constantly threatening us.

Next to knowing the exact capacity of each man on his own side, the best thing is to know that of the men who are opposed to him, so that he may foil the points of strength in his enemy just as he nurses them on his own side. Obviously his knowledge in this respect must be limited and difficult to acquire. The captain of acute perception, however, will seldom be at a complete loss in this matter. Opportunities to acquire such knowledge present themselves, and should be eagerly accepted. Newspaper reports are not always reliable, but something may constantly be gained from them as to what are the points of strength in a team whose merits are for the time being unknown, but which will have to be encountered in the due course of the season. Gossip and the comparing of notes with the members of other teams may be expected to furnish more valuable information, and chances of coming by such knowledge should at all times be eagerly sought. It is the captain's business to be something of a scout in this way, and to use every means in his power of acquainting himself beforehand with the formidable and the weak features of his future foes, so that he may counteract the one and play on to the other when his own time comes.

Again, the play in the first few minutes of a game will often reveal the entire characteristics of the opposing side, and when they are not known to him, the captain should be most acutely observant during this period. The knowledge that he gains in the first spell may be of inestimable advantage in the second, and it should never, or very rarely, happen that anybody else is able to point out to him something in the play of his opponents that he had not discovered for himself. And after a match he should file in his mind all the essential facts concerning the play of the opponents on this occasion, for reference and use the next time that the teams meet.

And this consideration leads us on to that of tactics. It is the most obvious truism to suggest that the captain must be a master tactician. All that we have said in this book and all that we have not said upon the subject of tactics must be at his fingers' ends. When his side have taken the field, on him devolves the onus of putting into practice much of this fine theory of the game. If he does not do it there are few others. Generally speaking, he will have prepared his plans for the day before he leaves the dressing-room, and will have thoroughly discussed them with the other members of the team, and have gained their complete sympathy with him in his various projects. On such occasions he must show himself not only ready but eager to listen to the suggestions and advice of others. Two heads are at all times better than one, and it is possible that another player may have thought of an idea for this particular occasion which might be of immense value from a tactical point of view. Some captains are disposed to be somewhat arrogant in these matters, and, without saying it, to give their subordinates to understand that they know how to play the game very much better than anyone can teach them. This is a fatal fault in a captain. Not only in his stupidity does he refuse to avail himself of much excellent thought on the part of his men, but he creates a feeling of resentment in them which is certain to have a very baneful influence in the ensuing play. The man who has thus been slighted is disposed to show this superior captain of his, whenever an opportunity presents itself, that he is not quite so wise as he thinks he is, and it may frequently happen that the process of this demonstration is one which is most expensive to the side, although the revengeful player had no intention of its being so. Such a desire to be "even" is very reprehensible in a subordinate; but it comes from simple human nature, and it is not to be disposed of in any other way than by removing the cause.

Going on to the field, then, with his plans prepared in

view of the features of the play of the other side, of the exact composition of his own, of the state of the weather, and of the various other circumstances and necessities of the case, the captain must be ready with alternative tactics to be put into operation at a minute's notice, according to the development of the game one way or the other. He must be prepared with every conceivable form of attack and defence. These are almost infinite in number, and the captain must never be so resourceless as to say to himself, after trying all kinds of schemes without success, "I have done everything; I can do no more." How often have we seen a good captain, a seasoned general, pull a game out of the fire by a sudden change of tactics at the last moment. Personally, we remember some astonishing cases of sides being many points down a few minutes from the end, and winning easily by the aid of nothing else but this sudden change of tactics on the part of the captain. We have known him to allow a weak forward team in opposition to secure the ball during the whole of a spell from his own strong forward division, and in the meantime merely play to keep the other backs from scoring. In the second spell he has given the command to action to his own forwards, still as fresh as daisies, and they have completely overwhelmed the opposition. Had he put his backs to attack at the outset, nothing is more certain than that they would have been completely bottled up while the other defenders were fresh, and would have been rendered comparatively impotent in the after-part of the game.

The longer a captain occupies this office, the more will he realise that he can never drag a hopelessly beaten team upwards to the pleasant heights of success; but the times when such a team is so hopelessly beaten are not numerous comparatively, and he must be very slow to admit them. Above all, even when the conclusion as to the hopelessness of the situation has been forced on his own mind, he must be very slow indeed to communicate the smallest suspicion of his state of feeling to his colleagues. No good purpose could be achieved by his doing so, and it is in the highest degree likely that harm would be done. We once heard the captain of a country team say to his men, " It's no use, boys ; we can't play them and the crowd too"; and it struck us as the most foolish thing we had ever heard a captain say, and one which at once showed his complete disqualification for his high office. It is easy enough to captain a winning team ; but when a side is many points down, is playing a severely uphill game, or is in disfavour with an exacting crowd, it is then that the skill of the cool, calculating, hopeful general will come to the aid of his fluttering team. Knowing his men, he knows when civil words of advice will lead and when an authoritative one will drive.

This is no place for the further consideration of any particular form of tactics, and the educated captain will not need to be told that, having won the toss, he must be careful to take advantage of a strong wind, if there should happen to be one in evidence, and that he must nurse his forward division in a skilful way during the first half while still playing a fast open game. It will also be obvious to him that in the second spell, when the wind is against him, he will have to rely on the forward division to make most of the ground by short close rushes up the touch-line. Too many forward divisions are often too much hustled, and have all the steam knocked out of them by the reckless handling of their captains, in the mistaken idea that they must get the last ounce out of them while the tide is on the flood. If the course of procedure as to the choice of ends when the toss has been won is not so obvious, the captain should always take one or two members of the team into consultation with him before deciding. Here again two heads are a great advantage, and we never advise the captain to make such a momentous decision on his own responsibility. There are also several small details that the captain should attend to before actual play is commenced. He must see to it, for example, that the referee knows the length of the spells to be played, and he should assure himself that the dead-ball lines are properly marked.

The good captain will exercise a fatherly kind of superintendence over his men at all times. He will encourage them to do their training regularly and thoroughly, and he will put the spur to a man whom he suspects of being something of a laggard. On tour, in a variety of ways he will do his utmost to maintain the health of his men at a high standard. A captain can do far more in this respect than some of those who hold the position imagine. He will see for himself that the players' boots are properly studded, and in a hundred other ways he will exercise efforts in the direction of leaving as little as possible to chance, or, what often amounts to the same thing, to the care of others who are not to the same extent bound up heart and soul with the success of the side. Apart from the great gain accruing from personal attention to all these matters, the circumstance of his giving so much time and attention to them has a great moral effect on his men. They see their captain doing so much for them and for their club, and they feel ashamed not to do their utmost as some kind of return. Their enthusiasm is sharpened, and when there is this devoted allegiance and this perfect comradeship among the fifteen, they are a dangerous side to tackle. And, lastly, the great captain is a broad-minded, generous man who bears himself modestly, and is charitable to his opponents when he has vanquished them, and who is consequently deserving of sympathy in the hour of his own defeat, which hour must come sometimes.

You see that the captain—the ideal captain that is—should be possessed of a multiplicity of virtues as seems impossible of association in the person of one individual; but the player who holds this position of chief officer in his team may at least strive to perfect himself for his most responsible duties. It is possible that such suggestions as have been offered in this chapter may bring home to him the fact that in one or two respects he has not fully appreciated the possibilities of his captaincy, and something substantial is gained when a man is brought to such a contemplation as this. A really good captain, possessing, say, a fair majority of the qualifications that we have mentioned, is priceless to his club. One would say that he is worth two men to his side, and even that from a great captain, skilled in all these arts of generalship, one might tolerate individual play that was below the standard. What was lost in the one respect would be far more than gained back in the other.

Captaincy is an art that has not been cultivated as it should have been, and there are reputations to be made with it that will endure when the great feats of players, and even of clubs, will be in the way of being forgotten. Happy is the man who, when his football days are over and his part is merely that of the watcher from the stand, or of the critic in the committee room, knows that it is said of him that it was he who made a certain famous team of long ago, and that it was he who inspired fourteen other men to deeds of which, without him, they were quite incapable. They will speak of it as his team, and to have his name thus linked with that famous combination as its master and its leader is the greatest honour that can ever come the way of the Rugby footballer.

WALLACE CONVERTING

CHAPTER XV

GOOD RULES

Discuss the plan of the game—Don't be late on the field—Practising specialities—Watching the ball—On codes—Codes should be changed—On new ideas and inventions—The reliability of old-fashioned things—The selection of a ground—Advantage of sandy soil and coarse grass—The methods of your opponents—Bad temper—Quack medicines—The possibilities of a new position—The mark—Removing wet things—The incidents of the match—A day off and the best way to spend it—The half-hearted player—Justifiable blame—An injured opponent—Allowances cannot be made—Talking to opponents during play—Don't play if you don't feel well—If chances do not come your way—Playing to the whistle—On shouting for a pass—After the match—Ask questions—On playing to the gallery—Quickness of decision—Attention to the boots—Be spick and span—The studs—Play a clean game—On speculation—When hurt in play—When you have missed your man—Never be idle or neglectful—On guarding a vacant position—Backing up a colleague—" My ball."

ALWAYS discuss the plan of action very thoroughly with your colleagues just before going on to the field, so that there shall be a very complete understanding all round as to what is to be attempted, and how. Throughout our British tour we made a great point of this preliminary conference, and found it of the utmost advantage. Too often does a side feel the necessity for such consultation after the match has begun, when, alas! there may be no opportunity for it.

Never be late in arriving on the field and getting ready to start. Such faults are very bad form, and exceedingly unfair to your punctual opponents, who naturally get into a great state of irritation at the delay. In New Zealand we have very strict rules in this matter. When a match is about to take place, three warnings are given to the players, and if a side is not ready to kick off when the third one is given, it is deemed, in the absence of some extremely satisfactory excuse, to have lost the match.

If you are a player with any valuable specialities of your own, or even if you only suspect that you may have such specialities, practise them for all you are worth, even for long after you feel that you have attained as much perfection as is practicable. Specialising pays very well, inasmuch as it is not easy to imitate, and is most difficult to play against. A man with a really good speciality—and not at all necessarily a complicated one—is always a very valuable adjunct to a team if he remembers that he must not be all speciality, but must do the ordinary business just as well as ever.

Either when you are immediately concerned with the movement in operation, or are for the time being only a spectator of the doings of others, always remember that it is your first duty and necessity to keep your eyes on the ball. When you do so you always know where it is, and can never be caught napping. The man who only momentarily looks for faces on the stands, speaks to a friend round the rails, or allows his thoughts to wander while he looks up at the sky, is sure to be taken unawares sooner or later, and he will both feel and look a very miserable footballer then.

One would advise every team to adopt a code for giving instructions to each other on the field, and to make a practice of using it, even though at first, through simplicity of tactics or for any other reason, some scepticism may be entertained as to its advantages. It can never be a good thing to let your opponents into the secrets of your future movements, even though these partake of the obvious.

GOOD RULES

Codes should be changed occasionally. It is a point to bear in mind that when an opponent deciphers your code instruction it is likely to impress itself more on his mind than when he merely heard one shouted in open language. He may therefore be keener to frustrate the proposed plan of action. The remedy is evident — take care that your opponents do not decipher your codes. It is particularly essential that there should be a code in operation between the scrum half and the backs, and that this should be changed from time to time.

It is better not to be eager to experiment with new ideas and inventions in the way of patent boots, patent balls, and so forth. It is rarely that there is much good in them, and, generally speaking, our experience has not been satisfactory. Their advantages are usually merely fanciful, and on some occasions these new fads might let you down very seriously. The longer one plays and the more inventions one sees, the more conservative in such matters is one inclined to be. Football, after all, is a very simple game so far as implements are concerned, and it hardly admits of the application to it of inventive genius.

When a new club is in search of a ground, it has not generally very much choice in the matter, especially when it has its headquarters in a large town, and for the sake of convenience, and to encourage the spectators, it does not want to go very far out. But when there is any choice it should pay attention to matters of drainage and the quality and nature of the soil and grass. It makes all the difference in the standard of play, and the comfort and enjoyment of the players, according to whether the playing arena is regularly muddy or regularly dry. It need hardly be pointed out that high-lying land is better than low, and that sandy or gravel soil is better than clay, and that a short but tough and strong kind of grass is better than fine stuff that would squash under one's heavy boots like silken threads.

Every player in every match should make a particularly careful study of the methods of those of his opponents with whom he must come into contact in the course of the game, in order that the next time he plays against them he may know all their tricks and specialities from the beginning, and may lose no time in counteracting them. Nothing is more aggravating to a captain than to be obliged to point out to one of his men something that an opponent of long-standing is doing constantly and gaining by, but which only needs mentioning to be effectually checked.

A little bad temper will neutralise a lot of very fine skill. A reputation for the former will overshadow a reputation for the other, and a player of magnificent ability may find his prospects ruined by his disposition. Be a sportsman.

Don't tinker about with patent pills and tonics in the belief that you are going to make yourself feel better and stronger and so forth, particularly on the eve of a match. More often than not the effect is the reverse of that hoped for, and there is a great liability temporarily to upset the digestive organs, which is a very bad thing for one's play.

If you think there is a likelihood of your being called upon to fulfil before long a different position in the team than that you at present occupy, or a position in another team, take every opportunity of studying the methods and the tactics of the present performer in it. Do your best to assimilate the good features of his play, and to improve upon those that are most obviously faulty.

Never forget the mark which it is often so advantageous to make and claim. Remember that it is particularly useful to your side when you are within easy distance of the opponents' goal posts, and consequently be on the lookout for miskicks by your opponents' backs.

After the match, get wet things off you as quickly as you can. You may be an exceedingly strong person, and not in the least subject to colds of any kind, but such neglect as this has killed some of the very strongest persons in an exceedingly short space of time, and it is the height of folly to run such unnecessary risks.

Think over all the incidents of the last match in your leisure hours, and particularly try to recall some of the most successful and the most unsuccessful tactics, and draw the morals from them to the best of your ability. This private study is very beneficial, and tends to make a player use his head more when he plays the game.

When you are left out of your team, or otherwise have an off day, make a point of availing yourself of this rare opportunity of being a spectator at the best match in the district that day. Watch every movement with the utmost care, and try to divine the secret of every point of tactics. A player will be surprised at what he will learn in one afternoon in this way.

Besides having a thorough knowledge of the rules, take care to study all the different interpretations that have been placed upon them officially from time to time. A quantity of this case law will be found in the appendix to this volume. Sometimes an official ruling places a different construction on a rule from what the player had regarded as the proper one.

Do not enter half-heartedly into any particular manœuvre or form of tactics ordered by the captain or initiated by one or more colleagues, because it is your own private opinion that it is useless and is foredoomed to failure. It is quite likely that you may be wrong; and remember that if the movement should fail, your colleagues would be thoroughly justified in declaring that it did so, not because the design was poor or wrong, but because one of the men—you—did not do his best to carry it through. The man who even on the very rarest occasions does not do his very best is a danger to his side, and is not worth his place in the team.

The situation is sometimes tantalising when a man injured on the other side insists on continuing to play, though at a great disadvantage and possibly in pain. What are you to do when he has the ball, and it is your duty to take it from him? Take it from him. You must without doubt treat him exactly as if you were unaware of his injury or indisposition, and tackle him just as forcibly. The simple rules of war must of necessity apply to all such cases. The man who remains on the field must be treated as a combatant. If he is unfit to play he has no business to continue to do so, and must accept all the risks involved in his persistency. If a player were to make the slightest allowance for an injured opponent, he might some day find himself shot at by a man who had flown the white flag. Rugby football matches must be conducted on sound business principles, and sentiment can have no place in them.

Don't discuss the game with your opponents while you are on the field. You can give a much better point to your remarks when the match is over. The opponents whom you talk to may regard you as an unmitigated nuisance, and you are certainly not doing justice to yourself or your side by these conversational efforts. You cannot think hard about the game and talk at the same time.

GOOD RULES

It is better not to play at all if you don't feel that you want to play very much. You mustn't play Rugby "just for the exercise." Be keen as a knife, and play for all you are worth.

Don't be despondent if, being a wing three-quarter, chances do not come your way. You are still doing your duty, and you may have more than enough work to do before long.

Play right up to the whistle. Remember that what may appear to you to be a breach of the rules may not appear so to the referee.

Never shout for a pass unless you are in a better position than the man with the ball. You may be very anxious to do something, but you will get into trouble by such displays of over-eagerness.

Talk the game over with your colleagues when it is all over. Discuss thoroughly the tactics employed, and do not hesitate to ask for opinions as to whether you did right or wrong in a certain case when you have a doubt in your own mind. It is only by asking such questions, and gaining the advantage of the opinions and experience of others, that you will be quite sure about what to do in the same circumstances next time. This point is of more importance in the proper development of a player than might appear at the first glance.

Never play to the gallery. You have quite enough to do to play your proper hard game, and any player (except perhaps a full back) who remembers comments made by people in the crowd has certainly not been as keen during the match as he should have been.

Be quick in your decision, and be quick to act upon it. To be caught in two minds is fatal. The hesitating player a danger to his side.

Always scrape and clean your boots on the evening of the match, and do not put off this task until the following morning. By so doing you will preserve them in shape, and improve their wearing qualities.

Make a rule of being "spick and span" when you go on to the field. It may be true that you won't remain in that state very long, but nothing looks worse or conveys a worse impression to spectators than a player who leaves the dressing-room in dirty, ragged garments.

Be particular about the studs in your boots, and, if possible, visit the ground beforehand on the day of the match to see whether any modification of them is desirable. For a hard or frosty ground they should be short and stumpy. For fair ordinary turf three-quarter inch studs are best, and they should be slightly longer when the ground is wet and sodden.

Never play "dirty" or "foul" Do to others as you would like them to do to you. Nevertheless, when you tackle a man, tackle him hard, and see that you put him down. Accidents resulting from real hard tackling are very rare.

Never "speculate"—at least not in your own twenty-five. Ninety-nine successful fly-kicks do not atone for one failure.

If hurt during the game, never play on if you feel that your condition will prevent you from playing your best game to the advantage of your side. Inform your captain of the state of things, and take his advice as to whether you should change your position (if you feel you might do that) or retire from the field. If you made a mess of things in your injured state, the latter is not readily taken as a complete excuse, and your side might be very much better without you than with you.

If you miss your man, or fail to prevent him passing, don't give up hope, but double back by the shortest possible route to the point where you think you will intercept the play.

When you have passed the ball on attack, if you are a back, don't stop at this point with the idea that you have done all that is required of you, but back up quickly to a point where you think you may be of assistance, possibly in the way of taking another pass. A half or a five-eighth should make for a point straight up the field with the object of accepting a cross punt or a pass-in, or he may cut across behind the passing rush, to be there to recover a dropped or misdirected pass, or to act as a defence behind the attacking line in case of a pass being intercepted by an opponent.

Any back following up a punt or a drop-out by a colleague should sing out to the nearest player of his side, " I'm following this," and it is then the duty of that player, whether back or forward, to safeguard the vacancy. Most teams see that this is done when a player follows up his own kick, but they sadly neglect the precaution when he is following up the kick of a colleague, though it is obviously quite as necessary.

When a colleague is about to take or field the ball, particularly if he is your full back, and your last line of defence, always try to be at hand, if at all convenient, to back him up. The moral support you give him by letting him realise that you are at hand means much to him.

When your side are lined out for your opponent's drop-out, kick off, or free kick, the player who observes by the flight and angle of the ball that he can take it, should immediately call out "My ball," and when he has done that no other player should upon any account attempt to field that ball. A golden rule in this connection is never to oblige a colleague to come back to take a ball when you can take it as safely, or more so, by going forward. "My ball" should be sung out plainly, and the warning should be acted on immediately. Only in this way may be prevented the humiliating occurrence of two players between them misfielding an easy catch, which would have been a certainty for either of them "on his own."

CHAPTER XVI

TWO DANGERS TO THE GAME

Referees and refereeing—The independent critic—Blame on the official for declining popularity—A game that is being strangled—Splendid opportunities for Rugby—A grand game—Its local patriotism—Advantages over the Association game—Not so attractive as it might be—The game is made too slow—Fast play in New Zealand—Tedious play in a great international match—Disappointment of Association spectators—Referees who are too fond of the scrum—More free kicks should be given—Little things that might be overlooked—Different interpretations placed upon the law—The need for conferences of referees—Neglected points—The off-side rule—When the ball goes clean through the scrum—Why order it to be put in again?—Do referees like scrums?—The referee's attire—Does it conduce to efficiency?—Laggard referees—They must keep up with the game—A rule that would be wise—But it is easy to blame the referee—Difficult duties—People who could always perform them so much better—On arguing with the players—Answering a captain's civil questions—Concerning professionalism—Our own status—Players out of pocket—The New Zealand Union's risk—The best principles—Professionalism in the Association game—Does professionalism necessarily mean better play?—The Northern Union—Some of its captures—The game must be made more attractive—The size of the scrum—On future developments.

THE subject of referees and refereeing is one which we approach with some diffidence, and if we make a few pointed criticisms in connection with this department of the game as it is conducted in Britain, we hope that it will not be considered that we are meddlesome. They are made in a disinterested spirit, with a genuine desire to give any hints that may be useful for the further development of the game, and it often happens that the independent critic from outside is better able to judge of the merits of a matter than those who have been closely concerned with it all their lives, and who have become so accustomed to its faults that they have ceased to regard them as such.

With such an apologetic preamble, then, let it be said that it is our firm opinion, after having had a thorough experience of British referees of all sorts and all nationalities, old and young, radicals and conservatives, but always men of reputation, in the course of our thirty-two matches in Britain, that a not small proportion of the fault for the decline in popularity with the public of the Rugby game lies at their door, and that unless their methods are changed it will be useless to expect to win back from soccer very many thousands of the sport-loving spectators who have given their allegiance to that form of football, just as it will be equally hopeless to expect a much larger proportion of the rising generation of athletes to attach themselves to Rugby when there is more excitement to be had out of Association. Rugby in Britain, it is our honest opinion, is being largely strangled by the referees. There can be no doubt in the mind of any impartial man who has studied both codes and seen them in practice, that in itself it is a much finer game than Association as at present played. The opportunities for the development and display of science and skill are much greater, the varieties of attack and defence are more numerous, and the combined evolutions of the players on the field much more picturesque, while there is certainly nothing in soccer to equal the enthusiasm which a brilliant run right down the field by a Rugby three-quarter will create, swerving, dodging, leaping, and all the while travelling at something not very much over even time. Soccer is an excellent game so far as it goes, but to our minds it is to Rugby pretty much what draughts is to chess.

Moreover, it is our opinion that the referees are also largely to blame for the circumstance that those of the British public who do not understand the game, and who consequently give their patronage to soccer, have long since made up their minds that it is so complicated that they never could understand it. Rugby, as played in Britain, has the enormous advantage of being clean and untainted so far as professionalism is concerned. It is a pure, honest game, played for the sheer love of the thing, and despite all the hundreds of thousands of people who go to see Association League matches and Cup ties on Saturdays, it is difficult to believe that Rugby under amateurism would not come into chief favour if the game were made more strenuous and more attractive. One is paying a poor compliment to the character of the British people if it is suggested—as it has been—that, given equality in all other respects, they would rather watch professional players brought in from outside to play for them at so much a week, than they would watch the men of their own towns and villages, kinsmen and colleagues in work, who play the game for the love of it, and do their utmost to win the match for their side because of the spirit of local patriotism that runs high in them, and not because they are promised so much extra remuneration if they win, and by great distinction will command higher wages from some other club. It is impossible that that can be the British feeling, and if such circumstances have brought it about temporarily, there has been neglect somewhere and disease has been encouraged.

Undoubtedly Rugby in Britain, on the lines on which it is guided at present by the referees, is not by any means so attractive as it might be; indeed, it would not be much of an exaggeration to say that many matches cannot be attractive at all to spectators, even when they have the finest knowledge of all the points of the game, while at the same time they are far less interesting to those who take part in them than they ought to be. The British referee is a very slow man, and he seems to like a slow game. At all events, he takes very good care that it is slow. If he were to see the games that we play in New Zealand, he would wonder whether it was really Rugby that we play, so fast are they from start to finish, and so few and far between are the tedious interruptions that are such a prominent feature of the game as played in Britain. It is the same with the important games as with the others. Take, for example, the last game of all that we saw before we sailed for home, a game of the highest importance, and one in which we were more impartial than usual—if we may put it that way—inasmuch as we were in mufti, and playing the part of spectators. The reference is to the International between England and Wales at Richmond, and to the extraordinary succession of scrums that were ordered at the same spot towards the close of the second spell. Somebody had perpetrated a small mistake to begin with, and a scrum was ordered, and because something went wrong with that scrum it had to be done all over again, and again, and again, and again. How are players or people to tolerate this kind of thing? The referee had it in his power to set the game going at once by giving a free kick, and no good purpose whatever could possibly be achieved by all this constant scrumming. This kind of thing was quite enough to make any soccer adherent, who had turned up at Richmond that day to see what sort of a game it really was that had begun to be talked about, go home firmly decided that he did not want to see any more Rugby.

The British referee is undoubtedly far too fond of the scrum. He will insist on calling a scrum for the most trifling infringements, which do not affect either side, and which might very well in the interests of the game be allowed to let go. For example, when the ball is thrown in from touch, if it does not happen to be sent in a dead straight line, away goes the whistle, and a scrum is the result. In nine cases out of ten this is most exasperating. We strongly advocate a referee giving a free kick if he finds a man deliberately throwing the ball in in such a manner as to gain an unfair advantage. But small and purely technical breaches of the law, for the most part accidentally committed and giving material benefit to neither side, might certainly be overlooked with advantage to all concerned, and the game is then made brighter and faster to both players and spectators.

The playing of the game should be regulated according to the spirit of the law. It is then necessary that there should be an exact and general understanding as to what that spirit is, and there should therefore be a common interpretation of the rules. It is very evident that there is no such understanding and no such common interpretation in Britain, and it seems to us essential that one should be arrived at with as little delay as possible. One referee puts a certain interpretation upon a particular rule, and conceives that the spirit of the law is to a certain effect, while another referee reads quite a different meaning into the same law. This is very bad for the game, and unfair to the players. The remedy is fairly obvious. Some pains must be taken to bring all the referees into line, and the only way to do that is to hold frequent conferences throughout the country, where referees may assemble and discuss the particular penalties that are to be exacted for particular infringements. It is the only way. Before a referee can conscientiously demand a certain penalty for a certain infringement, he must know why he does so, and it is to be feared that in too many cases he has no such clear understanding of the situation. In Britain the referees are very loth to allow the advantage which accrues to a player from an opponent's knock-on, and when such a thing is done they generally whistle for a scrum. They are quite in order in allowing the player who has benefited from his opponent's knock-on to retain his advantage, and in not doing so they are unfair to him, and they make the game slower at the same time.

Then there is the case of a man taking the ball from a pass forward by a member of his own side when the former is off-side. In New Zealand the referees have no hesitation in ordering a free kick for such an infringement of the rules, but in Britain it is always a case of another scrum. Why? We think that our reading of the rule is the only one possible in the circumstances, and we quite fail to see how the scrum is justified. The result is that, the penalty being so light, these infringements of the off-side law are encouraged; but one still sees the scrum ordered when there has been a case of deliberate waiting off-side for the ball. There is another phase of the off-side law that needs to be more carefully considered by the referees. It is the written rule that "an off-side player shall not play the ball, nor during the time an opponent has the ball, run, tackle, or actively or passively obstruct, nor may he approach or wilfully remain within ten yards of any player waiting for the ball." How many times is the penalty for this infringement enforced in England or Scotland? Now on page 29 of the Welsh Handbook we read (extracted from the suggestions to referees as made by the International Board) in reference to this particular point: " It is important that referees should more strictly enforce these penalties, and it should be observed that a referee must award a free kick if he thinks a fair catch would have been made had not an off-side player, through his proximity and not retiring beyond the ten yards limit, have rendered such catch more difficult. For instance, a player waiting to receive the ball fails to catch it properly, and it falls from his hands to the ground. An opponent who is off-side, and who is standing or has approached within ten yards of him, immediately pounces upon him, and prevents him recovering and playing the ball. A free kick should be awarded, as it was the duty of the off-side player to have retired beyond the ten yards limit. Referees too often give offending players the benefit of unintentional off-side instead of inflicting the free-kick penalty." There is no excuse for referees not enforcing the proper penalties.

Reverting again to the scrum, where the failures of the referee are most in evidence, one reflects that over and over again during our tour three scrums were called for to get the ball properly scrummaged when there should have been only

TWO DANGERS TO THE GAME

one. When front rankers obstruct the passage of the ball into the scrum, a free kick should at once be given against their side. It is the only proper penalty, and when the ball is not fairly put in, the same penalty should be exacted from the offending side. It is inadequate and unfair merely to order the thing to be done over again. Again, many a time the ball is ordered to be put in again after having gone right through the scrum. In ninety per cent. of cases this is quite wrong. The ball has been put in fairly enough, and it is merely through the circumstance that the weight of the opposing forwards and their pushing power have been evenly distributed and balanced that the ball has gone through and neither side has been able to hook it. This is almost as much as to say that the state of things as between the two contending sides at that particular moment has been almost ideally equal, and that neither held the smallest advantage over the other. Then why should there be another scrum, as there generally is? Is this not a really very curious anomaly? The referee will have it that one side or the other must be asserting its superiority at the time the ball goes in. When it is thrown fairly into the scrum and it goes clean through, play should be allowed to proceed just as if it had been heeled. Many hard things are said about referees; but of all of them we do think that those which have reference to their partiality for scrums are most deserved. This partiality is almost incomprehensible. One can only conclude that for reasons of their own these officials do not like fast games, and that they enjoy watching scrums. It is to be urged that in these criticisms of the referee we are not making the slightest insinuation as to their capacity for judging fairly on points of fact. What we think is that in far too many cases they give decisions which cannot be supported by the laws of the Rugby code.

Another matter that calls for mention is a little more personal. Is it quite necessary that referees should almost invariably be attired, when officiating, in ordinary and more or less dainty walking-out costume—high collar, very likely cuffs, and no studs on their boots? It looks very well for a time at all events, and may, in the minds of some people, seem to confer a little halo of dignity on the man with the whistle. But does it conduce to efficiency? On the other hand, does it not frequently make it next to impossible for the referee to conduct his duties properly? In most respects a referee should be on an equality with the players if he hopes to keep up with a fast game. He should be both fit and properly dressed. He should see to it that he is always in good condition, and he should be a fast runner. If these requirements are not fulfilled, he cannot keep up with the game, and if he does not do that he cannot hope to give proper decisions in all cases. To be just, he must be on the spot. For example, suppose there is a passing run among fast backs, and the referee is left in the rear, as will inevitably be the case unless he too is a fast man and is equipped for travelling at a fast pace. When that referee is some fifteen or twenty yards in the rear, or even more than that, one sometimes hears his whistle go for a pass forward. How can he with any degree of certainty say whether there had been such a pass forward or not? One suspects that too often in such cases he is influenced merely by the appeal from the other side. It should be a rule that referees should be attired in sweaters, and if players find it necessary to have studs in their boots in order to enable them to run fast enough on the somewhat slippery turf, one fails to see how it is that they are not equally necessary to referees.

But after all it is very easy to blame the referee for this, that, and the other thing. He is the natural objective of the grumbling player, and we should not like it to be thought that we have no proper appreciation for the difficulties of his task—in Britain as everywhere else. We have the very greatest appreciation of the fact that these men give up their time, and often put themselves to the greatest inconvenience, in order to be of service to the game that they love like all

TWO DANGERS TO THE GAME

of us. We know from long experience on the football field that the referee's lot is never a happy one, and that it is very difficult to please both sides. And there are sometimes five or ten thousand people round the field, a majority of whom seem to be of the opinion that they could perform the duties of referee much more satisfactorily than the gentleman appointed. Players should always side with the referee against unfair criticism on the part of the spectators. The clever persons round the rails and on the stands who think they could do so well if they had the whistle, would never want a second experience if they were afforded a first. It would be likely that if they had such an experience they would never again want to see a football ground as long as they lived, and if perchance they did ever find themselves at a match, it is quite certain that wild horses would never be able to drag them on to the field of play to officiate as referee again. No referee is infallible, and the best of them are bound to make a mistake at some time or another, none of them being supplied with eyes in the backs of their heads to enable them to look both ways at once. It should be remembered that lookers-on in the position of spectators are often able to see more of the game than anyone else, and they should make the necessary allowances for the circumstance.

Both players and public alike respect a man who gives his decisions in a cool, clear, and business-like manner. Never under any circumstance should a referee argue with any player who sees fit to question his decision. Once he condescends to this sort of thing, he loses his command over the men, and the remainder of his task will be one of extreme difficulty. The referee is an autocrat, and he should remember that he is one; but, so far from being derogatory to his position, it is merely a wise act and one of common courtesy to explain his reading of some particular rule upon which he has just acted when the captain of a side invites him to do so in a gentlemanly way. He will lose nothing, but will gain in the confidence that he will inspire.

Now we have incidentally mentioned professionalism, and though it may be held to be none of our business to go any further into the matter as it affects Rugby football in Britain, there are one or two aspects of the case concerning which we beg pardon for intruding our opinions. In the first place, let it be said that we come into any discussion of this business with clean hands. In New Zealand we have very pronounced ideas on the subject of professionalism, and it is quite certain that it does not exist, even in the most modified form. Many dark insinuations have been levelled against the team that toured through Britain, and letters have been written to the papers suggesting fairly plainly that we were not pure amateurs, that we could not possibly afford to make such a tour as this, and that we must be paid, and probably paid well, for our services out of the large gate receipts in which we have had a share. We should therefore like it to be placed on record that the arrangement made with the members of the team not only precluded any possibility of profit, but made it quite certain that, one and all, they would be out of pocket, in some cases very considerably. Most of us have lost salaries and wages for the whole time that we have been away, and for this we receive no recompense.

When the tour was arranged, there was no idea of its being a financial success to the New Zealand Union, who promoted it. The Union promoted it at great risk of loss, and the extent of that risk may be appreciated from the circumstance of the authorities declining to give us the £200 guarantee for which we asked in the case of the international match against Scotland. At the first glance £200 may seem a lot of money; but it must be remembered that there were some thirty men to keep in comfort, and with travelling expenses for the bulk of them it may be reckoned that the cost of this international match to us could not be very far short of that sum. If, then, our drawing powers were regarded here in Britain as being so very poor that we could not make enough out of a big international match to pay our expenses, it must be evident that our prospects financially for the whole tour were very black, and that our Union was indeed taking a risk. Happily our success soon removed all danger in this respect. However, the point is that the arrangement with us was that we should be paid bare hotel and travelling expenses and the inevitable washing. Beyond that we have had nothing whatever. The Union takes the funds, and no doubt will apply them to the good of the game in our country.

The amateurism of Rugby in New Zealand is beyond suspicion, and we cannot help saying that what we have seen of the results of professionalism in Britain, and the spread that it is making, has had a deep impression upon us, and will certainly stiffen us in our determination to resist it if it should ever make an attack on our game in New Zealand. It seems to us that unless something is done, and the public is aroused to a proper sense of the danger of the situation, there will be less and less of amateurism in Britain in the future. Everybody must admire Rowland Hill's manful battle for it,—and he has no greater admirers anywhere in the world than in the colonies, where his name is a household word,—and it is sincerely to be hoped that so much splendid effort will never prove to have been wasted. It was a great pleasure to the Australasian colonies to hear that the moral support which they gave to the English Rugby Union at the time of and after the secession of the Northern Unionists, was of great value to it. If the game in England has degenerated a little as a spectacle for the public, the clubs and the players have at least the satisfaction of knowing that their principles are the best, and that when they play they are confident that each side is out to win, and out to win for the mere love of the thing. It is a painful thing to read, as we have read, articles written by men of authority in the Association football world, solemnly advising the Rugby Union to adopt professionalism as a cure for all its troubles. Leaving all other aspects of the matter on one side, and sinking the question of sport, what is the future of all these professionals when they have ceased to be of any use to any club? Some of them may go on all right, but is it too much to regard the lives of the majority as ruined? We think not. If it came to that, it is better that a game should be played badly, and that no one should go to see it, than that the price should have to be paid for professionalism as has to be in departments of football that are outside the pale of the Union.

And is it so certain that professionalism necessarily means better play and more attractive games? Take the case of the Northern Union. Its stronghold being those northern counties that are the homes of many a famous Rugby player, it is a serious menace to the Rugby Union, and we hear great stories of how they play the game in these days. During our tour many letters appeared in the sporting papers, written by prominent Northern Union people, which amounted to challenges to us to play them, and it was stated that we should then, and only then, meet the flower of English Rugby football, while at the same time it was very plainly insinuated that we should meet our doom. Of course we could do nothing of the kind, as it would have involved our becoming professionals ourselves, and it would have taken much more than a challenge from the Northern Union to have induced us to abandon our status. Their chief consideration being their gates, these clubs have unlimited amounts of money at their disposal to snap up any likely amateur player whom they may covet, and their offers at times are so tempting that poor working men can hardly resist them. Well, we have the names of three of their latest acquisitions in this way, one a Devonian and two Welshmen. One cannot fail to be apprehensive of the future of these men. They are long past the meridian of their success. We formed a very poor opinion of the play of one of them, and we seriously doubt whether either of the Welshmen would have been considered good enough to get into any Welsh team against us. Then, if this class of man is typical of the flower of the Northern Union, we may merely remark that if we had played a team drawn from that Union, we do not fancy that in such a match we should have received any check.

The English Rugby Union has undoubtedly a difficult task still in front of it, and one can only hope that it will continue to fight determinedly against this canker of professionalism, and that sooner or later there will be a revulsion from the present state of public feeling, and that professionalism will become distasteful to the people who want to see games played on Saturday afternoons. All that can be done should be done to make the game more attractive to players and spectators. It has been pointed out that our formations and systems make it opener and faster, and it has been suggested by some critics that even more might be done on the same lines. In the light of what has happened in the past, it would be dangerous to prophesy as to the future, and one could certainly not go as far as to suggest that either in Britain or in New Zealand we have attained the farthest point of the development of the Rugby game towards perfection. At the same time it is difficult to see in what direction future developments will lie.

Someone has suggested that as we in New Zealand have cut down the scrum from eight to seven with apparently beneficial results, it will be cut down still more in the future, and it has been put forward in print that five forwards are enough for the scrum, or that even fewer would be ample and the game would be all the faster. This would not do. After all, the scrum is one of the chief features of Rugby, and as it is worked at the present time it is capable of the application to it of an enormous amount of skill and science. You could not possibly make a proper scrum out of five forwards, or even six. Seven appears to be the absolute minimum. Apart from this view of the matter, what could be done with the men who were taken out? We have found that with seven forwards we have quite enough men in the back division for our utmost needs, and any more would only interfere with our present system of attacking movements, and be an embarrassment. One must guard against any tendency thus to crowd up the back division, for such a course of procedure would defeat the object of making the game faster and more interesting. In the attainment of this object, one must permit developments to take place as they force themselves on the game, and while, as has been said, it is too dangerous to prophesy, it may at least be put forward with some confidence that we shall not see fewer than seven in the scrum for a very long time to come. The game as it is played in New Zealand at the present time is fast enough and interesting enough for anyone.

GOAL!

ONE OF WALLACE'S CONVERSIONS – IN THE DEVON MATCH

CHAPTER XVII

PROSPECTS OF EXPANSION

> The "games of the world"—Spread of the British games—The games of the future—Their features—Climatic conditions—Rugby football in France—An increasing aptitude for the game—In Europe generally—Cricket as a universal pastime—Its disadvantages—Needs to be bred in the player—The advantages of football—The superiority of Rugby—The value of tradition—Its colonising properties—An amateur game—Simplicity of organisation—Bad examples—The evils of red tape, and their consequences—The status of Association football—Bright prospects of Rugby—An Imperial council—Rising colonies—The game in Australia—Customs in Sydney—The next menace to the supremacy of the mother country—The game in South Africa—Excellently suited to the country—Football in the United States—Suffering from want of good tradition—A very bad state of affairs—Description by an authority—A change required—A chance for Rugby.

ONE of the most interesting speculations with regard to the future of the game is as to the place that it will occupy among the games of the world in days to come. We use the term "games of the world" advisedly, for, with the greater facilities for intercommunication among peoples, their closer association with each other, and the tendency to break down sharp divisions of customs, habits, and even thoughts, and to make the features of life everywhere more general than particular, it is inevitable that games also should become less exclusive to particular countries than they are at the present time, and indeed every year we see them becoming less so. And just as the English language is spreading everywhere, and showing a disposition to become more the universal language than any other because the British people are the greater multitude and are themselves spreading all over the globe more and more every week and every month, so the games of the Britishers are spreading also and forcing themselves on the attention of foreign countries, who, after a preliminary lingering hesitation, sometimes adopt them whole-heartedly. Hitherto there may be said to have been more national games than countries; but with the closer association of nations and a closer community of interests there are certain to be fewer, and those that are the fittest and that are played by the greatest majority will inevitably survive. This is almost as much as to say that it is the British games that will endure and spread, and that not only because they are good games, and are played by the British people in so many different parts of the world, but because they have been consolidated and perfected by many generations of players, and have traditions attached to them which must give them an enormous advantage over all others. No games are so well adapted to become universal as are the British, although in some respects they appeal to a particular class of temperament. But, on the whole, their employment is less restricted in this way than other games. Other countries have had their favourite pastimes for hundreds of years, but where these have only a comparatively small vogue, and where they appeal most particularly to peculiar temperaments, they will gradually disappear and their place will be taken by the games which show the tendency towards universality. Thus, while we were in London we had an opportunity of witnessing an exhibition of the Basque ball game, pelota, and it is certainly one that has many strong features and which demands a great measure of skill on the part of the players. But neither this nor any other game of its class can ever make a strong appeal to British people. Its principles are altogether unsuited to their temperaments.

The universal games of the future as spread by the Britishers can only be their old games. There will be no new ones. They will all be, so far as games to be played in daylight are concerned, games requiring large spaces for movement, games for the open air, games in which hardihood and courage will count for something, and in which there must be a close association among large numbers of players on each side. Except in one or two very rare cases, such as golf, there is no bright prospect for the games that are individual rather than collective. They do not seize and hold on to the imagination of the people. British games, moreover, have for the most part the great advantage of being peculiarly adapted to such average climatic conditions as rule in most parts of the world where people most want to play games.

Therefore, while we think that in the future there will most certainly be a closer cohesion among the games of all the English-speaking peoples, other nations will be attracted by their example, and as the result of international friendships and other such influences the universality will be made more and more complete. In this connection we could not help but be greatly impressed by the enthusiasm of the French people for Rugby football as we witnessed it on the occasion of our brief visit to Paris at the conclusion of our tour through Britain. On the face of things, Rugby football hardly seems the kind of game most adapted to the Frenchman,—at least to the Frenchman whom we have, so to speak, carried about in our minds for so many years,—a man of great delicacy and gentleness in all his habits, and of such a hot, thin temperament as to make his participation in our rough-and-tumble sports seem almost an absurdity. But not only has this popular conception of the Frenchman in his unsuitability to strenuous athletic games been quite erroneous, having largely been built on international prejudices in the past, but the rising generation of the French people is showing an increasingly strong disposition towards such vigorous exercises as are favoured by our own countrymen. They are showing an adaptability and an enthusiasm for them that augur an almost certain success in the future

At the present time the Rugby football of France can hardly be said to have attained a very high level; but we were much surprised at its being anything like so good as we found it to be; and the French are so thorough in these matters, when they give their minds to them, that we are strongly of opinion that the game will spread in their country, and that in course of time they will be able to put a team in the field which will command the utmost respect of any other. Such enthusiasm as theirs must tell in the long run, even though it may be necessary for it to be bred through two or three generations, and to become natural, as is our own, instead of made. And in Germany and throughout the middle of Europe the prospects of the missionaries of British games are highly favourable.

When the games of the world come, then, to be reduced in numbers and a few British specialities are to be made almost universal, which are they to be? If cricket is always to be regarded as the premier game of England, it would nevertheless appear to be less calculated than others to spread. It does not attract continental peoples at all, and while it has gripped Australia, has some hold on South Africa, and is played to a small extent in America, it almost appears to have reached the limit of its expansion; while, in considering its prospects in this direction, it cannot but be regarded as most significant that even at home in Britain it is only popular in England, and has comparatively little vogue in Scotland, Ireland, and Wales. Cricket not only has the disadvantage from the point of view from which we are looking at it of being a game which is very largely dependent on fine weather, but it is a game which by its very nature needs more breeding into a people than possibly any other; and to a people strange to it, it would take too long to make any satisfactory start to inspire them with any enthusiasm for it. Cricket is a magnificent game without any doubt, but there is no overlooking the fact that it is to a large extent an acquired taste, and a taste that takes a long time to acquire if it has not been bred in a man. That is why the Englishman who does not follow cricket, and who did not play it at school, is so very indifferent to it as a rule—far more indifferent than he is towards other games he has never played and of which he may know next to nothing. Golf and even lawn tennis appear to have far greater attractions for outsiders and foreigners.

For a game to be played in cold and often wet weather, such as may almost be said to predominate in those medium high northern and southern latitudes where vigorous outdoor games are most in favour, a form of football seems to have more to recommend it than any other, and at the same time seems to have greater colonising properties, and so has the best prospects of something in the nature of the universality of which we have been speaking. And of the two chief varieties, Rugby and Association, it is hardly to be doubted that, outside the United Kingdom at all events, the chances of complete supremacy are in favour of the former. Its backing in the way of history and tradition is the stronger; while it has been so refined that it is now the most complete science, it has still in it more of the elements of the primitive game of the mediæval Briton, and these considerations count for much when the modern Britain is taking a game away with him to play in some other land.

Moreover, it has a solider backing from the public schools and the Universities. Reference to the inception and the history of British games played in the colonies will show that the old public school boys and University men constantly take the lead, and their influence is far more frequently in favour of Rugby than it is of Association. Public school boys had more to do with the original development of football in New Zealand than any other class. And while one has no desire to introduce any controversial matters at this point, it would be idle to overlook the fact that the present conditions under which Association football is played in Britain do not predispose people abroad towards it. When a game is started abroad, and pioneers have heavy work to do, they do not want a game that is regarded chiefly as a spectacle for the entertainment of scores of thousands of people who have never kicked a football in their lives. They want a game to play, and particularly they want a game that will cultivate in them all the best qualities of sportsmanship. Therefore they would prefer that they were not associated with a pastime which in the land of its birth is almost entirely in the hands of the professional element, who, despite any argument to the contrary, cannot possibly be imbued with the same feelings of the keen sportsman when they play the game, as those players who participate in it solely because they love it and not because they have any hope of pecuniary gain from it. Nor, to the outsider in want of a game and taking stock of those that are played elsewhere, does the idea of one that is controlled by such an intricate red-tapeified organisation make any appeal to him. In all games the maximum of simplicity of organisation should be aimed at. For the purpose of championships, of competitions, and even to make practicable matches between different clubs existing in different parts of a country, and to preserve an equitable arrangement between them in regard to many different points, some kind of controlling and legislative body is usually necessary and desirable; but it will always be found that those games have succeeded best in which this machinery has been of the simplest possible character, and that, on the other hand, some sports have been entirely ruined by over-legislation and meddlesomeness on the part of individuals with whom such tinkering is a hobby, and who very likely are themselves non-participants. For simplicity of control look at golf and cricket, and yet in regard to what games are there fewer difficulties? It has usually been the case that the more intricate and comprehensive this legislative machinery and the greater its meddlesomeness, the more determinedly has professionalism sprung up under it. The Rugby Union may not be perfect, but at all events it is a simpler, healthier body than some others, and there are not a multitude of hangers-on attached to it who every week are holding committee meetings under all kinds of names all over the country, always suspending someone or other, fining others, closing grounds, banishing officials, and generally tampering with the game, until the followers of it hardly know where they stand. There are far too many of these hangers-on, who spend too much of their time in travelling about meeting each other and holding committee meetings. They may to some extent be necessary in the present state of things, but the necessity has been created by themselves in the first place. Such is the government of professionalism.

When the Englishman goes abroad to settle, his ways of life tend to become simpler than when he lived at home, and he is simpler and more natural in his thoughts. And this kind of machine-managed game for professional players and scores of thousands of spectators becomes odious to him—more so, perhaps, than it would ever have done if he had stayed at home. There is no getting over the fact that, despite its popularity in Britain, the status of Association football among the games of the world to-day is low, and is likely to remain so. Nothing but a practical extinction for a time, and then a complete regeneration on strictly amateur lines, will raise it. There is proof of our contention in the fact that Association has had nothing like the influence on the colonies that Rugby has; and this leads us to the conclusion that the winter game for the future, the game that will become most general everywhere, is Rugby football as at present played, or some such modification of it as is brought about in the ordinary course of time. No game in the world has better prospects—none so good. It behoves those who are at the head of affairs in these circumstances to be careful in their actions and to appreciate the responsibility that is cast upon them. There must be some kind of close cohesion between the authorities at home in Britain and the subsidiary authorities in the colonies, who acknowledge—and are glad to acknowledge—the supremacy of the mother Union. In this connection one is glad to hear of the movement that is apparently on foot for the establishment of something in the nature of an Imperial Council, a movement which we believe is suggested chiefly by our friends in New South Wales. Such a Council or Board might do much towards stimulating interest in the game in the colonies, and in course of time it might lead to a kind of Universal Union, for if countries like France continue to develop the game as they are doing, and to play it under our rules as they must almost necessarily do, they will naturally desire some kind of official connection with the controlling authority.

The necessity for some more definite and complete arrangement of imperial management may not be so striking to the British footballer as it is to his brother in the colonies, because he has not a proper idea of the playing strength of those colonies. The capacity of New Zealand seems to have come as a considerable surprise to him, and unless we are much mistaken there are more such surprises in store. The prospects of the game in New South Wales and Queensland, as we can say from intimate personal experience, are of the brightest possible character. The game is going ahead in these quarters very rapidly, it is in a thoroughly healthy state, and we might confess that the players are if anything keener to perfect themselves and their system than we are. They have put into practice some very interesting ideas in Australia. For example, in Sydney they have annually, we think, what is called a country week, when all the clubs from the country districts come up to play, and make a thorough football festival of it. During this week these various country clubs play one against the other until one of them has established itself as the premier country club, and then that club plays the pick of the Metropolitan Union for supreme honours. This is by way of being a test match, and coming, as it often does, just before the engagement

PROSPECTS OF EXPANSION

with Queensland or New Zealand, forms a good trial for those matches. We play New South Wales once every two or three seasons. They have a better chance than we. They are better supported financially. Australian Rugby foot ballers could give a very good account of themselves in a tour in Britain at the present time, and unless we are very much mistaken they will be the next menace to the supremacy of this country. Of course in Victoria and South Australia they play under Victorian rules.

One cannot but think also that the prospects of the Rugby game in South Africa are very excellent. It does not seem possible to imagine a game that is more suited to the climate and conditions of that country, or to the habits and the temperament of the people who occupy it, than this one, and we believe that it is making the very best progress there. There is something about the climate and the country that makes one feel instinctively that here is a place where Rugby football would thrive if it would anywhere in the world. One of us has had a fair experience of the country, and this thought recurred over and over again.[1]

But the future progress of the game is not likely to be confined to our own colonies, or even to some of the continental nations. Those people who take any interest in this aspect of the game cannot have failed to notice with some concern what has been going on in the United States recently. The history of football in the United States has been curious and not altogether happy. After a very vague sort of beginning, something in the nature of a regular game of football was developed on lines which more nearly corresponded to the Association game than any other. The game was practically confined to the college teams. Shortly afterwards, about 1875, an effort was made to introduce the Rugby game into the country, the other one not having been wholly satisfactory. Harvard took the initiative in this matter, and at length persuaded Yale not to adopt the

[1] I acted as a scout during the Boer war.—D. G.

Rugby game out and out, but to make a kind of compromise between that and the American game as then in force. Some of the rules of the new blend were very peculiar, as for instance, that which ordered the ball to be thrown into the air whenever a foul was committed. By and by the American element was dropped out and more of the real Rugby introduced, so that eventually the game became very much like Rugby. But from that point there was a relapse. America had no ties with Britain, and, so far from being influenced by British sports, there was something of a natural desire to be independent and original in all such matters. And so the game in America drifted in an entirely different direction from the course of development that was being pursued in the home of the game.

The history of the game in America is a very striking example of the value of sound traditions to a game, or rather of the danger of loss of balance when these traditions are absent. When these traditions are behind a game in a country, the spirit of progressiveness is always wisely tempered by a certain conservatism which is born in the players. They have a regard for the great events of the past, and a respect for their great players, and they feel that they prefer to play the same kind of game, or one something like that which their fathers and grandfathers used to play. Certain developments are inevitable; but the main principles remain the same. This steadying influence counts for a great deal, and prevents any such wild and revolutionary changes as would spoil the game or make an entirely new one from it. A game that has been slowly evolved during four or five hundred years is not to be suddenly improved out of existence in a single generation. But the American player has been without these traditions and steadying influences. He has had no point to which to revert when going along too fast, and we have the result, with a great moral attached to it, in the frightful and chaotic state of affairs which has at length been brought about. In the game as is played in

America now, brute and bloody force counts for far more than it ought to do in any game, and it is appalling to hear that in consequence of the methods employed there were killed on the football fields of the States from the beginning of the season up to the middle of December 1905, no fewer than twenty players, and thirty-six were severely injured. Players go on to the field wearing all kinds of weird head protections, and after a little while the game develops to such a furious state that life and limb are counted as of next to no value. The following account by a leading authority in an American newspaper may serve to convey to people who have the privilege of not having witnessed such a game some idea of the revolting character of the proceedings:—

"I have witnessed most of the great college games during the past seventeen years, and have enjoyed various phases of every one of them. The skilful punting, the artful drop kicks, the long-dodging runs, the general opening out into field play, and even the excitement of an occasional fumble, tend to induce the spectator to close his eyes to the overwhelming brutality of the rest of it.

"And the rest of it is about ninety-nine per cent. Players have been deliberately jumped upon when lying isolated in the field, and their bones broken. Players when punched in the face have begged the umpire not to put the offender off the field, in order that they might 'get even.' Players have been knocked out repeatedly by foul blows. It is a part of the game to cripple the strong men of the opposing side, and put them off the field if possible. Any truth-loving coach will admit these things.

"But this is not the only bad feature of it. With a contest under present rules, running fairly and smoothly, there is a 'down' about once a minute. The spectators see but little more in these line-plays than masses of men piled indiscriminately on top of each other. To the average onlookers it is a senseless proceeding, repeated over and over again.

"They do not know who has the ball, where he struck the line, who jammed him through, who tackled him, or why it is necessary for twenty-one men to pile on top of him if they can do so.

"Of course there is a certain amount of science in these scrimmages just as there is science in a big battle or a prize-fight, but of what use is it? There is science in the opening of a hole in the line, and in the 'interference,' which is warding off the opposing players with knees, arms, shoulders, and elbows, but that it is a brutal science as it stands cannot be gainsaid. It is a science which means an injured player for almost every ten yards the ball is advanced.

"In every scrimmage an appalling amount of sheer brute force is expended, and the huge pyramids of players are the result of it. What goes on in the heart of these scrimmages, nobody knows, not even the players themselves. A player with the ball in making a plunge against the line feels himself hurled forward by an addition to his own impetus, in the shape of two or three of his muscular fellows selected for that very purpose. He sees the opposing line mass and bunch against him. Those pressing behind do not care how he gets through, so long as he can lie down his own length along the sward, with his head to the enemy's goal, while the two teams pile helter-skelter on top of him.

"He feels the crush of a knee into his solar plexus, the smash of a foot into his ribs, the impact of a fist against his jaw, and when the scrimmage is disentangled he lies there dead to the world. This is repeated time after time with a steady and persistent brutality that is amazing. The sufferer does not know that he is wilfully attacked, and it may be granted that in most cases he is not. But the requirements of the game are such that no human battering-ram, however strong, can withstand the strain for any length of time and come out of it unharmed.

"Such mass plays are not only dull and uninteresting, but they form the most brutal feature of the game, within the limits of the rules. They are unnecessary. They speak well for the courage of American college boys, but argue ill for their judgment, and their love for real, exhilarating pastimes. Such scrimmages place a premium on bull-necked force. Agility counts for little. Speed goes for naught. Artful dodging, in such a mess, is a negligible factor.

"The game as it stands is altogether on the side of the heavy and experienced rush line which ploughs through its opponents foot by foot and yard by yard to the goal, no matter how many may be killed and injured. The lighter players as a rule are not wanted.

"For real engrossing interest to the spectators, save for an occasional punt down the field or an occasional kick over the goal bar, the game, according to present rules, might almost as well be played with a red rag as a football. To the uninitiated it resembles nothing so much as the game of 'Who has the button?' with an ingredient of manslaughter mixed in."

The Americans have too much sound sense not to realise the enormous mistake of tolerating a "game" of this kind, and at last there has been a general outcry against it, with the result that it is threatened with either a very radical alteration or complete extinction. At the time of writing, the latter course seems to be the one towards which the best feeling most generally inclines, and we are told that the colleges and the players are at last sick of the whole thing, and are looking round for a new game to adopt and to start fresh with from the beginning. Rugby football has already been mentioned, and there is reason to believe that a serious consideration is being given to the possible adoption of the game and the laws of the English Rugby Union, with an understanding that after such adoption there shall be complete adherence to them and to their subsequent modifications, the States, for the time being at all events, taking their time from the home of the game.

These contemplations may have a more important bearing on the future history of Rugby football than may appear at first. If they took up the game, the enthusiasm and the thoroughness of the American students may be taken for granted, and they would not be satisfied until they had achieved a position of distinction.

Having all these various considerations in mind, one is led to believe that there is a great future of popularity in store for the game, of which those who only follow it at home in England are not in the best position to judge.

CHAPTER XVIII

HOW THE "ALL BLACKS" PREPARED FOR THEIR TOUR

>A dream of old—A previous effort—New Zealand not united—Opposition from Otago—English Union would not entertain the proposal—All for the best—The colony united—Visit to Britain arranged—Excitement in New Zealand—Selecting the team—Trial matches—An avalanche of criticism—Eleventh hour selections—The team's last matches in New Zealand—Embarkation on the *Rimutaka*—Conferences on tactics—Methods brought into line—Entertainments during bad weather—Some disquieting experiences—The calm—Monte Video—Hard practice on board ship—Training rules—The daily programme—A very thorough system of preparation—Forwards and backs hard at it—Huge appetites—Tropical heat and cessation of work—Players in the stoke-room—Prizes won at the ship's sports—Arrival at Plymouth—A little nervousness—Headquarters at Newton Abbot—We witness a match—More confidence—Hard practice on the field—An Englishman's prophecy—How we won our first match—Welcome back to Newton Abbot—The British sportsman—The campaign begun.

TO those who were not of our party, our little band of brothers, the tour of the New Zealanders through England, Scotland, Ireland, and Wales towards the end of 1905 may have been, and very probably was, but an incident, even if the leading one, of a season; but to the "All Blacks," as we came to be called, and everybody who has at heart the best interests of Rugby football in New Zealand, it was at the same time the coming true of an old dream, the fulfilment of a great ambition, and the consummation of the work, the endeavours, and the study of long years. Much was written about the events of that tour as they transpired; but perhaps we may be pardoned for the belief that now, when the facts are being condensed and put away into history, some comment, and occasionally some new intelligence, from our side may not be unacceptable, since others, and not merely ourselves, acclaim this team of "All Blacks" as having established a more wonderful record than any other team had ever done before them, coming as it did within but a veritable ace of absolute perfection. We were pleased to think also that we did something to rouse the interest in this great game among people who were evidently not paying the attention to it that they should do. Such impartial notes and comments as we make here could not be made before, for very much the same reason as that which prevented us from telling to everybody the smallest details of our methods, while, as it seemed to us, the secrets were still of some value. We did not believe in our officers being war correspondents to the journals of the enemy while hostilities were still in progress, and the rule against the procedure was maintained through the tour.

As suggested, the idea of this tour, and of our being matched against the best football talent of the mother country, was no new one, and it is not to be supposed that, just because the trip had to be postponed until last year, this was the earliest occasion on which we felt ourselves able to undertake such a task without fear of disgrace. We should probably have been able to give a very fair account of ourselves some years ago. A long time since, during a period that is now lapsing into the dim past, the New Zealand footballers made an official and very strenuous effort to persuade the British authorities to receive a team from the antipodes. At that time, however, our New Zealand Union, though in being, was not complete, and this proved to be the stumbling-block. Some of the provinces up to then had not joined the Union, and, as often happens in such cases, they were not only not with us, but against us; and when it was proposed in the name of this Union, and standing for New Zealand, that a team should visit England and challenge her best to play them, there were some very strong comments

HOW THE "ALL BLACKS" PREPARED 241

made in the colony, and feeling in the matter ran high. The chief of those outside the pale was Otago, and when the New Zealand Union persisted in laying the proposal officially before the authorities at home, and at the same time presented for their inspection a plan of the country marked in red and blue to show what an insignificant portion of it lay outside the influence of the Union, Otago took occasion to be represented at the meeting, and strongly and successfully opposed the scheme. In all the circumstances that obtained at that time, it was, no doubt, just as well that the team that was then suggested did not sail. Neither the Unionists nor the people of Otago would have felt satisfied that it was quite the real thing from New Zealand, despite the fact that a very strong combination could have been got together. It was better to wait, gather the whole of the colony under the banner of the Union, and then send out a side whose doings would stir the interest and arouse the warm sympathy of all the people in the colony from one end to the other. In due course Otago joined the Union, New Zealand was as one, and then in 1903 the complete authority again approached the English Rugby Union in the matter of a proposed visit, it being a considerable point that in the meantime a good British team had visited us and found plenty of sport. On this occasion the English Union received our addresses with cordiality; but as it was then too late to make satisfactory arrangements for a visit during the season of 1904-5, we were advised to defer it until the early part of the following session. We were glad to assent to the proposal.

Then New Zealand football was very greatly stirred. Players had a new ambition to achieve, one that was greater than any that had been held before them in former seasons. A band of the best men had to be chosen to sail nearly half-way over the world to play, with the badge of the fern leaf on their jerseys, in the name of their homeland. As a preliminary to the serious consideration by the authorities as to who should go and who should not, the various provincial unions throughout the colony were asked to submit the names of players who might be regarded as suitable candidates for final selection. The long list that was forthcoming was boiled down to one hundred and fifty before it was placed before the special selection committee, which consisted of two experts from the North Island and two from the South Island. The committee then got to work, and after some time they succeeded in reducing the number to fifty, and inquiries were then made as to character in the first place, and physical soundness in the second, a doctor's certificate upon the state of each man being asked for and given. Then a further reduction was made, and some clear idea was formed at this stage of what the composition of the New Zealand team was likely to be. A trial match, North $v.$ South, was played in the presence of the committee, and after that a team for Britain was chosen, with the necessary reserves, or rather alternatives.

The team as originally selected consisted of twenty-four players, nineteen of whom left New Zealand early in July to play three matches against New South Wales before the final departure from Wellington on the first of August. Playing at Auckland beforehand, they were severely pressed, and only just managed to gain a victory owing to the superiority of their backs, though it had to be taken into consideration that Gallaher, Tyler, and Mackrell, three of the chosen for Britain, were included in what would even without them have been a very strong Auckland combination. This match, as was to be expected, was followed by a perfect avalanche of criticism upon the manner in which the selectors had done their work, and it was stoutly maintained that they had not chosen nearly the best side that the colony was capable of putting into the field. The position of the selection committee was made still more uncomfortable by the accounts that came over from New South Wales of what was happening there. Our men did pretty well in the first two matches, which they won by large margins of points; but in the third

HOW THE "ALL BLACKS" PREPARED 243

and last match the score stood at eight points (two potted goals) to three (one try) against us when only three minutes were left for play. Some magnificent rearguard movements, however, resulted in Smith obtaining a splendid try, which Wallace converted by an even more splendid goal kick, and thus the New Zealanders were able to make a draw of it right on time.

It was quite evident that there was something wrong with the team, and by this time expert opinion was fairly general that it was in the forward division that things were not what they ought to be, and, specifically, that what was wanted was a lock. In New South Wales, also, a good wing forward was sorely missed; but as Gallaher had not made the trip, this was a trouble for which there was a remedy waiting in due course. For the improvement of the side in other respects, Cunningham, one of the best lock forwards New Zealand has ever had, and Abbott, wing three-quarter, were added to the team. The wisdom of the inclusion of the former was amply demonstrated by results in Britain, for Cunningham played in fifteen matches without a break, and by the end of that time he had so educated Newton up to the peculiarities and necessities of the position of lock, that the team's selection committee had no hesitation in playing him in the English and Welsh international matches.

Before they took ship, the team was matched against three of the provincial teams, one of which, Wellington, beat it by three points to nothing. It was a wet day. Although we could not be expected to be working very well together so soon, and were opposed in these cases by teams who, so far as knowledge of each other was concerned, were in perfect combination, these results serve to indicate that we left a lot of very fine talent behind us, and it is not to be supposed that the New Zealand team, although, as we think, the best that the colony could put into the field, was so vastly superior to what was left behind as to be unrepresentative of the whole. Wellington beat us by three points to nothing, and then we sailed over the sea and won our next match, against Devon, by fifty-five points to nothing, and were not again beaten until we tackled Wales, who did just what Wellington had done before we sailed.

When we embarked we had the best wishes of the whole colony for our success in the homeland, as England is always called out there. Then for the first time did many of the team see and know each other. At the first glance this may seem a surprising state of affairs; but it must be remembered that men were chosen from the extreme north and from the extreme south, and between these points there is a distance of twelve hundred miles. We had been reckoning on entering upon a system of physical training and doing something to perfect our scrum formation and make it work in a scientific manner as soon as we left New Zealand; but when the good ship *Rimutaka* was bearing us away southeast towards Cape Horn, so boisterous and cold was the weather, that we had to come to a decision to suspend these training operations for a fortnight, until we got clear of the dreadful antarctic storms. In the meantime we occupied ourselves by discussing the possibilities of our tour, and there were held at set times the most serious conferences on tactics and rules. At these conferences the whole team assembled, and there were lively discussions as to what would be the best methods to adopt in ordinary and in particular circumstances. The necessity of such conferences lay in the fact that, as was indicated at the beginning of this work, there are in the colonies several variations from the standard system of play, and several of our men had been accustomed to different variations. It was therefore imperative that we should come to a common understanding as to what our particular tactics were going to be, and eventually we agreed upon the system practised through the tour, which was the most popular in our colony. Apart from this, we studied the game very deeply, and made ourselves thoroughly sympathetic with each other in all matters.

Much entertainment of all kinds was forthcoming during those tedious days when we were kept indoors. Two enthusiastic bridge players introduced the game to the party, and thereafter much time was spent in this diversion, while several concerts were organised, and we got up impromptu debates, in which our fellow-passengers joined. During this period we laid the foundation for a fine good-fellowship among all the members of the team, so that as time went on we were all just like brothers in one large family. It was a good advantage to have this perfect understanding so soon. We passed the Horn on our third Sunday out, and were very glad to pass it, for on the two previous Saturdays we had had what were really terrifying experiences of the antarctic storms, which make this route such a dangerous one to mariners. If by any stretch of imagination there could be said to have been a humorous side to these experiences, it might have been discovered in watching the different facial expressions of the various members of the team. They were mostly representative of abject misery and despair, and one thinks that we were all unanimous in one thing at that time, and that was in a devout longing for dry land. It may safely be said that the majority of us would gladly have foregone the anticipated pleasures of our tour if in exchange we could have felt ourselves once more safe in New Zealand.

But after the storm the calm, and as we glided up the east coast of South America the weather each day showed a great improvement, until, after nineteen days' steaming, we anchored at Monte Video in beautiful tropical weather. Here a large batch of first saloon passengers and a supply of coal were taken on board. Monte Video was very interesting to those of us whose first experience it was of anything Spanish, but it was not altogether pleasing to the nasal sense, and the crude system of sanitation was not quite the same kind of thing that we had been used to in New Zealand. When we left the capital city of Uruguay, we felt proud that we were of British heritage, and we had not developed a very high opinion of the colonial Spaniard.

Now that we were in good weather, a fortnight's hard practice was put in by the whole team. Everybody was eager, and it was partly through this eagerness, and partly because we had not got used to making allowances for the movements of the ship while we were engaged in our training exercises, that several minor accidents took place, resulting in one or two men retiring from action for a short period. Before we enter into a detailed description of our training and practice, we must make some expression of our indebtedness to the captain of the ship for the excellent facilities that he granted to us, in the way of providing us with a clear deck, and netting off a large open space for our practice at handling and passing the ball. Henceforth training rules were strictly enforced.

Breakfast was at half-past eight, and it was optional whether each man had a run about before then or not. Some few enthusiasts did so regularly; they would miss no chance of attaining the most complete fitness. At ten o'clock all hands appeared on deck in football costume. The first part of the programme was a jog trot round the deck for about a mile and a half under the direction of Smith. Then, under the direction of Gallaher and Cunningham, the forwards were put through half an hour's good solid scrum work. The men were tried in every possible place in the scrum, and no hooking was attempted until we had done ten days of this kind of preliminary examination of our forces. While the forwards were thus practising the various tactics of scrum work, the backs, under the direction of Smith, were just as thoroughly practising sprinting along the fore deck, where a very fine length of about forty yards was always clear for us. Then all hands were mustered together again on the hurricane deck, where, under the direction of Gallaher, a vigorous course of physical drill was gone through. After that passing was practised two at a time, while on another part of the

HOW THE "ALL BLACKS" PREPARED 247

deck Sandow's developers, boxing gloves, and a punching ball were available, and were patronised systematically by all the men. All this made up a very good morning's work, and by the time we had bathed and rubbed down it was time for one o'clock lunch, and never before in any saloon had such an array of powerful appetites been in anxious readiness for the ministrations of the stewards. On such a long voyage as ours, all perishable victuals had, of course, to be kept in the freezers, and the stewards were always engaged in a procession to these freezers to withdraw from them supplies over and above what had been considered sufficient for each meal.

This sort of training went on steadily for a fortnight, and then we ran into such tropical heat that any kind of physical exertion was really out of the question, and training operations were suspended for a week; but after that we got in another week's training before our arrival at Plymouth. It is worth mentioning that many of the heavier members of the team paid periodical visits to the stoke-hole, where they performed the ordinary duties of stoker, and it was reported that they were so efficient and so energetic in this capacity that the engineers constantly found it necessary to blow off steam when they were at work! Despite these various means of keeping in condition, nearly every man put on weight. One of us who write (Stead), who was only ten stones and the lightest man in the team on leaving the colony, actually put on twenty pounds during the voyage, and, more marvellous still, played at eleven stone four all through the tour. The same thing, though not quite to such a marked extent, happened to other members of the party.

A committee representing all the passengers on the ship drafted a sports programme, which included several events, with prizes offered to the winners. Various members of the team managed among them to annex most of the prizes. We assisted to the best of our ability—which was not small— at the concerts that were periodically held, and we invariably supplied the music when there was dancing on deck. When we left the *Rimutaka* we felt that we were bidding good-bye to a very old friend, and, judged by the way in which the captain, officers, and even many of the passengers, looked us up while we were on tour, it seemed that the feeling was reciprocated.

Although it was very early in the morning when we arrived at Plymouth, we were given a most gratifying welcome by representatives of British Rugby football. A strange feeling of exultation possessed us at being at last in dear old England; but at the same time, a great anxiety came up in our minds as to how we should get on in competition with the great sides that were waiting to be matched against us. Now we realised that the time of our trial was at hand, and we were to be called upon to justify all the care and wisdom of our selectors, and to make the name of New Zealand football respected. A little nervousness at such a time was perhaps excusable. Mentally and verbally we ran over all the old arguments for and against our success. We had confidence in our system on account of the manner in which it had fared against the British team that had come out to play us; but, on the other hand, there was the possibility that that team did not adequately represent the flower of English Rugby football. One and all we were eager to begin, as indeed was sufficiently indicated by the circumstance that within an hour of being fixed up at our first headquarters the whole team was out practising in real earnest.

Newton Abbot, in South Devon, where we were first domiciled for a seven days' preparation for our first match at Exeter against Devonshire, was an ideal spot for the purpose. It was quiet and healthy, and was central for the little sight-seeing that we all desired to do, and which was quite irresistible in the circumstances. We shall always have a pleasant recollection of the beautiful autumn afternoons that we spent on the moors and at the seaside resorts of this beautiful county. It was midday on Friday, September 7,

TACKLING PRACTICE BY THE NEW ZEALANDERS
(DUNCAN COLLARING BOOTH; NEWTON ON THE LEFT)

when we arrived at Newton Abbot, and although it was raining hard, we spent the whole of that afternoon in running and in kicking practice. On the following day we went by invitation to Devonport to witness a match between the Albion and Torquay, and to obtain, if possible, some kind of notion of what we were about to be called upon to do. We went away after that match with some reduction of the feeling of nervous anxiety that had possessed us from the time of our landing, for, after making full allowance for the earliness of the season, and the consequent excusable want of combination on the part of the Albion, whose splendid record we had to bear in mind on the other hand, we felt convinced that, with ordinary luck in matters affecting the health of our men, we should win a majority of the club and county games.

On the following Monday and Tuesday we were at it in grim earnest at ten o'clock each morning. Picking sides, we played a really vigorous game, giving and receiving hard knocks. As a matter of fact, Harper and McDonald were so knocked about that they were not available for the first three matches on our programme. Such very serious work might at the first glance appear to have been rather unwise; but we hold that it is necessary to be more than merely fit in wind and limb to attain the real acme of fitness for Rugby football. A man must be able to stand the hard knocks, and to be able to stand them he must have had some practice and some intimate and recent personal experience of them. It is wonderful what good a little knocking about will do for a man, and it was this vigorous practice in which we indulged at the start that made us, when we turned out against Devon, feel as if we had already played a couple of real hard games, instead of this match at Exeter being the first one of the new season.

We fully expected to win the match against Devon after what we had already seen, but no one anticipated that we should be blessed with such a fine and easy victory as came our way—55 points to 4. The result was all the more gratifying to us, as it demonstrated our thorough fitness to last out a hard and fast game, and it was really a splendid testimonial to the sound preparation on natural and sensible lines to which we had submitted ourselves. An interesting incident before the match is worthy of mention. We fell into conversation with a prominent resident of Newton Abbot, who was a great Rugby enthusiast, and who indeed was a referee, and he tried to extort from us what was the full extent of our anticipations in connection with this match. When he saw how the Devon team was constituted, he kindly gave us his opinion as to what was likely to happen. He was not very encouraging. "You might worry them a bit at the start," he said, "because you are in so much better condition; but Devon, with their superior passing and potting, will be all over you at the finish." One need hardly say that we were highly elated at the result of our first venture on British soil. We won so easily because the Devonians were so utterly at a loss as to how to counteract our system of attack.

The same evening we were given a practical illustration of what a truly sporting people the English are, and our bosoms swelled with pride at the reflection that we were of the same blood and the same race. It was a quarter to twelve when we got back to Newton Abbot from Exeter, and we expected to find the little place all still and quiet, and its inhabitants all in bed. Instead of that they had turned out *en masse* to welcome us back and to cheer us after our victory. There were bands playing, men, women, and children shouting in thousands, and everybody doing their utmost to show their pleasure at our success. They seemed to have regarded us as belonging to Newton Abbot. And we were given this reception after having beaten the pick of their county! We were not a little astonished, but much more delighted, and our hearts warmed towards our English brothers then. We saw that the people of Devon, whether defeated or victorious, were always of that glorious type known all the world over as the British sportsman. We knew a little more of our countrymen that night than we had ever known before, and until we go over to the great majority the welcome that was given to us then, and indeed throughout our tour, will never be effaced from the memories of any of us.

But now our campaign had begun in real earnest, and there was much to think about. We felt that great feeling of satisfaction that comes of being in action after a long period of waiting, when we fell asleep in the small hours of the morning.

CHAPTER XIX

THE GREAT CAMPAIGN OF 1905

The match against Cornwall—Another easy victory—Third victory at Bristol—Good work by our halves—At Northampton—A criticism—169 points to 4—The Leicester match—Gift of boots—In London—The Middlesex match—Anxious to make a good show—Points of our play—Engaged against Durham—A hard game against the champion county—The Hartlepools—A gigantic score—One try every five minutes—A telegram from Mr. Seddon—Ordeals before us—The Northumberland match—The men who scored the tries—Gloucester—Good combined attack—Wallace's fine run—The game against Somerset—Devonport Albion—The first team to attempt to play a winning game—Backs short of pace—The Midland Counties—A good lot of forwards—The thirteenth match—The Surrey match at Richmond—Too many free kicks—The Blackheath match—A team of many internationals—Seven forwards in the scrum—The University matches—Richmond—Bedford collect a side—Necessary change in our plans—The international match against Scotland—Trying conditions—Scoular not to blame—An unfair accusation against us—West of Scotland—Gloomy prophecies—Staleness in the team—A great responsibility—An enjoyable visit to Ireland—Tactics in the international—Splendid forward play by the Irishmen—Match with Munster—The international match against England—A great crowd at the Crystal Palace—Disappointing conditions—A poor game—Could England have chosen a stronger side?—Entertained by the Rugby Union—At Cheltenham—The match against Cheshire—Against Yorkshire—Northern Union spectators—The great match against Wales—Staleness prevalent—Dashing play by the Welshmen—Most of our backs off colour—The only defeat—Glamorgan opposed at Swansea—The Newport match—A remarkable match at Cardiff—A narrow escape at Swansea—All over—Return to London—A trip to Paris—A great time—Happy remembrances—Great British players—British sportsmanship—Hopes for a future visit.

THE second match of the tour, which was against Cornwall, and which was played at Camborne on September 21, resulted in another very easy victory for our men, for with four goals and seven tries we won by 41 points to 0. Hunter obtained three tries, Smith two, and Nicholson,

Wallace, Mynott, McDonald, Abbott, and Deans one each, while Wallace did all the converting. The last-named, while playing at back, had really nothing to do, and often went up with the three-quarters, where he showed himself formidable in attack. The Cornishmen were a good enough side, but they were not capable of withstanding our system of play; and, like the Devonians, they saw very early on in the game that defence would be their portion, but at the same time were at a loss as to how to make it effectual. They simply did not know, and consequently when the game got into full swing we did pretty nearly as we liked. Two days later we appeared at Bristol, and there, curiously enough, we beat the Bristol club by exactly the same score as that by which we had overcome Cornwall. We scored 41 points to none, our total being made up on this occasion of seven goals and two tries. Smith, Hunter, and Thompson credited their side with two tries each, and Roberts, Stead, and Seeling with one, while as before Wallace kicked all the goals. Our halves did very good work, and their swerving seemed to impress the onlookers very much, judging by the things that were said and written about it. Close attention was also now being paid to our scrum formation; and, while at the outset of our tour the British people appeared rather to treat the idea very lightly and to think that it would fail against the orthodox British formation, they were now disposed to reconsider the matter, and to ask themselves whether there was not something in it. Out and out suggestions were made that the best way of playing against us would be to have only seven forwards in the scrum, and to give a roving commission to the other man, who should be fast. Gabe, Llewellyn, and other prominent Welsh players witnessed this match.

After this we left the west and journeyed up into the Midlands, turning out against Northampton on September 28. In this match we made our first experiment with the team, putting Gillett to play as wing forward instead of

Gallaher. Generally, the team was slightly weaker than before, in view of a specially hard match with which we were threatened when we should be opposed to Leicester almost immediately afterwards. In the circumstances our men did very well to win by 32 points to 0—four goals and four tries. A. O. Jones of Leicester came over to watch the match, and the conclusion that he arrived at was that our superiority, such as had been demonstrated, was due to individual excellence, and that our tactics were of quite secondary importance. Of course we thought that in these early matches, as in all others, our individual form carried us a long way, and it is possible that in the match against Northampton our tactics had not such telling effect as they had at other times; but to say that our tactics were of quite secondary account, as a generalisation, was quite wrong. We who employ them know very well that they are of the supremest importance to us. So far we had scored 169 points to 4.

Our match with Leicester on the first day of October was very interesting to us. It was particularly so from the fact that Leicester were undoubtedly strong forward, and they gave a practical demonstration of the fact that had been or ought to have been suspected by other opponents, that if they could beat us forward we were relatively not too solid on defence. A. O. Jones was still impressed with our individualism as against our collectivism. We won by five goals and a try (28 points) to nothing, so that we were now within three points of our second century, while the only score against us was the dropped goal that Devon obtained when we were blooded at Exeter. While we were at Leicester we were each presented with a pair of football boots, to our own design and measure. All the players we met, with whom we talked football and who took stock of us, were surprised at the light boots that we wore. We admired the splendid ground, and the perfect arrangements that were made for our comfort.

"ALL BLACKS" ATTACKING
(NEW ZEALAND v. MIDDLESEX)

THE GREAT CAMPAIGN OF 1905

We were back in London again on the 4th, opposed to Middlesex at Stamford Bridge. We looked forward to this match with some eagerness, as we had been threatened with all kinds of things when we ran up against a forward team that could secure the ball from us. Apart from this, we were anxious to make a good show, as the London New Zealanders' Society had taken one of the stands and filled it with Maorilanders, among whom were the captain and officers of the good ship *Rimutaka*. It was certainly a strong side that was put in the field against us, and on the whole we gave one of our best all-round exhibitions so far, winning by 34 points (five goals and three tries) to 0. On this occasion our backs gave a taste of what they could do, scoring three tries without once receiving the ball from the scrum. If really Middlesex had been expecting to find a weakness in us here, they must have been undeceived. We were rather glad to think in the circumstances that British authorities were noticing the better points of our play, and were very willingly according us credit for them. Thus in this case, J. E. Raphael, the International, pointed out how our passers and takers were both always going at full speed when the ball was transferred from one to the other, the advantages of which we have strongly urged in what we may call the business section of this book, and which Raphael himself saw without being told. Another International in H. Alexander urged upon English sides to do something to counteract our system of leaving half of our opponents' scrum with nothing to push against. Every team that we met now were playing right on to us, purely on the defensive. On the 7th of the month we were north again, engaged with Durham, the champion county, whom we found to be a very good team, mostly drawn from the working population, as we were informed. It was a wet day, and we were given a very hard game on a greasy ground. The champion county, through Clarkson, were the first in Britain to cross our line. We won at the finish by 16 points to 3, our score now being 247 points to 7. In this match, besides kicking the goals, Wallace obtained two of the tries.

Three days later there was a great event at West Hartlepool, where we played the Hartlepools, and from our lowest score of the tour so far went straight to our highest, and the 63 points that we ran up against our opponents stood as the record for the whole tour. This score was all the more remarkable in the circumstances, as the Hartlepools were considered to have a good chance of extending us; but we think we may fairly say for ourselves that it was one of the finest exhibitions of the real game of Rugby football that New Zealanders have ever played, and we who played it were very highly satisfied, particularly as, though the side we put into the field was certainly a strong one, it was not the strongest we were capable of, as we were resting two or three men whom we wanted for stiff work shortly. We were not the only ones to be pleased with our work, as there were several members of the Scottish selection committee present, who did not hesitate to express their admiration for it, while the twenty thousand spectators who were present — and who constituted an exceedingly fair crowd — were apparently delighted with what they saw. In the compilation of this wonderful score, which was made up of nine goals and six tries, Hunter had a big share, getting four tries, while Abbott scored three, Smith and Roberts two each, and Stead, Wallace, Deans, and O'Sullivan secured one apiece, and Wallace did all the goal-kicking as usual. Our fifteen tries meant that we scored at the average rate of a try about every five minutes. Altogether we rather enjoyed our visit to the Hartlepools. We were shown over the shipyards,—where, by the way, the men were given a half holiday to see the match,—and were generally made much of. A cablegram in very kind and congratulatory words was received about this time from Mr. Seddon, the New Zealand Premier, who all along had taken the very keenest interest in our trip. Mr. Seddon said that he was not

THE GREAT CAMPAIGN OF 1905   257

surprised that the British public should be amazed at such skill as we had exhibited, and he confidently anticipated that we should prove equal to the strongest teams that would be matched against us. As indicating public interest in New Zealand, he said that information concerning the various matches was waited for almost as eagerly as was news of the war in South Africa when it was in progress. Everybody had received the results with the greatest enthusiasm. Mr. Seddon said to the British public that the natural and healthy conditions of colonial life produced the stalwart and athletic sons of whom New Zealand and the Empire might be justly proud. Such a message braced us up again, if indeed we needed any bracing up, and we meant to make a big effort to make our record the finest ever set up, even though the life of the tour was still young, and many of the severest ordeals were still before us.

Our next match was against Northumberland on the 14th, and for this we were rusticated at Tynemouth. The game was a rather trying and unpleasant affair, for there was half a gale blowing, it was wet and the ball was greasy, and under such conditions we could not hope to show anything like our true form. In such adverse circumstances we gave one of our poorest displays, but managed to win by 31 points to 0, Hunter getting five tries. Though we constantly make mention of the men who scored the tries, we did not set too much account on these details while we were on tour, because we always reckoned that every man in the fifteen had had a hand in the scoring of every try, and there was certainly never any such selfishness as some might fancy these large scores by particular individuals suggested. They simply showed that these particular men, like all their colleagues, were in the right place at the right time, and that then they did their duty as well as it was possible for it to be done. South again on the 19th, opposed to Gloucester, we were ourselves again. We had been led to believe that this would be one of our toughest matches, and accordingly we put a very strong team into the field. And although we won at the finish by 44 points to 0 (7 goals, 3 tries), the home side for a great part of the game put up a really hot fight against us. We played a strong game, and on reflection we should be inclined to bracket this match with that against Blackheath as those in which we gave our best exhibitions of combined attack among both forwards and backs. The ground and other arrangements were magnificent, and we enjoyed the match. One of its chief features was a remarkable run made by our ubiquitous Wallace, who covered himself with glory. This happened just before the end of the first spell, when the ball having been sent out to the backs it passed from one to the other until it came to Wallace at the right-hand end of the three-quarter line, for on this occasion he was playing wing three-quarter. In a second he realised that here was a situation for a display of individualism which, if his speed were sufficient, would very likely be rewarded with success, and so, instead of passing back, he made off with the ball at top speed. He had his lightning heels on him on this occasion, and he showed them to the opposing backs in great style. He ran round them and sprinted clean away, so that when he grounded for a most magnificent try he had them all ten yards in his rear. The spectators cheered in the most frantic fashion. The game against Somerset at Taunton on the 21st was a rather insipid affair. The ground was rough, and we put a rather mixed-up team in the field in view of the match with Devonport Albion, which was the next on the list. After a poor exhibition, we ran out winners by 23 points (three goals—one penalty, one dropped, and three tries) to 0.

For the game against the Albion we returned to Newton Abbot, our original quarters, where we received a great reception. The people at this pleasant little place seemed to claim us as their own, and it certainly appeared to be like going home to go there. The game was a rattling, splendid affair from start to finish, and it did us all a lot of good to play it. The Albion were the first team who attempted to play a winning game against us, and they did it in good style, for they attacked most determinedly in the first half and took a lot of keeping out. We scored a useful try at the beginning, and towards the end of the match we changed our tactics, went in a little more than usual for individualism, and eventually won by 21 points to 3. Both teams were as fit as fiddles, and the Albion were as keen and determined as they could be. We think that their weak point—perhaps the only respect in which they were deficient—was that their backs had not enough pace. Wallace was out of the team on this occasion. Our score was made up of three goals and a couple of tries. The penalty goal which the Albion obtained in this match brought the combined score of all our opponents for the twelve matches played so far to 10 points.

We had another very fine game when we opposed the Midland Counties at Leicester on October 28. The side put into the field against us comprised the best lot of forwards we had encountered so far, and they were well backed up by individual excellence among the backs. They scored a try —which was converted—as the result of good cross punting and following up, our full back being smothered. For our part we seemed to be showing signs of wear and tear, and there was a haunting fear among us that something like staleness was setting in in some quarters. There was some superstition among some of our men as to the result of this match, as it was the thirteenth on the list. However, though the margin of victory was not quite so large as usual, as was not to be expected considering the strength of the opposition, no very evil luck befell us. We won by 21 points (three goals, two tries) to 5. McGregor, who had been laid up since his arrival, turned out for the first time on this occasion. At Richmond on the first day of November we were pitted against Surrey, and the match belongs to the category of those that were disappointing. The weather was wet, and to make matters worse for us, the referee completely upset all our plans by penalising us every time we hooked the ball. The result was that we had to let our opponents have it so that we might play the forward game against them, and in this way we won by 11 points (one goal and two tries) to 0. Surrey did not make a very bold bid for victory, and one may be excused for thinking that the peculiar circumstances of the match, as just indicated, had more to do with the comparatively narrow margin than anything else. Six free kicks were awarded to Surrey in the first twenty minutes, and the explanation which the referee is alleged to have given—that we were not playing the game, and that our hookers were handing the ball out of the scrum, screened by their bent knees—was preposterous.

We looked upon the Blackheath match on November 4 as some kind of a criterion as to the strength of the international teams we should have to face, as Blackheath had seven international players on their side. As it happened, we gave one of the three best exhibitions we gave during the tour, and won by 32 points (five goals, three tries) to 0. In the second half Blackheath played seven forwards in the scrum, and it was generally considered that they did better with them than they had done with eight.

The two University matches followed. First we went to Oxford, to tackle the Dark Blues, and, making a very good display of football, were returned winners by 47 points (four goals, nine tries) to 0. Hunter did some very brilliant individual work in this match, his dodging and swerving enabling him to get through on his own account more than once. The students treated us very well, and we were dined in the evening at Trinity Hall. We were now just half-way through our programme, and our total score at this stage was 540 points to 15 for the sixteen matches. The Light Blues played a fine sturdy game against us at Cambridge, and made one or two excellent passing rushes; but we were rather handicapped by our two wing three-quarters being crippled early in the game. With a goal and three tries, we gained the match by 14 points to 0. Back in London, we played Richmond on the 11th, and the only remark that need be made about the game, which we won by 17 points to 0 (one goal, four tries), is that for the second time on this ground we had a greasy ball to deal with.

The circumstances of the nineteenth match, which was against Bedford, were rather curious, and to a certain small extent irritating at the time. Three days after this game we were to play the first of our international engagements, this being against Scotland, and accordingly we had a long journey before us as well. This being so, we were naturally desirous of putting as weak a team into the field as we dared, so as to reserve some of our best men. We should have been able to do this, as Bedford under normal circumstances were surely not one of the strongest sides that we were called upon to meet. However, with a desire to give a great account of themselves, Bedford called upon all and sundry to come to their help, with the result that the team that was got up to face us was a very formidable one, with a flavouring of internationals. There was nothing for it but to strengthen up our own side, and although Wallace, Smith, and Cunningham were left out, we had a very useful fifteen on duty for the day, and they were all inspired with a great desire in the circumstances to run up as big a score as possible. They had just turned the forty corner when the whistle blew, while Bedford had not scored. Our 41 points were made up of four goals and seven tries.

And so at last, on November 18, the first of the four internationals came to be played at Inverleith. To cut the story as short as possible, the game was played under very difficult and trying circumstances, and, after being given a distinct fright, we managed to snatch a victory towards the close by 12 points (four tries) to 7. The ground was frost-bound and slippery, and the ball was generally covered with frosty rime. It was quite impossible for us to play anything like our best game under these conditions, and our backs could never get going in their usual way. However, it is not our part to make any excuses, as if we were not satisfied with a narrow victory, for to beat Scotland at all was a thing of which any colonial side had reason to be proud, and we were undoubtedly very elated at achieving victory in our first international engagement—all the more glad as Scotland led us by a point at half time, and for the greater part of the game. When only seven minutes were left for play, we were a point to the bad and in our own twenty-five. We would like to say here, as we have said before, that we don't think Scoular was to blame for allowing Smith to get past him and score, as so many severe critics made out. The only other comments that we have to make are, that we were very unjustly accused of rough play. About the accusation, and beyond the mere recording of our resentment, the less said the better. And the referee, though fair and skilful, could not keep up with the game. The Scottish Rugby Union must have felt very disappointed with one aspect of this match. We have mentioned before, how when this fixture was arranged this Union did not seem to think very much about the New Zealanders or their drawing power, and declined to give the guarantee of £200 for which we asked. They preferred to make an arrangement by which we were to take the whole of the gate money after expenses had been deducted. As it happened, the receipts came to over £1000. Little wonder—as some people said—that the Scottish fifteen got no caps for this engagement. Before crossing over to Ireland for the second match of the international series on the following Saturday, we encountered a West of Scotland fifteen at the Queen's Park, Glasgow. We were greatly impressed with the ground, and there were twenty thousand people on it; but the match was a rather dull thing, and we won easily by 22 points (two goals, four tries) to 0.

The next few weeks were big with fate for the "All Blacks," as we had got used to be called. We had three international matches still in front of us after we left Scotland, and while all British people had by this time a very kind respect for our play, we could not disregard the fact that with the past all spread out before them many of the best judges thought that we should lose at least one if not two of these internationals. It was prophesied that the cross-channel trip would upset us, and that Ireland had a distinct chance of victory. And they were waiting for us in Wales. At the beginning of the tour, when we were told that we had all the stiffest matches at the end of the programme — which was none of our arranging — we were rather inclined to treat the matter lightly, on the principle that sufficient for the day was the evil thereof. Things were going very well then, and there was no need to worry about the future. But now, as the date of our invasion of Wales was drawing near, we began to realise the truth of it all. There is no doubt that by this time a considerable amount of staleness had crept into the team. The men were as willing and anxious as ever—in fact, they were more anxious— but it is not in human nature to go through such a heavy campaign as we had been doing for more than two months, with two hard matches every week, without showing some very noticeable signs of it. Moreover, our record began to weigh upon us. With not a single defeat upon it, it had become a very severe responsibility, and a burden as well as a matter of pride. At the outset of the tour we hoped to do nothing more than render a thoroughly good account of ourselves and win a good majority of our matches. With that we should have been satisfied. But as time went on and success followed success, it was inevitable that we should begin to cherish our clean sheet, and the farther we progressed it naturally happened that the greater did our desire become. As we entered upon the closing stages of the campaign, we became distinctly uneasy about it, and were led into being anxious when, in the light of past experience, there was no cause for anxiety. This was while we were off the field. We should be sorry to suggest or admit that when we were on it our play suffered through any consideration of this kind.

We enjoyed our visit to Ireland. The Irish people proved to be as hospitable as their reputation suggested, and they gave us a thoroughly good time, while the Irish fifteen played good, honest, dashing football, which gave us a great deal of trouble, but which we were very glad to have played against us. There was no half-heartedness in the Irish attacks. The team which we put into the field at Dublin was an experimental one, and it was fortunate that the experiment was entirely successful. As it happened, Gallaher (sent to bed by the doctor on account of the bad turn taken by a hack on the shin received when in Scotland, and which now required constant fomentation) was unable to play, and Gillett was up as wing forward, while Mynott was tried at wing three-quarters for his defensive capacity. It worked very well indeed. There was any amount of devil in the Irish forwards, who put more "go" into their game than any other forward division we had encountered. They made the pace very hot indeed for the early part of the game. In the circumstances we thought that the best thing to do would be to let them run about as much as they wanted and tire themselves out. We could bide our time. These tactics were entirely successful, and so we won by 15 points (three goals) to 0. If the Irish forwards had been supported by a better back combination, the result of the match would have been very problematical. We would like to pay our tribute to the refereeing of Mr. Crawford Findlay. It was excellent. When this match was over he made a frank confession that on the first occasion when he refereed in one of our matches he was puzzled by our methods, and was often taken unawares by the rapidity and novelty of some of our movements. But he said that now that he understood them, he appreciated the correctness of many things about which he had had doubts before.

The match with Munster, played at Limerick, which we

THE GREAT CAMPAIGN OF 1905

won by 33 points (four goals, five tries) to 0, was, like the West of Scotland match, not part of our original programme as it was arranged when we left New Zealand. These two engagements were inserted in the list while we were on our way over, and though in the circumstances we were practically obliged to fulfil them, we did so with some regret, as we should very much have preferred to have had a clear week between each of the three internationals, which were bunched together at this period. The Munster match cost us a very valuable man, for Smith hurt his shoulder so badly that he was only able to turn out once afterwards, and that against Glamorgan County when nearly all was over.

As the international against Scotland had been played under trying conditions, so also was that against England at the Crystal Palace, though in this case they were of another sort. The ground was in a dreadfully sodden state, and the circumstances of the greasy floor and greasy ball were all against anything like a good exhibition of the game. It was at all times difficult to get going in the slush, and any of the finer movements, such as swerving, were almost out of the question, while the ball could scarcely be held. This was very disappointing, for more reasons than one, for there were fifty thousand people present — by far the biggest attendance of spectators we had ever seen at a Rugby match; and as the Crystal Palace ground — a splendid ground with arrangements to match—is usually given over to the soccer enthusiast, we were anxious to give a really good exhibition of the game, and do something towards converting any of the soccer people who might happen to be present. One must fear that they could not have formed a very high opinion of the game from what they saw of it on this occasion. It was a poor match, and not worth description. We won by 15 points (five tries) to 0. One cannot help thinking that England might have picked a stronger side. By this time we had had considerable experience of the class of player to be found in the towns and shires, and we certainly did not think that the fifteen who were put up against us at the Crystal Palace were fully representative of the best men to be found in the country. During the tour it had been our object to avoid as much as possible the feasting here, there, and everywhere to which we were kindly and hospitably invited; but we were very delighted with the dinner given to us at the Trocadero the same evening, when Mr. Rowland Hill, the President of the English Rugby Union, presided and warmly congratulated us on our success, which he hoped would have the effect of wakening up the game in Britain.

This was on December 2, and on the 6th we had a very pleasant day at Cheltenham. The club we encountered was a young one, but they put a very fair side into the field, and gave us some most unexpected opposition. On our side we had put several of the junior members of our party into the team to give the others a rest, and among those who were looking on were Smith, Wallace, Hunter, Gillett, and Seeling—a pretty solid lot to put on the reserve list at the same time. We only scored four tries, three of which Harper converted by magnificent kicks right from the touch line. So we won by 18 points to 0. It was a perfect day, and the crowd was of thoroughly typical English sporting character. Only two other matches remained to be played before we went into Wales for the concluding part of the tour. First we had Cheshire to play at Birkenhead Park on December 9, and our attack being in good working order we got ten tries, two of which were converted, winning by 34 points to 0. At Leeds on the 13th we met a Yorkshire team and obtained ten more tries, Wallace this time converting five of them, making 40 points. Yorkshire failed to score. This was really the first opportunity that was afforded to the bulk of Northern Unionists to see us play. Their criticism was very lofty. According to them, the Yorkshire side was the weakest that ever played

NEW ZEALAND V. WALES AT CARDIFF

THE GREAT CAMPAIGN OF 1905 267

for the county, and of course they, the Northern Unionists, could have made a terrible example of us if they had had the opportunity. When we left England for Cardiff we had 801 points to our credit, and 22 had been scored against us, in the twenty-six matches played.

At last, on December 16, we played the great match of our season, and Wales inflicted upon us the single defeat of the tour. Their margin of victory was narrow enough, and our spotless record was spoiled by the single try that Morgan scored. It is not our place now to make excuses for this defeat that stung so much at the time. It is enough to say that the game we played did not entirely deserve a much greater reward than it was vouchsafed. The worst fear we had came true. We had of late been thinking too much about this match, and at last the thoughts went on to the field with us and paralysed the efforts of many of our men. This, we are certain, would not have happened if we had not approached so near to the end of our tour and remained still unbeaten; and again, it would not have happened if there had been no staleness in the team. We had by this time got into that state when every match we played made us very much worse, and though we ran up scores good enough in each of them, there is no doubt that the concluding matches on English soil did much to establish very thoroughly this canker in our systems. Then, when we made an ineffectual start, and the Welshmen from the beginning showed a wonderful amount of dash and fire, something very much like nervousness crept into our side. Our usual coolness vanished, and if not the whole of our machinery, the biggest part of it was thrown very badly out of gear. Pass after pass went wrong. The forwards, indeed, were sound enough, in fact throughout this trying ordeal and despite that we were beaten, it is not too much to say that they played a magnificent game, and that no share of the blame for our only defeat belongs to them. But, with perhaps the single exception of Roberts, the backs were hopelessly off colour. Names of delinquents need not be mentioned, and it is enough to say that in the light of reflection the excitement that prevailed and the twenty-seven matches that had gone before were excuse enough. The Welshmen were excited too, but their passing and their play generally were very good. They were a strong side, probably just about as strong as we expected to find them, and in their ranks were contained some of the finest masters of the Rugby game. For some days beforehand they had been perfecting their plans for the match, and stepped on to the field with a very complete programme of tactics. Among them was the adoption of our scrum formation, to which Gwyn Nicholls expressed himself as a complete convert, and he observed, after the game was over, that on account of our superior speed he was confident that they would have been unable to have coped with our attack if the backs had been eight to seven. Thus the verdict in the case of this historic encounter was against us to the extent of 3 points to 0.

Although four matches remained to be played, and they proved to be the hardest and the most interesting from the point of view of equality of the whole tour, they came as something in the nature of an anticlimax after the Welsh international, and they may be dismissed in a very few words. On December 21 we played Glamorgan in the presence of a very unsympathetic crowd at Swansea, and with three tries won by 9 points to 0. Another defeat had been prophesied for us. Two days later we encountered Newport, and with a try and a penalty goal against a penalty goal won by 6 points to 3. It was one of the best contested matches of the tour, and was fought out in a good sporting spirit. But staleness was more than ever in evidence, and it was palpable that the "All Blacks" could not last much longer. It was well that the end was near. Even apart from staleness, so many men were suffering from injuries of one kind and another, that it was very difficult now to put

THE WELSH TEAM THAT DEFEATED THE "ALL BLACKS"

THE GREAT CAMPAIGN OF 1905

a sound team into the field. On Boxing Day we had to go through the severe ordeal of a match against Cardiff, and, to make matters all the worse for us, we were handicapped to the extent of having to play a man short for the last fifty minutes, O'Sullivan being very seriously injured. The match was rather remarkable. Each side scored two tries, and the only difference, so far as the registration of points was concerned, was that both of ours were turned into goals by Wallace, whereas one of Cardiff's remained unconverted. So victory was with us by 10 points to 8. But we are obliged to admit that Bush made us a present of our second try. We had kicked the ball past their three-quarters, and Bush reached it as it went over the goal line. There was nobody troubling him, and he had any amount of time to touch down, but he dallied, and then, as Nicholson went running up, he attempted to kick dead, missed the ball, and before he knew what had happened Nicholson had scored. At the time that this happened the scores were level—a goal each. It was a bit of bad luck for Cardiff, but served to balance matters in respect to our loss of a man. In the last match of all, at Swansea, we had a very narrow escape, and were credited with a somewhat lucky win by 4 points (a dropped goal by Wallace) to 3. However, we missed any number of chances in the second spell. When the referee's whistle went for time, the general feeling among us was "Bravo! It's all over." It had become very hard work towards the end. The final gross score was 830 points for us and 36 against.

The same night we went back to London, crowds gathering at several railway stations to give us a cheer and wish us good-bye, and from London we went straight on to Paris, where on the Monday we played a French team, who proved to be really good sportsmen. Of course we won the game, for Rugby football has hardly got going in France yet, but the Frenchmen played up well, and were plucky enough for anything. It delighted them greatly when they crossed our line. Then back to London, and at last, on January 20, after many entertainments and much British hospitality on the final days, we took train at Waterloo for Southampton, and there embarked for New York, the New Zealand Government having kindly come forward with an invitation to go home by San Francisco.

And so it was all over. We had a great time, and one which none of us will ever forget. Our remembrances of all with whom we came into contact will always be of the happiest, and we hope that our tour may to some extent have served a good purpose, and that we shall have the opportunity of welcoming back to New Zealand before long a team bent on winning back from us some of the points we have taken home.

Our impression of Britain is of the dear motherland, loved as much by those who saw her for the first time during this tour as by those who as babies nestled upon her bosom; of the deeply venerated parent of the game that we glory in —perhaps of a parent in the prime of life, who is inclined to take things a little too easily; of many great players, who have no warmer admirers than the "All Blacks," wearers of the silver fern—Gwyn Nicholls, L. M. McLeod, Basil MacLear, Gabe, E. T. Morgan, Vile, Dicky Owen, E. D. Simson, Gent, Jago, Winfield, and Jackett are a few of the names that come uppermost haphazard in one's mind; of weak selections made from such talent; of well-meaning and scrupulously fair, but frequently slow and stubborn, referees; of sportsmen everywhere, real British, and particularly round the arena, giving a fair field and no favour, and cheering us, their kinsmen, to the echo when we pleased them with our play, even when in so pleasing them the bill of costs had to be settled by our opponents, the home team, the pets of those crowds round the rails. We were impressed by this feature of our tour, and we hope that some of us at least will come back again.

APPENDIX

PLAN OF THE FIELD.

```
                    DEAD-BALL LINE.
            ┌──────────────────────────┐
  TOUCH-    │         IN-GOAL.         │   TOUCH-
  IN-GOAL.  │                          │   IN-GOAL.
            ├──────────────────────────┤
            │        GOAL LINE.        │
            │                          │
            │       G.P. |   | G.P.    │
            │                          │
            │      25 YARDS LINE.      │
            │                          │
  TOUCH     │      10 YARDS LINE.      │   TOUCH.
  TOUCH     │      HALF-WAY LINE.      │   TOUCH
  LINE.     │      10 YARDS LINE.      │   LINE.
            │                          │
            │      25 YARDS LINE.      │
            │                          │
            │       G.P. |   | G.P.    │
            │                          │
            │        GOAL LINE.        │
            ├──────────────────────────┤
  TOUCH-    │                          │   TOUCH-
  IN-GOAL.  │         IN-GOAL.         │   IN-GOAL.
            └──────────────────────────┘
                    DEAD-BALL LINE.
```

The field of play should not exceed 110 yards in length nor 75 yards in breadth, and should be as near those dimensions as practicable. The maximum extent of the dead ball line is 25 yards.

It is recommended that the posts and flags marking the centre and 25 yards lines should be kept well back from the touch lines. The touch lines and goal lines should be cut out of the turf, or otherwise well defined.

THE LAWS OF THE GAME OF FOOTBALL AS PLAYED BY THE RUGBY FOOTBALL UNION.

(As Revised for the Season 1905-1906.)

I. INTRODUCTION.

Introduction.

1. The Rugby Game of Football should be played by fifteen players on each side. The field of play shall not exceed 110 yards in length, nor 75 in breadth, and shall be as near these dimensions as practicable. The lines defining the boundary of the field of play shall be suitably marked, and shall be called the goal lines at the ends and the touch lines at the sides. On each goal line and equidistant from the touch lines shall be two upright posts, called goal posts, exceeding 11 feet in height, and placed 18 feet 6 inches apart, and joined by a cross bar 10 feet from the ground; and the object of the game shall be to kick the ball over this cross bar and between the posts. The game shall be played with an oval ball of as nearly as possible the following size and weight, namely—

Length	11 to $11\frac{1}{4}$ in.
Length circumference . . .	30 ,, 31 ,,
Width circumference . . .	$25\frac{1}{2}$,, 26 ,,
Weight	13 ,, $14\frac{1}{2}$ oz.

Hand sewn and not less than 8 stitches to the inch.

II. GLOSSARY—DUTIES OF OFFICIALS—SCORING.

Glossary. of Terms.

2. The following terms occur in the laws, and have the respective meanings attached to each:—

Dead-Ball Lines.—Not more than 25 yards behind and equidistant from each goal line, and parallel thereto, shall be lines, which shall be called the Dead-Ball Lines, and if the ball or player holding the ball touch or cross these lines the ball shall be dead and out of play.

In-Goal.—Those portions of the ground immediately at the ends of the field of play and between the touch lines, produced to the dead-ball lines, are called In-Goal. The goal lines are In-Goal.

Touch.—Those portions of the ground immediately at the sides of the field of play and between the goal lines, if produced, are called

APPENDIX

Touch. The touch lines and all posts and flags marking these lines, or the centre, or 25 yards lines, are in Touch.

Touch-in-Goal.—Those portions of the ground immediately at the four corners of the field of play, and between the goal and touch lines, if respectively produced, are called Touch-in-Goal. The corner posts and flags are in Touch-in-Goal.

A Drop-kick is made by letting the ball fall from the hands, and kicking it as it rises.

A Place-kick is made by kicking the ball after it has been placed on the ground for the purpose.

A Punt is made by letting the ball fall from the hands and kicking it before it touches the ground.

A Tackle is when the holder of the ball is held by one or more players of the opposite side.

Held is when the player carrying the ball cannot pass it.

A Scrummage, which can only take place in the field of play, is formed by one or more players from each side closing round the ball when it is on the ground, or by their closing up in readiness to allow the ball to be put on the ground between them.

A Try is gained by the player who first puts his hand on the ball on the ground in his opponents' In-goal.

A Touch Down is when a player touches down as above in his own In-goal.

A Goal is obtained by kicking the ball from the field of play, by any place kick except a kick-off, or by any drop kick except a drop-out, without touching the ground or any player of either side over the opponents' cross bar, whether it touch such cross bar or either goal post or not.

Knocking-on and *Throwing-forward* are propelling the ball by the hand or arm in the direction of the opponents' In-goal; a throw out of touch cannot be claimed as a throw-forward.

A Fair Catch is a catch made direct from a kick or knock-on, or throw-forward by one of the opposite side; the catcher must immediately claim the same by making a mark with his heel at the spot where he made the catch.

Kick-off is a place kick from the centre of the field of play; the opposite side may not stand within 10 yards of the ball, nor charge until the ball be kicked, otherwise another kick-off shall be allowed. If the ball pitch in touch, the opposite side may have it kicked off again.

Drop-out is a drop kick from within 25 yards of the kicker's goal line; within which distance the opposite side may not charge, otherwise another drop-out shall be allowed. If the ball pitch in touch, the opposite side may have it dropped out again.

At kick-off the ball must reach the limit of 10 yards, and at drop-out must reach the 25 yards line. If otherwise, the opposite side may have the ball re-kicked, or scrummaged, at the centre or in the middle of the 25 yards line, as the case may be.

Off-Side.—See Laws 7 and 8.

<small>Referee and Touch Judges.</small> 3. In all matches a *Referee* and two *Touch Judges* must be appointed, the former being mutually agreed upon. The Referee must carry a whistle, the blowing of which shall stop the game; he must whistle in the following cases:—

    (*a*) When a player makes and claims a fair catch.

    (*b*) When he notices rough or foul play or misconduct. For the first offence he shall either caution the player or order him off the ground, but for the second offence he must order him off. If ordered off, the player must be reported by him to this Union.

    (*c*) When he considers that the continuation of the play is dangerous.

    (*d*) When he wishes to stop the game for any purpose.

    (*e*) If the ball or a player running with the ball touch him, in which case it shall be scrummaged at the spot.

    (*f*) At half-time and no-side, he being the sole timekeeper, having sole power to allow extra time for delays, but he shall not whistle for half-time or no-side until the ball be held or out of play.

    (*g*) When he notices any irregularity of play whereby the side committing such gain an advantage.

    (*h*) When he notices a breach of Laws 5 and 15.

    (*i*) When he wishes to enforce any penalty under Law 11.

    (*j*) When a goal is kicked.

    (*k*) When the ball goes into touch-in-goal.

<small>Powers of Referee.</small> The Referee shall be sole judge in all matters of fact, but as to matters of law, there shall be the right of appeal to this Union.

<small>Duty of Touch Judges.</small> The Touch Judges shall carry flags, and shall each take one side of the ground, outside the field of play, and the duty of each shall be to hold up his flag when and where the ball goes into touch, or touch-in-goal, and also to assist the Referee, when kicks at goal from a try, fair catch, or free kicks are being taken, each standing at a goal post.

<small>Rules.</small> 4. The captains of the respective sides shall toss for the choice of In-goals or the kick-off. Each side shall play an equal time from each In-goal, and a match shall be won by a majority of points; if no point be scored, or the number be equal, the match shall be drawn.

<small>Scoring.</small> The following shall be the mode of scoring:—

A Try	equals	3 points
A Goal from a Try (in which case the Try shall not count)	,,	5 ,,
A Dropped Goal (except from a Mark or a Penalty Kick)	,,	4 ,,
Goal from a Mark or Penalty Kick . .	,,	3 ,,

APPENDIX

5. At the time of the kick-off all the kicker's side shall be behind the Kick-off ball; if any be in front, the Referee shall blow his whistle and order a scrummage where the kick-off took place. The game shall be started by a kick-off—

  (*a*) After a goal, by the side losing such goal, and
  (*b*) After half-time by the opposite side to that which started the game.

III. MODE OF PLAY—DEFINITIONS.

6. When once the game is started, the ball may be kicked or picked Mode of Play. up and run with by any player who is on-side, at any time; except that it may not be picked up—

  (*a*) In a scrummage.
  (*b*) When it has been put down after it has been fairly held.
  (*c*) When it is on the ground after a player has been tackled.

It may be passed or knocked from one player to another provided it be not passed, knocked or thrown forward. If a player while holding or running with the ball be held, he MUST at once put it fairly down between him and his opponent's goal line.

7. A player is placed off-side if he enters a scrummage from his Off-side. opponents' side, or if the ball has been kicked, touched, or is being run with by one of his own side behind him. A player can be off-side in his opponents' In-goal, but not in his own, except where one of his side takes a free kick behind his goal line, in which case all of his side must be behind the ball when kicked.

8. An off-side player is placed on side—

  (*a*) When an opponent has run 5 yards with the ball.
  (*b*) When the ball has been kicked by, or has touched an opponent.
  (*c*) When one of his side has run in front of him with the ball.
  (*d*) When one of his side has run in front of him, having kicked the ball when behind him.

An off-side player shall not play the ball, nor during the time an opponent has the ball, run, tackle, or actively or passively obstruct, nor may he approach or wilfully remain within 10 yards of any player waiting for the ball; on any breach of this law, the opposite side shall be awarded, at their option—

  (*e*) A free kick, the place of such breach being taken as the mark.
  (*f*) A scrummage at the spot where the ball was last played by the offending side before such breach occurred.

Except in the case of unintentional off-side, when a scrummage shall be formed where such breach occurred.

9. If a player makes a fair catch, a free kick shall be awarded, even Fair Catch.

though the whistle has been blown for a knock-on or a throw-forward. Any player on the same side may take the kick or place the ball.

Free Kicks. 10. All free kicks may be place kicks, drop kicks, or punts, but must be in the direction of the opponents' goal line, and across the kicker's goal line, if kicked from behind the same. They may be taken at any spot behind the mark in a line parallel to the touch lines. In all cases the kicker's side must be behind the ball when it is kicked, except the player who may be placing the ball for a place kick, and it is the duty of the Referee to see that the ball be kicked from the parallel line. In case of any infringement of this law, the Referee shall order a scrummage at the mark. The opposite side may come up to, and charge from anywhere on or behind a line drawn through the mark and parallel to the goal lines, and may charge as soon as the kicker commences to run or offers to kick or the ball be placed on the ground for a place kick, but in case of a drop kick or punt the kicker may always draw back, and unless he has dropped the ball the opposite side must retire to the line of the mark. But if any of the opposite side do charge before the player having the ball commences to run or offers to kick, or the ball has touched the ground for a place kick (and this applies to tries at goal as well as free kicks), provided the kicker has not taken his kick, the charge may be disallowed.

IV. PENALTIES.

Penalty Kicks for 11. Free kicks by way of penalties shall be awarded if any player—

Intentionally handling Ball or falling in scrummage. (*a*) Intentionally either handles the ball, or falls down in a scrummage, or picks the ball out of a scrummage.

Not putting Ball down when held. (*b*) Does not immediately put it down in front of him, on being held.

Not getting up or allowing to get up. (*c*) Being on the ground, does not immediately get up.

(*d*) Prevents an opponent getting up, or putting the ball down.

Illegally Obstructing, etc. (*e*) Illegally tackles, charges, or obstructs as in Law 8.

(*f*) Wilfully holds an opponent who has not got the ball.

(*g*) Wilfully hacks, hacks over, or trips up.

Unfairly putting Ball down. (*h*) Wilfully puts the ball unfairly into a scrummage, or, the ball having come out, wilfully returns it by hand or foot into the scrummage.

APPENDIX

(*i*) Not himself running for the ball, charges or obstructs an opponent not holding the ball. — Illegal Charge.

(*j*) Shouts "all on side," or words to that effect, when his players are not on side.

(*k*) Not in a scrummage, wilfully obstructs his opponents' backs by remaining on his opponents' side of the ball when it is in a scrummage.

(*l*) Wilfully prevents the ball being fairly put into a scrummage.

(*m*) If any player or team wilfully and systematically break any law or laws, for which the penalty is only a scrummage, or cause unnecessary loss of time.

(*n*) Being in a scrummage, lift a foot from the ground before the ball has been put into such scrummage.

The places of infringement shall be taken as the mark, and any one of the side granted the free kick may place or kick the ball.

On breach of sub-section (*j*) the opposite side shall be awarded at their option—

(*a*) A scrummage where the ball was last played.
(*b*) A free kick at the place of infringement.

V. GENERAL.

12. The ball is in touch when it, or a player carrying it, touch or cross the touch line; it shall then belong to the side opposite to that last touching it in the field of play, except when carried in. One of the side to whom the ball belongs shall bring it into play at the spot where it went into touch, by one of the following methods:— — Ball in Touch.

(*a*) Throwing it out so as to alight at right angles to the touch line, or
(*b*) Scrummaging it at any spot at right angles to the touch line, 10 yards from the place where it went into touch.

If the Referee blows his whistle because the ball has been thrown out so as not to alight at right angles to the touch line, the opposite side shall bring it out as in (*b*).

13. When the side has scored a try, the ball shall be brought from the spot where the try was gained into the field of play in a line parallel to the touch lines, such distance as the placer thinks proper, and there he shall place the ball for one of his side to try and kick a goal; this place kick is governed by Law 10 as to charging, etc., the mark being taken as on the goal line. It is the duty of the Referee to see that the ball is taken out straight. — Try at Goal.

The Referee shall award a try, if, in his opinion, one would undoubtedly have been obtained but for unfair play or interference of the — Unfair Play. Allowing or Disallowing a Try.

defending side. Or, he shall disallow a try and adjudge a touch down, if, in his opinion, a try would undoubtedly not have been gained but for unfair play or interference of the attacking side. In case of a try so allowed, the kick at goal shall be taken at any point on a line parallel to the touch lines, and passing through the spot where the ball was when such unfair play or interference took place.

Ball held in In-goal.
14. If the ball, when over the goal line and in possession of a player, be fairly held by an opposing player before it is grounded, it shall be scrummaged 5 yards from the goal line, opposite the spot where the ball was held.

Drop-Out.
15. After an unsuccessful try, or touch down, or if the ball after crossing the goal line go into touch-in-goal or touch or cross the dead-ball line, it shall be brought into play by means of a drop-out, when all the kicker's side must be behind the ball when kicked ; in case any are in front, the Referee shall order a scrummage on the 25 yards line and equidistant from the touch lines.

Knock-on, Throw-forward.
16. In case of a throw-forward or knock-on, the ball shall be brought back to the place where such infringement occurred, and there be scrummaged, unless a fair catch has been allowed, or the opposite side gain an advantage.

Pass or Carry Back over own Goal Line.
17. If a player shall wilfully kick, pass, knock, or carry the ball back across his goal line and it there be made dead, the opposite side may claim that the ball shall be brought back and a scrummage formed at the spot whence it was kicked, passed, knocked, or carried back. Under any other circumstances a player may touch the ball down in his own In-goal.

Hacking, Tripping.
18. Hacking, backing over, or tripping up are illegal. The Referee shall have full power to decide what part of a player's dress, including boots and projections thereon, buckles, rings, etc., are dangerous, and having once decided that any part is dangerous, shall order such player to remove the same, and shall not allow him to take further part in the game until such be removed.

Irregularities in In-Goal, not otherwise provided for.
19. In case of any law being infringed in In-goal by the attacking side, a touch down shall be awarded, but where such breach is committed by the defending side, a scrummage shall be awarded 5 yards from the goal line, opposite to the spot where the breach occurred.

Other Irregularities not provided for.
But in the case of any law being broken, or any irregularities of play occurring on the part of either side not otherwise provided for, the ball shall be taken back to the place where the breach of the law or irregularity of play occurred, and a scrummage formed there.

(*Attention is drawn to the Recommendations of the International Board, Case Law, and other sections of this Appendix for a completer elucidation of these rules.*)

BYE-LAWS OF THE RUGBY UNION.

1. The name of the Society shall be THE RUGBY FOOTBALL UNION, and only Clubs entirely composed of amateurs shall be eligible for membership; and its Headquarters shall be in London, where all General Meetings shall be held.

2. Any Club willing to conform to the Rules of the Union shall be eligible for Membership, but before being admitted, such Club must be duly proposed and seconded by two Clubs belonging to the Union.

3. The Annual Subscription, payable in advance, of each Club belonging to the Union, shall be £1, 1s. There shall be no Entrance Fee for two Seasons from 29th September 1904. The Annual Subscriptions of all Clubs shall fall due in September. Any Club whose subscription has not been paid before 1st March shall be struck off the Union List.

4. The Annual General Meeting shall be held in May in each year for the election of Officers, the consideration of the Bye-laws, Laws of the Game, and Rules as to Professionalism, and other business.

5. Each Club shall be entitled to send one representative only to any General Meeting, exclusive of the Officers and Committee of the Union.

6. The Committee, who shall be elected annually, shall consist of the following Officers, namely :—a President, two Vice-Presidents, an Hon. Treasurer, a Secretary, and other members. All past Presidents of the Union, who shall have attended two regularly convened committee meetings during the previous year, shall be members of the Committee. Seven shall form a quorum; the Chairman shall have a casting vote in addition to his first vote. No past President shall be entitled to vote on the selection of teams unless he has been chosen to act on the Sub-committee elected for that purpose. Any vacancy in the Committee occurring during the year shall be filled up by the Committee.

7. The Committee shall be elected by Clubs belonging to this Union :—

   (a) One Committeeman by Oxford University, one by Cambridge University, one by the Central District, and one by the Eastern Counties and Sussex County combined, providing the University, District, or Combination so electing has ten colleges or clubs, including itself, subscribing to this Union; one Committeeman by any County which plays in the County Championship Competition, which is a member of this Union, and which has six clubs, including itself, subscribing to this Union—such Counties being Cheshire, Cornwall, Cumberland, Devon, Durham, East Midlands, Gloucestershire, Kent, Lancashire, Middlesex, Midland Counties, Northumberland, Surrey,

Somerset, and Yorkshire. No Metropolitan Club shall change its County or District for voting purposes without the sanction of the Rugby Union Committee.

(b) As soon as any of these Counties, or the Central District, has forty Clubs subscribing to this Union, it shall be entitled to a second representative.

(c) The Central District shall consist of all Clubs, Counties, and Unions — home, colonial, and foreign — not included in any elective body specified in (a).

(d) The Committee shall have the sole power of admitting new Counties to play in the County Championship Competition, or of eliminating any of those at present taking part, and upon the Committee shall be thrown the responsibility of ascertaining that each County has the requisite number of *bonâ fide* Clubs; the Committee shall also determine when a County has the requisite number of Clubs to entitle it to a second representative.

All such elections shall be in the hands of the Secretary by 1st April; if not, the New Committee shall fill up any vacancies.

The manner in which the above seats are distributed may be altered at any Annual General Meeting, provided notice of such proposed alteration be given to the Secretary not later than 1st April, any alteration to take immediate effect.

8. There shall be sent to each Club, not later than 8th April in each year, a list of the representatives so elected, together with the Committee's nominations of Officers for the ensuing year, namely :—a President and two Vice-Presidents nominated from the above representatives, and an Hon. Treasurer, not necessarily from the above representatives. Any Club has the right to make further nomination of Officers only, but any for President or Vice-President must be from the elected representatives; any such nominations must reach the Secretary by 15th April, and a complete list of all nominations must be sent to each Club with the circular calling the Annual General Meeting.

9. The election of Officers shall take place at each Annual General Meeting, and shall be decided by a majority of those voting. In case the Hon. Treasurer be elected from the elected representatives, then such representation shall become void, and the county, university, or district shall elect another representative to fill such vacancy. In case a district has to make another election, such must be done within fourteen days of the Annual General Meeting; if not so made, the Committee shall fill the vacancy.

10. No Bye-law, Law of the Game, or Rule as to Professionalism shall be altered, rescinded, or added to, without the consent of at least two-thirds of those present at a General Meeting.

11. Each Club shall be furnished with a copy of the Bye-laws, Laws of the Game, and Rules as to Professionalism, and be bound thereby. In case of infringement thereof by any club or player, such club or player may be punished or expelled by the Committee, subject to appeal to a General Meeting, except on a matter of fact, when there shall not be any right of appeal.

12. Notice of any amendment or alteration in the Bye-laws, Laws of the Game, or Rules as to Professionalism, together with the names of the proposing and seconding Clubs, shall be given in writing to the Secretary not later than 1st April, and a copy of such notice shall be sent to each Club not later than 8th April; notice of any amendment to such amendment or alteration must be in writing signed by an official of the Club making it, and must reach the Secretary by 15th April, after which each Club shall be advised by circular of the date of the Annual General Meeting and of all proposed alterations and amendments.

13. The Secretary shall convene a Special General Meeting at any time on receiving a requisition to that effect signed by the secretaries of not less than forty Clubs belonging to the Union, and stating specific notice of motion. No Special General Meeting shall be called to alter the distribution of seats.

In case of a Special General Meeting, such must be held within one month of receipt of requisition, preliminary notice must be sent out by the Secretary within ten days of such requisition, and notices of amendment must be received by him within seventeen days of receipt of requisition.

14. The Committee shall have sole control of the funds of the Union. The accounts shall be audited by two Auditors, appointed at the previous Annual General Meeting. A printed copy of the signed balance-sheet shall be sent to each Club, along with the notice calling the Annual General Meeting.

15. The Committee shall appoint three Trustees, in whose names they may from time to time invest any funds of the Union; which investment shall be held by the said Trustees solely for the furtherance of Amateur Rugby Football.

16. Any League or Combination of Clubs shall be under the authority of, and shall obtain the consent of the Union, to its formation; and shall be required to submit its proposed rules, and any subsequent alterations thereof, for approval to the Rugby Union Committee, who shall have power—

- (a) To forbid the formation or continuance of such League or Combination of Clubs in their absolute discretion.
- (b) To discharge from membership or suspend any Club contravening this Bye-law.
- (c) To suspend any Club which shall play a match with a Club which

has been suspended or discharged from membership under the Bye-law, or with any Club which has been formed out of the nucleus of any suspended Club.

17. There shall be an annual close time, during which it is illegal to play football where gate money is taken, such close time being between 21st of April and the 1st of September. In the event in any year of the Tuesday in Easter Week falling later than 21st April, for such year the close season shall commence from the Wednesday in the Easter Week.

18. Any difference of opinion arising as to the meaning of any of these Bye-laws shall be decided by the Committee, but if it occurs at a General Meeting, by the chairman thereof; any such decision shall be recorded in the minutes and shall be accepted as the true meaning of the Bye-law until otherwise interpreted at a General Meeting, after due notice has been given.

REGULATIONS AUTHORISED BY THE RUGBY UNION ON COUNTY QUALIFICATIONS.

1. A man may play—

(a) For the County in which he was born, or
(b) For the County in which he has resided for the three months previous to the time of playing, or
(c) For the County in which he is residing at school or college, either as pupil or master, at the time of playing, provided his residence at the school or college be in the same County.

2. A man shall still be qualified to play for a County, having previously qualified for and played for that County, and not having subsequently played for any other County.

3. No man shall play for more than one County during the same season.

4. A man who has resided for three months previous to the time of playing in a County in which there is no County Club playing matches, shall be qualified to play for any County adjoining the County in which he resides. Residence by Members of the University at Oxford and Cambridge shall not afford a qualification under this Regulation. This Regulation shall not apply to the County of Monmouth.

5. Should any question arise as to qualifications, the same shall be left to the decision of the Rugby Union Committee.

APPENDIX

REGULATIONS FOR DECIDING THE COUNTY CHAMPIONSHIP.

1. There shall be two Divisions—(I) Northern, (II) Southern.

(I) The Northern Division shall consist of one group, comprising Cheshire, Cumberland, Durham, Lancashire, Northumberland, and Yorkshire.

(II) The Southern Division shall be subdivided into—

  (a) South-Western Group, comprising Cornwall, Devonshire, Gloucestershire, and Somersetshire.

  (b) South-Eastern Group, comprising East Midlands, Kent, Middlesex, Midlands, and Surrey.

  It shall be left to the Rugby Football Union Committee to define the area from which players are to be chosen for the East Midlands.

2. (I) The Northern Division winner shall be ascertained by means of matches between each member of this group and the others.

(II) The Southern Division winner shall be ascertained by means of—

  (a) Matches between each Member of the South-Western Group and the others.

  (b) Matches between each Member of the South-Eastern Group and the others.

  (c) A Match between the Counties at the head of these groups (a) and (b).

3. The winner of the Championship shall be ascertained by means of a match between the two Counties at the head of the Northern and Southern Divisions respectively.

4. Each match shall be decided by points. A win shall score two points, and a drawn game, one point to each side. If, in the case of matches referred to in Regulation 2 (I), 2 (II) (a), and 2 (II) (b), owing to two or more counties scoring an equal number of points, a winner of a group is not ascertained, another match or matches to be played, and, in default of mutual agreement, where two counties are concerned, the visiting team in the prior match that season shall have choice of ground in the second match, and, where three counties are concerned, each county shall have one home match to be settled, if necessary, by drawing lots; should a draw again occur, the matches shall again be replayed, but on the grounds of the last visiting teams.

5. The matches referred to in Regulation 2 (II), (a) and (b), must be played by the 31st January; and the matches referred to in Regulation 2 (I) and (II) (c), must be played by the 20th February; the date of the match for the Championship shall be fixed by the Rugby Football Union Committee should the two counties interested fail to agree.

6. The final match for the Championship shall be played in the North of England if North v. South has been played in the South, and *vice versâ*, the home County having choice of ground.

7. In case of a draw between the two counties at the head of 2 (11) (*a*) and 2 (11) (*b*), or in the final match, the selection of the ground for the second match shall rest with the visiting team in the first match.

8. All replayed matches under these Regulations shall be treated as separate matches, and shall have no effect on fixtures in future seasons.

9. In the final match and all replayed matches the expenses of the two teams shall be paid out of the net proceeds of the gate, such net proceeds to include the use of the ground, the grant for which shall be determined, if necessary, by the Rugby Football Union Committee ; no dinner shall be given out of the proceeds of the match, and any surplus shall be equally divided. If the net proceeds of the match are insufficient to pay the expenses of both teams, any deficit shall be met equally by each of the competing Counties.

10. In the event of the teams journeying to the ground, and the Referee deciding that it cannot be played owing to state of ground, fog, etc., the match, if necessary to decide a group or ultimate winner, shall be played on another day in the County in which it was originally fixed to be played, the visiting team to receive the expenses incurred by them in their first visit.

11. In the event of International or other matches played under the management of the Rugby Football Union Committee being postponed to a date on which County Championship matches have been arranged, such County matches may be postponed, unless it is mutually agreed by the Counties interested to play.

12. In all Championship matches at least thirty-five minutes, and in the final match forty minutes, each way, shall be played, if in the opinion of the Referee it is possible to do so.

13. The fact of the removal of a County from one group to another shall not break the continuity of the Championship scheme.

14. In the case of two Counties which have never met in the Competition, the place of the match shall be settled by drawing lots, and the Rugby Football Union Committee shall not interfere in the matter of one County giving to the other a donation towards expenses.

15. County matches played outside the County Championship Scheme shall have no effect in deciding the ground on which County Championship matches shall be played.

16. Any question which shall arise, and is not above provided for, shall be decided by the Rugby Football Union Committee.

17. The Rugby Football Union Committee may delegate to a sub-committee of their body the exercise of all or any of the powers conferred on them by the above regulations.

BYE-LAWS OF THE INTERNATIONAL BOARD.

1. The Board shall be called THE INTERNATIONAL RUGBY FOOTBALL BOARD.

2. The Board shall consist of twelve representatives, six from the Rugby Union and two each from the other Unions. The Chairman, who shall have a casting vote, shall be appointed at each Meeting in regular rotation from the different Unions, in their order of seniority.

3. The Annual Meeting of the Board shall be held on the day preceding, or on the morning of the date of the England and Scotland International Match in the city or town in which such match may be played. In the event of no match being played, a meeting of the Board must be held not later than the 30th of April in each year. Such meeting, and all other meetings of the Board, shall be held in London, unless otherwise agreed by the four Unions, at such time as the Honorary Secretary shall appoint.

4. All International Matches shall be played under the Laws approved of by the Board.

5. In case of disputes about International Matches, or otherwise, between two countries, a Committee of the Board, consisting of two representatives appointed by each Union, shall have absolute and exclusive jurisdiction. The Board shall have no power to interfere with the game as played within the limits of the different Unions.

6. Notice of any proposed alteration in the Laws of the Game, or in the Bye-laws of the Board, shall be sent to the Hon. Sec. at least four weeks before the Annual Meeting, and the Hon. Sec. shall intimate these proposals to the Unions at least three weeks before Meeting.

7. The Hon. Sec. shall, at any time, convene a Special Meeting of the Board on receipt of a requisition from the Secretaries of at least two of the Unions: the purpose for which the Meeting is desired shall be intimated to the different Unions at least three weeks before the Meeting.

8. If the Chairman, entitled for the time being to preside, shall, on the occasion of any appeal, happen to be a representative of either of the disputing Unions, his Chairmanship shall be postponed in favour of, and take order next after, the Chairmanship of the first neutral Union entitled by rotation to furnish a Chairman.

9. The referee at any Match shall be ineligible to act as a representative at a meeting called to settle any dispute arising out of that Match.

10. No alteration in the Laws of the Game or the Bye-laws of the Board shall be made at any Meeting called for that purpose, unless by a majority of at least three-fourths of the delegates present.

11. All expenses incurred in connection with the Board shal be equally defrayed by the Unions, but, in case of a Committee appointed

under Bye-law 5, all hotel and travelling expenses shall be equally defrayed by the disputing Unions.

12. All decisions of the Board or Committee shall be accepted as final.

The International Board at a Meeting held on 9th March 1901 passed the following resolution:—

That it be an instruction to Referees in International Matches, that in case of an injury to a player the game shall not be stopped for more than three minutes.

The International Board at a Meeting held on 21st March 1903 passed the following resolution:—

That Referees in International Matches be directed to strictly enforce Law 3 (*b*), as to rough or foul play, or misconduct.

The Rugby Football Union Committee have decided to ask all Societies of Referees to carry out the above resolutions.

The Laws of the Game of the Board are identical with those of the Four Unions.

DELEGATION OF POWERS.

The Rugby Union Committee have delegated to the following recognised governing bodies, namely, to the Counties of Northumberland, Durham, Cumberland, Yorkshire, Lancashire, Cheshire, Middlesex, Kent, Surrey, Sussex, Hampshire, Gloucestershire, Somersetshire, Devonshire, and Cornwall, to the Universities of Oxford and Cambridge, to the Midland Counties', East Midland, and Eastern Counties' Unions—

The following powers to act for them, namely:
A. Under Rule 11 in the "*Rules as to Professionalism.*"
Under Rules 2, 3, and 4, all powers except—
  (1) The power of re-instatement after suspension.
  (2) The passing of sentence of expulsion.
    If individuals or clubs are found guilty under 2 (1) *A*, *H*, *I*, *L*, *M*, *N*, and *O*, or 2 (2) *A*, *D*, *H*, *I*, *L*, *M*, and *N*, they must be at once temporarily suspended, and reported to the Rugby Union.
Under Rules 4 (1st clause), 5, and 6, all powers.

The Rugby Union Committee solely have the power of expelling. The Rugby Union Committee also solely have the power to re-instate after suspension.

APPENDIX

B. Under the Laws of the Game, the following powers:
Law 3 (*b*).

The above powers are only delegated to recognised governing bodies, when all individuals and clubs involved are under the jurisdiction of one governing body.

While delegating the above powers, the Rugby Union Committee wish it to be distinctly understood that the above recognised governing bodies have not the power or right to further delegate any of these powers.

The Rugby Union Committee have ruled that where the words "expelled or suspended club or player," or words to this effect are used in the "Rules as to Professionalism," they shall be read to include any professional club or player.

The Committee wish to specially draw the attention of County and Club Committees to the fact that recognised governing bodies have no power to sanction the formation of Leagues, or combination of clubs, and also to the alterations in Bye-law 17, as to Leagues having to submit any alteration in or addition to their Laws or Rules, to this Union, and as to the power of this Union to forbid the continuance of any League.

The Committee have delegated to the New Zealand Union and the South African Board the power to carry out their regulations, and have given them the right to delegate such powers to other Bodies in New Zealand and South Africa.

RULES AS TO PROFESSIONALISM.

Adopted at Rugby Union Meeting, September 1895, to take the place of the Rules as to Professionalism, the "Insurance Laws," and the "Transfer Laws," which were in operation previously, and altered in conjunction with the Welsh Union in 1899–1900.

1. Professionalism is illegal.
2. Acts of Professionalism are—
    (1) By an individual—
A. Asking, receiving, or relying on a promise, direct or implied, to receive any money consideration whatever, actual or prospective; any employment or advancement; any establishment in business; or any compensation whatever for—
   (*a*) Playing football, or rendering any service to a football organisation.
   (*b*) Training, or loss of time connected therewith.

(c) Time lost in playing football or in travelling in connection with football.
(d) Expenses in excess of the amount actually disbursed on account of reasonable hotel or travelling expenses.

B. Transferring his services from one club to another in opposition to Rule 4.
C. Playing for a club while receiving, or after having received from such club, any consideration whatever for acting as secretary, treasurer, or in any other office, or for doing or for having done any work or labour about the club's ground or in connection with the club's affairs, unless such work was done before the receiver became a football player.
D. Remaining on tour at his club's expense longer than is reasonable.
E. Giving or receiving any money testimonial. Or giving or receiving any other testimonial, except under the authority of this Union.
F. Receiving any medal or other prize for any competition except under the authority of this Union.
G. Playing on any ground where gate money is taken—
(a) During the close season.
(b) In any match or contest where it is previously agreed that less than fifteen players on each side shall take part.
H. Knowingly playing with or against any expelled or suspended player or club.
I. Refusing to give evidence or otherwise assist in carrying out these rules when requested by this Union to do so.
J. Being registered as, or declared a professional, or suspended by any National Rugby Union or by the Football Association.
K. Playing within eight days of any accident for which he has claimed or received insurance compensation, if insured under these rules.
L. Playing in any benefit match, connected directly or indirectly with football ; but this shall not prevent this Union giving permission for a *bonâ fide* charity match.
M. Knowingly playing or acting as referee or touch judge on the ground of an expelled or suspended club.
N. Receiving money or other valuable consideration from any person or persons as an inducement towards playing football.
O. Signing any form of the Northern Union.

(2) By a club or other organisation—
A. Paying or promising payment, or giving, offering, or promising any inducement as to employment, advancement, or establishment in business, or any compensation whatever to any player for—

APPENDIX

(a) Playing for that club.
(b) Training or for travelling expenses to or from any training resort, or for loss of time in connection with training.
(c) Loss of time while playing or travelling in connection with football.
(d) Hotel or travelling expenses in excess of the sum actually and reasonably disbursed.

B. Receiving as a member a member of another club in opposition to Rule 6.

C. Receiving or continuing as a member any one it may pay or have paid for either regular or occasional services.

D. Paying for any of its teams, players, officials, or members on tour longer than a reasonable time ; or paying for more than a reasonable number.

E. Giving from its funds, subscribing, or playing a match for any testimonial.

F. Giving any medal or other prize for any competition except under the authority of this Union.

G. Taking gate money at any ground—

(a) During the close season.
(b) At any match or contest where it is previously agreed that less than fifteen players on each side shall take part.

H. Knowingly playing or allowing its members to play with or against any expelled or suspended player or club.

I. Refusing to produce its books or documents, or to allow its officials or members to give evidence or to assist in carrying out these rules when requested by the Union to do so.

J. Knowingly playing or admitting as a member, without the consent of the Union, any member or an expelled or suspended club, or any expelled or suspended player, or any person registered as or declared a professional or suspended by any National Rugby Union or by the Football Association.

K. Knowingly allowing a player to play in its matches within eight days of any accident for which he has received or claimed insurance compensation, if insured under these rules.

L. Playing or allowing its ground to be used for any benefit, or charity match, connected directly or indirectly with football, except permission to play which has previously been obtained from this Union.

M. Knowingly allowing its members or teams to play on the ground of any expelled or suspended club.

N. Refusing to pay, within any time ordered by this Union, any costs or expenses ordered by this Union for inquiries held under these rules.

3. For offences under 2 (1) *A, H, I, L, M, N,* and *O,* an individual shall be expelled from all English clubs playing Rugby football, and shall not be eligible for re-election or election to any club. For offences under 2 (1) *B, C, D, E, F, G, J,* and *K,* an individual shall be suspended during the pleasure of this Union.

For offences under 2 (2) *A, D, H, I, L, M,* and *N,* a club shall be expelled from this Union. For offences under 2 (2) *B, C, E, F, G, J,* and *K,* a club shall be suspended during the pleasure of this Union. Any club disregarding a sentence of suspension shall be liable to expulsion.

But when this Union is fully satisfied that any offence under 2 (2) *A, D, H, I, L, M,* and *N,* was of an accidental, trival, or technical character, they may suspend instead of expel.

4. When a player wishes to join a new club he may do so; if this Union request it, he shall produce a letter from his old club stating that they have no objection; on receipt of such letter this Union shall give the necessary permission, unless they believe there may have been collusion, or that illegal means have been employed to induce the player to join the new club, in which case they shall hold an inquiry. In case any club or clubs refuse to give such written permission, this Union must hold an inquiry, at the request of the player or of the club he wishes to join. If from any cause an inquiry be held, this Union shall have full power to order the payment of the costs of such inquiry, and of the clubs and witnesses, as it may think fit.

In case an English player wishes to join a Welsh club, or a Welsh player an English club, he may do so; if requested by either Union, he shall produce a letter from his old club, stating they have no objection; on receipt of this letter, the Union requesting such shall, if satisfied, give the necessary permission; if not satisfied, they shall ask the other Union to hold a joint inquiry, such inquiry to be held by a joint committee of two representatives of each Union. The chair shall be taken alternately, but no chairman shall have a second or casting vote. In case of disagreement, a member of the Scottish Union shall be asked to arbitrate, or, failing such, a member of the Irish Union. Any such joint committee or arbitrator shall have power to order the payment of expenses as they think fit, and all findings shall be final.

This Union may grant power to recognised governing bodies to increase the stringency of this rule, provided such proposed alterations be submitted to and approved of by it.

5. A county or club may insure its players either through—

A. A recognised insurance company, or—

B. A fund entirely set apart for insurance, the accounts of such fund to be yearly audited by a professional auditor. Such audit to be made at the close of each season, and to be concluded, and the auditor's certificate lodged with this Union, not later than the 20th May in each year, provided that—

APPENDIX

(*a*) Any injured player does not receive more than 6s. per week day while injured.

(*b*) Payments are only made on the certificate of a registered medical practitioner.

(*c*) Any player does not play football within eight days of his accident; if he does so, no insurance compensation shall be paid.

(*d*) Proper books of accounts be kept.

6. This Union may hold inquiries into any alleged breaches of these rules at its pleasure, and shall do so when requested by any club or member of a club, provided any such club or member make a preliminary deposit of £10, or such smaller sum as this Union may determine, to be accompanied by a preliminary written statement of the chief known facts. After any such inquiry, this Union may return the preliminary deposit, wholly or in part, and may order the expenses of such inquiry, of clubs and members implicated, and of witnesses, to be paid as it may determine.

7. At all inquiries under Rules 6 and 8, correct notes must be taken.

8. Any club, member, or player affected by any decision given by a county, union of counties or university, under delegation of powers contained in Rule 11, may appeal direct to this Union; such appeal must be made within ten days, and must be accompanied by a deposit of £50 and a written statement of the grounds of appeal. After any such appeal this Union may return such deposit, wholly or in part, and may order the expenses of such inquiry, of clubs and members implicated, and of witnesses, to be paid as it may determine.

9. This Union may delegate to recognised governing bodies, such as counties, union of counties, and universities, powers to act for it in such cases and under such regulations as it may determine. All powers so delegated, and the bodies to whom such delegation be made, shall be published annually in the official guide of this Union.

BYE-LAWS OF THE NEW ZEALAND RUGBY UNION.

1. This Union shall be called THE NEW ZEALAND RUGBY FOOTBALL UNION, and shall consist of such local Unions of the colony as are already affiliated, and of any others that may be admitted as hereafter provided.

2. It shall affiliate with the English Rugby Union, and shall adopt the rules of football as from time to time fixed by that body.

3. Its objects shall be to foster and control Rugby football throughout the colony, to make preliminary arrangements for teams visiting this

colony, and take the management of New Zealand representative teams leaving the colony; to be the Court of Appeal in the colony for all cases of dispute which may be submitted to it; to consider and suggest to the English Union any alterations or additions to the rules of football which may seem desirable; to control inter-island matches; to foster inter-Union meetings, and to provide referees when requested, the expenses to be paid by the home Union.

4. The affairs of the Union shall be managed by a Council, a Management Committee, and such other sub-committees as may from time to time be appointed under these bye-laws.

5. The Council shall consist of the delegates of the affiliated local Unions, together with the officers. The written statement from the Secretary of any affiliated Union to the effect that any person present at a meeting of the Council represents that Union shall be accepted by the chairman as conclusive evidence of appointment.

6. The Management Committee shall consist of the officers of the Union, and of seven delegates, who shall be elected at the Annual General Meeting of the Council—five to form a quorum.

7. The Council and the Management Committee shall have power to elect such sub-committees as may be deemed necessary from time to time to assist them in carrying out their duties.

8. The officers shall consist of—Patron, President, Vice-Presidents (one Vice-President to be nominated by each Union), Honorary and Assistant Honorary Secretary (the latter to have no vote), and Honorary Treasurer, who shall be elected annually at the Annual General Meeting of the Council. The Annual General Meeting shall be held on a date to be notified by the Secretary, of which at least one month's notice must be given the affiliated Unions.

9. The following shall be the basis of representation of affiliated Unions upon the Council of this Union :—

(a) Unions having under fifteen teams, one vote; fifteen and under twenty-five, two votes; twenty-five and under thirty-five, three votes; thirty-five and under forty-five, four votes; forty-five and over, five votes.

(b) The annual subscription of affiliated Unions shall be two shillings and sixpence per annum for each team of fifteen men affiliated to, or playing under the auspices of, such affiliated Union.

10. Delegates may be represented at any meeting of the Council during their term of office either in person, or by their written proxy, provided—

(a) That no delegate may hold proxies for more than one Union.
(b) That any one delegate may exercise all the votes to which his Union is entitled.
(c) That a Union may be represented by a separate delegate for each vote to which it is entitled.

APPENDIX

Appeals and Disqualifications.

11. There shall be an Appeal Committee, consisting of five members, who shall have continuity of office for three years. Such Committee shall be elected by the Management Committee; three members of the Appeal Committee shall form a quorum. In the event of any vacancy or vacancies occurring during the above period, the Management Committee shall have power to fill such vacancy or vacancies. The location of the Appeal Committee shall be fixed at an Annual General Meeting of the Council.

12. Its duties shall be to decide upon all questions in dispute arising out of the interpretation of the laws of the game, which shall have been first heard and determined by a local Union, and to answer questions forwarded, as provided for in the regulations of the Referees' Association of New Zealand.

13. Any decision of the Appeal Committee may be appealed against to the English Rugby Union, provided that such appeal be forwarded through this Union.

14. In all cases of misconduct by individual players, officials, clubs, or teams, travelling or otherwise, inquiry shall be held by the Union directly interested.

15. In all cases where an affiliated Union has passed a resolution disqualifying any player, official, team, or club, for any reason whatsoever, such resolution shall be reported to the Secretary of this Union for the purpose of being made general in its application throughout the jurisdiction of the other affiliated Unions. The Secretary shall communicate the terms of the resolution to all other affiliated Unions, and the resolution shall be observed by each affiliated Union from the date of the receipt of the advice, whether or not the terms are in accordance with the rules of any such Union.

16. Any such player, official, team, or club may lodge with the Secretary of this Union an appeal from the resolution not later than fourteen days after the passing thereof (accompanied by a deposit of £1, which shall be forfeited should the appeal prove frivolous), and this appeal shall be considered and determined by the Management Committee.

17. Should the Management Committee have reason to believe that any Union has failed to make searching inquiry into any case of misconduct, or into any matter likely to bring discredit upon football, they shall require the Union concerned to complete the inquiry, and, failing compliance with such request, it shall be the duty of the Committee to obtain evidence, and take such action as they may deem fit.

18. In all cases of misconduct by individual players, officials, or teams, while under the direct control of this Union, the Management

Committee should hold an inquiry and accord such disqualification as it deems suitable; and the ruling of the Management Committee shall be observed by each affiliated Union, whether or not it is in accord with the rules of such Union.

19. Pending decision of any appeal, all disqualifications accorded shall be operative.

20. The term "disqualification" includes any punishment accorded by resolution by any Union, or by this Union, in accordance with its rules; and as long as such disqualification remains in force, any player, team, club, or Union wilfully acting in defiance of the terms of such disqualification, shall be disqualified by the Management Committee.

COLOURS.

21. Each Union, upon affiliation with the New Zealand Union, shall register the colours worn by its representative team, which colours shall forthwith become the exclusive property of the Union first registering them, and may not be worn by any other Union.

ALTERATION OF RULES.

22. At any Annual General Meeting of the Council, any suggestion for alteration of the laws of the game may be considered, provided that not less than six weeks' notice of the intended motion shall have been forwarded to the Secretary in writing.

23. Should any such alteration be approved, it shall then be forwarded as a recommendation to the English Union.

MISCELLANEOUS.

24. No Union affiliated to the New Zealand Union, whose subscriptions and dues are not paid by the first day of July in each year, shall be allowed to have any vote at any meeting of the Council.

25. No Club or Union affiliated to the New Zealand Union shall play any Club or Union not affiliated, unless such affiliated Club or Union shall have first obtained the permission of the Management Committee.

26. All Unions desiring admission to this Union must be proposed and seconded by delegates of different Unions already affiliated, and shall then be balloted for, a majority of votes to elect.

27. Any Union disobeying any of the rules of this Union, or permitting any Club or individual under its jurisdiction to do so, may be suspended from membership at the pleasure of the Management Committee.

28. A Special General Meeting of the Council shall be called by the

APPENDIX

Secretary at any time on receipt of requisition from not less than two affiliated Unions. At such meeting a report from the Management Committee on the business transacted since the previous General Meeting shall be submitted.

29. That no rule of the New Zealand Union shall be altered except at a General Meeting. Notice of intention to move such alteration must be given at least six weeks previous to such meeting.

30. The Secretary shall give not less than one month's notice to affiliated Unions of all business which he proposes to lay before any meeting of the Council.

31. At any meeting of the Council representatives from not less than half the total number of affiliated Unions shall form a quorum.

REGULATIONS FOR THE REFEREES' ASSOCIATION OF NEW ZEALAND.

1. The Referees' Association shall be a body consisting of Branches associated with the respective Rugby Football Unions, the location of the Appeal Council of the New Zealand Rugby Union to be its headquarters.

2. The Branches shall be formed in the following manner:— Suitable persons shall first be appointed by the several Unions. Subsequent members shall be elected by ballot, and no person shall be elected unless three-fourths of those present shall have voted for him. Any person desirous of becoming a member shall be proposed and seconded at one meeting of the Branch, and elected or rejected at a subsequent meeting.

3. The objects of the Association shall be—
   (*a*) To secure the services of well-qualified Referees for all matches played under the auspices of the local Unions.
   (*b*) To take steps to punish any person who may offer insult to a Referee.
   (*c*) To encourage the exchange of views between Referees respecting the reading of the laws of the game, etc., or respecting rulings given at matches, and thereby secure uniformity in the interpretation of such laws.
   (*d*) To provide means for properly controlling the game, regulating the conduct of the players and the public, etc.

4. Any branch may at any time, by a three-fourths majority at a meeting, write off its roll any member for misconduct or incapacity as a Referee, provided that the notice of motion for such removal shall have been given at a previous meeting.

5. The officers shall consist of a General Honorary Secretary at headquarters, and an Honorary Secretary for each Branch.

6. Meetings of the members of the Branches shall be held at convenient intervals, of which notification shall be sent by the local Secretary.

7. The respective Branches shall pass resolutions fixing the number of members which shall constitute a quorum at their meetings.

8. Any member may submit any point in connection with the game for discussion at any meeting, provided that if the Chairman should rule that it is not a proper one for discussion it shall not be received.

9. Any question brought before a Branch shall be decided by a majority of votes, and such decision shall be accepted by all members of the Branch, unless it shall be overruled by the Appeal Committee of the New Zealand Rugby Union, or by the English Rugby Union.

10. Members shall vote in person only.

11. As long as there are any members of any Branch available for the position, no person not a member of the Association shall be selected to fill the post of Referee.

12. A Referee appointed for any match shall be paid by the local Union such expense as he has necessarily incurred in attending the match.

13. Referees who may be unable to act on any occasion when matches are to be played, shall give the earliest possible notification of the fact to the local Secretary.

14. The name of the Referee should be published with the names of the team whenever possible.

15. If any Referee shall, without permission of the Branch on which he is a member, fail to act, he shall be called upon for an explanation, and dealt with as his Branch thinks fit.

16. The local Secretary may, by resolution passed at any Branch meeting, apply, through the Honorary Secretary of the New Zealand Union, to the Appeal Committee of that Union for a ruling on any point not already in dispute.

17. Each Branch shall be supplied by the Honorary Secretary of the New Zealand Union with copies of all decisions of the Appeal Committee.

18. Whenever the New Zealand Union is asked to appoint a Referee in any match, any senior member of any Branch of the Association shall be eligible.

19. These regulations shall not be alterable except by a meeting of the Council of the New Zealand Union, and then only after one month's notice shall have been given to the Honorary Secretary of the New Zealand Union, provided that each Branch may pass such bye-laws as it may find necessary for the carrying out of these regulations.

APPENDIX

DECISIONS OF A CONFERENCE OF NEW ZEALAND REFEREES.

During the season of 1901 an important Conference of Referees was arranged by the New Zealand Rugby Union, for the purpose of arriving at a uniform reading of the laws of the game. It was held at Wellington, and was representative of Referees from all parts of the colony. Mr. F. J. Ohlson of Auckland presided over the Conference, which lasted two days. Mr. Ohlson said he considered that the time had arrived for New Zealand to draft laws to suit itself outside those of the English Union, and asked members for an expression of opinion with regard to a motion to this effect. It was decided to take no action, as the Conference would be going beyond its powers in interfering with the laws. Mr. Garrard proposed "That all rulings and decisions of the Conference be submitted to the English Rugby Union, but that they take effect as soon as decided by the Conference." This was agreed to.

The following interpretations of the laws of the game were adopted:—

Scrummage.—Question: Is the ball considered in the scrum when a bunch of forwards on the line-out get the ball and put it down between themselves and the opposite side?—Decision: The Conference decided that this was a matter which had to be left to the discretion of the referee. Question: When is the original formation broken up?—Decision: It was admitted that no hard-and-fast rule could be laid down on this question. Question: In the event of a scrummage overlapping the goal line, is it lawful for the defending forwards to heel the ball back, and if the ball is not clear of the overlapping part of the scrummage, can it there be made dead?—Decision: No.

LAW 2. *Try and Touch Down.*—So as to press the ball on the ground with the hand.

LAW 2. *A Fair Catch.*—If a referee anticipating a fair catch blows his whistle, but the fair catch is not made, a scrummage should be formed at the spot.

LAW 3 (Section B). *Referee and Touch Judges.*—Question: In the event of a referee neglecting to report a player or players whom he has ordered off the field of play, what action should be taken? Decision: It is competent for anyone conversant with the above facts to report such to the New Zealand Rugby Union, through the local Union.

LAW 3 (Section B).—It was decided that for continual appealing, referees should deal with offending players under this law.

LAW 3 (Section C).—Referees are instructed to strictly carry out instructions *re* "players hurt," as contained in late circular letter.

LAW 3 (Section F).—Time shall not be called until the ball is out of the field of play.

CASE LAW. *Referee having once given his decision cannot alter it.*—Question: A referee asks a touch judge's opinion, and then gives his decision, subsequently finding the touch judge in error on law. Was the referee justified in reversing his decision?—Decision: No; the onus is on the referee for not appointing competent touch judges.

Duty of Touch Judges.—The ball may be brought into play from touch, provided such be done according to law, even though the touch judge does not signal where the ball has gone into touch before the ball is thrown in again.

LAW 8 (Section B).—Even though an opponent touches the ball, an off-side player who is within the 10 yards' limit may not play the ball until he has been put on side.

LAW 9. *A Fair Catch.*—If a fair catch be obtained in the opponents' in-goal, the kick must be taken in the field of play.

LAW 10.—In all free kicks it is not necessary for the ball to reach a line drawn parallel to the goal line through the place where such kick was allowed. In all place kicks the kick is forfeited if the ball is not "placed" on the ground by the placer. If the kick be so forfeited—(1) when a try has been obtained, kick out from the 25; (2) when a free kick or fair catch has been awarded, a scrum where the mark was made. NOTE.—Dropping the ball on the ground while in the act of placing shall not be considered placing.

Referees are requested to more strictly interpret the law *re* "charging," as contained in circular letter from the English Union, dated 1900. Penalties should be inflicted at once for the slightest breach.

LAW 11 (Section E).—Referees should inflict penalty if a wing player in any manner handles an opponent not holding the ball. Players calling out for the purpose of intimidating an opponent may be dealt with.

Section F.—Referees are instructed to strictly enforce the penalty *re* wilfully holding an opponent who has not the ball.

Section H.—The ball may be put back in the scrummage by the foot.

Section J.—A wing player placing his hand on the scrummage shall not be considered part of a scrummage.

Section K.—If a player lift his foot before the ball be fairly put in, he "may" be penalised.

LAW 12 (Section B).—Referees are recommended to disallow the ball being brought into play from touch by drop kicks or punts.

LAW 14.—If opposing players simultaneously place their hands on the ball on the ground in in-goal, it shall be considered as held in-goal.

LAW 16.—"There put down" shall be interpreted as meaning "put down for a scrummage." NOTE.—This is the English Union's interpretation.

LAW 17.—See decision on Law 2.

APPENDIX

WING FORWARDS.

It was resolved that the Conference express the opinion that wing forwards should be abolished.

SUGGESTIONS AS TO HOLDING AN AUSTRALASIAN CONFERENCE AND REVISING CASE LAW.

A suggestion was made to the New Zealand Rugby Union that an Australasian Conference be held, consisting of not less than three delegates from each colony, such Conference to be held at the earliest possible period; also, that it be suggested to the same Union that its Appeal Committee revise all the New Zealand Union's case law.

SUGGESTIONS TO THE ENGLISH RUGBY UNION.

The following suggestions to the English Rugby Union were made by the Conference :—

1. That in the event of a scrum overlapping the goal line, it shall be lawful for the defending forwards to heel back the ball, and if the ball be not clear of the overlapping part of the scrum it can there be made dead.

2. That a fair catch be allowed if the player claims with his voice simultaneously with catching the ball.

3. When placer drops ball in act of placing, should not such place of dropping be the spot at which the scrummage should be formed?

4. That all charging of free kicks or kicks at goal be deleted from the rules.

5. Is it lawful to bring the ball into play from touch by drop kick or punt, the player himself being out of touch, provided the ball be thrown at right angles?

6. In the circular letter of 1899 the wording of the last paragraph (referring to Section 3, Law 12) is stated to have been altered so as to give the opposite side the right to bring the ball out if not originally thrown out straight. This Conference would like to know where the alteration from the previous rule is.

7. Is it a breach if the ball be kicked back into the scrummage by the player outside?

OPINIONS OF THE ENGLISH COMMITTEE ON POINTS SUBMITTED BY THE NEW ZEALAND UNION.

1. See page 6, Official Book, 1900-1901, "Circular International Board": "Heeling back over goal line shall be considered as wilfully kicking back."

2. Regard this as not a desirable alteration. Are of opinion that it would very much increase the difficulties of the Referee.

3. Consider the game should proceed as though the ball had been properly placed.

4. Are of opinion that this would not be an improvement. It would rob the game of what is distinctly scientific play.

5. No. The player must be out of touch when he catches the ball after bounding it in the field of play.

6. The wording of the old law: "If the ball be not thrown out of touch so as to alight at right angles to the touch line, the opposite side *may* bring it out, as in C." The present: "If the Referee blows his whistle because the ball has been thrown out so as not to alight at right angles to the touch line, the opposite side *shall* bring it out, as in C."

7. It is not illegal so to do.

                   (Signed)   G. ROWLAND HILL,
                                                Hon. Sec. R.F.U.

September 5, 1901.

NEW ZEALAND RUGBY FOOTBALL UNION.

DELEGATION OF POWERS.

By virtue of the powers vested in it by the English Rugby Union Committee, the Committee of the New Zealand Rugby Union hereby delegates to all affiliated Unions the following powers to act for it:—

1. In the laws of the game:—
   Under Law 3 (*B*) all powers.
2. In the rules as to Professionalism:—

    A. Under Rules 2 and 3, all powers except—
        (1) The power of re-instatement after suspension.
        (2) The passing of sentence of expulsion.
            If individuals or clubs are guilty under 2 (1) *A*, *H*, *I*, *L*, *M*, *N*, *O*, or 2 (2) *A*, *D*, *H*, *I*, *L*, *M*, *N*, they must be at once temporarily suspended, and reported to the New Zealand Rugby Union.

    B. Under Rule 4 (1st clause), 5, and 6, all powers.
    C. Under Rule 11, all powers.

NOTE.—The committee of the New Zealand Rugby Union solely has the power of expelling and the power to re-instate after suspension.

Wellington, *November* 30, 1904.

INTERNATIONAL BOARD'S RECOMMENDATIONS TO PLAYERS AND REFEREES.

Some four years ago the International Board addressed a circular letter to those gentleman who undertake the duties of Referees. Since then this Board and the various Unions have given rulings on various points of law, and the Board think it would be highly advantageous if such were brought together and explained, so that both players and Referee may in future fully understand them and also act up to them. This circular is therefore addressed to both players and Referees, and although it may appear to touch upon many points which are perfectly clear and simple, yet one or other of the Unions have had appeals on all the points raised.

INTRODUCTION.—Firstly, it is the duty of the visiting team to see that the ground complies with Law 1 as to size, and is properly marked, that the dead-ball line is distinct, etc. If they fail to see these points before the game begins, no appeal can afterwards be entertained in relation thereto.

GLOSSARY.—*A Rebound* is not a knock-on, and therefore no fair catch can be made therefrom or penalty given. This is important, as some Referees appear to regard a rebound as a knock-on.

A Fair Catch can only be claimed by the catcher making his mark *after* he has caught the ball; the mark, however, must be made as soon after the ball is caught *as possible*; and, in practice, Referees might allow a claim when the mark was simultaneously made with the catching. A fair catch can be made in a player's own in-goal.

If a player goes beyond the 25 yards to drop-out, or if he punts, the Referee must blow his whistle and order the player to take a new kick, which must be a drop within the 25 yards limit.

All grounds should be properly marked out, including the half-way, 25 yards, touch, goal and dead-ball lines, unless other boundaries form these latter, in which case flags at the half-way and 25 yards lines are unnecessary; if they be used, they would be set well back from the touch lines. Corner flags should be used, and should be at the junction of the touch and goal lines. If a player holding the ball touch one of these, the ball must be considered as in touch-in-goal. A player may himself be in touch-in-goal and yet play the ball with his foot if the ball be not in touch-in-goal, or he may touch it down with his hand.

Referee Whistling.—No power is given to a referee to whistle simply because a player is tackled with the ball, and this is one of the most important points to which the Board wish to direct the attention of players and Referees, as the present habit of whistling the moment a man is tackled is simply spoiling the game by slowing it down and taking away any advantage a side of quick followers up would otherwise gain.

When a player with the ball is tackled, and the ball fairly held, a Referee may only blow his whistle for one of the following cases :—

1. LAW 11 (*b*).—When such player does not *at once* fairly put the ball down.
2. LAW 11 (*c*).—When such player is on the ground and he does not *at once* fairly part with the ball, and either get up or roll away from the ball.
3. LAW 11 (*d*).—When a player of the opposite side prevents such player either putting the ball down or getting up.
4. LAW 3 (*e*).—When the Referee considers that the continuation of play would be dangerous.

This latter point must be left entirely to the Referee, but the Board wish to point out that if the tackled player played the laws in the spirit in which they are written, and at once fairly parted with the ball, very few cases of danger would arise, but by holding on a short time danger may arise. In such a case the Referee should blow and award the penalty of a free kick instead of simply ordering a scrummage on the plea of danger, as by so doing he deprives one side of an advantage and does not inflict a penalty on the other, both of which are deserved.

Player Hurt.—If a player be hurt, the Referee should not blow his whistle till the ball be dead, unless such hurt player is in a position that continuance of play might entail further danger.

While speaking of the Referee, the Board would like to point out that, once a Referee has ordered a player off the ground, he cannot allow him again to take part in the game, and must report him; and further, if a player with the ball touch the Referee in his opponents' in-goal, a try should be allowed at the spot where he so touched him.

Referee Touch Judges.—A Referee, once he has given a decision, cannot alter it, and his decision alone is final; he may, however, consult the touch judges in cases of touch and touch-in-goal play, and may ask them to assist him at kicks at goal. Under all circumstances the Referee's whistle must stop the game, even if blown inadvertently; and the Referee's decision as to time must be final, even if he has kept it inaccurately. On no account must a Referee consult with any outsider, except in the case of a failure of his watch, when he should in the first instance consult the touch judges.

Position of Players.—A player may play in any position so long as he is on-side and does not obstruct his opponents; he may come up to a scrummage and attempt to hook the ball out with his foot, provided his other foot is behind the ball.

LAW 8.—The Board desire that Referees should *more strictly* enforce these penalties, and would point out that a Referee should award a free kick if he thinks a fair catch would have been made had not an off-side player, through his proximity and not retiring beyond the 10 yards limit, have rendered such catch more difficult.

It is the opinion of this Board that Referees too often give offending players the benefit of unintentional off-side, instead of inflicting the free kick penalty.

LAWS 9 and 10.—In cases of tries and free kicks, any player may place or kick the ball; in cases of fair catches, the catcher only may place the ball, drop, or punt it.

In cases of players waiting to charge when a kick, after a try, fair catch, or free kick is about to be taken, they must remain behind the goal line or behind the mark with both feet, and any standing over the goal line or over the mark with one foot shall be considered to have charged, and the Referee shall blow his whistle and award no-charge. The Referee shall also be particular that any side waiting behind a mark do not gradually creep up beyond the mark; such shall be considered as a charge. When a player is placing the ball he shall not wilfully do anything which may lead his opponents to think he has put the ball down when he has not; if he does, the charge shall not be disallowed. Even when a charge has been disallowed, the would-be chargers may, provided they remain behind the mark, jump up and attempt to stop or touch the ball; if they so touch it, no goal can be scored.

If a Referee whistles to allow a no-charge just as a kicker takes his kick, such kicker shall have the option of another kick—that is, if he has kicked a goal, he can allow it to stand; if he has not, he can take a second kick.

After a charge has been disallowed, any player except the kicker may place or replace the ball, and he may alter the spot for the place kick.

Sub-section (*i*), lifting a foot in a scrummage, has been deleted.

New sub-section (*f*) has been added, which gives a free kick penalty for wilfully holding an opponent who has not got the ball.

RULE 11.—New sub-sections (*g*) and (*j*) have also been added, giving penalties of free kicks for (*g*) wilfully hacking or tripping up (although a penalty of a free kick is now given, the Referee should still caution a player, or even order him off the ground, if such hacking or tripping up constituted rough play), and (*j*) shouting on-side when his players are not yet on-side. This is intended to chiefly apply to a back having kicked the ball and while following up shouting on-side when he has not yet placed his side on-side—a most unfair practice.

In the Board's circular of 1897 it was pointed out in relation to sub-section (*k*), then lettered (*h*), that "this prohibits the habit of three-quarters and half-backs standing in front of the ball, so as to mark the opposing backs, and should be strictly enforced." The Board, whilst now wishful to emphasise this, would also point out that it is not intended thereby to penalise a half-back who unintentially overruns the ball in a scrummage.

RULE 12.—The wording of the last paragraph has been altered so as to give the opposite side the right to bring the ball out, if not originally thrown out straight.

If the ball has not been fairly bounded into play, or not bounded or thrown at the right place, the Referee shall order that the same side shall bound or throw in at the proper place.

A player may be in-touch and yet play the ball, if the ball be considered not in-touch.

A ball kicked over the touch line and blown back shall be considered as in-touch.

A ball from a kick-off having reached 10 yards, and then been blown back, shall be considered as in play, as also a ball having reached the 25 yards line from a drop-out. Also a goal is scored if the ball has crossed the bar, although it may be blown back afterwards.

RULE 17.—Heeling back over own goal line shall be considered as wilfully kicking back. If, when a ball is passed back, the would-be receiver fumbles it so that it goes over his own goal line, the Referee shall decide whether such fumble were intentional or not, and decide accordingly.

A kicker and a placer must be distinct persons, and the kicker may not under any circumstances touch the ball when on the ground, even though the charge has been disallowed.

In case of any dispute relative to a try, where it is possible an appeal may be made to this Board. Referees are recommended to allow a kick at goal, so that if this Board afterwards allows the try, the goal points may be added if the kick was successful.

Injured Player.— Game shall not be stopped for more than three minutes.

CASE LAW.

(*In the following decisions, given officially by the English and New Zealand Unions upon definite points raised, the ruling body is indicated by initials at the end of each decision.*)

LAW 1.

Firstly, it is the duty of the visiting team to see that the ground complies with Law 1 as to size, and is properly marked, that the dead-ball line is distinct, etc. If they fail to see to these points before the game begins, no appeal can afterwards be entertained in relation thereto.

The onus is on a side to see that their opponents do not play more than fifteen men, and if they fail to do so they must be sufferers thereby, and points scored must be counted.—E.U.

APPENDIX

If the referee notices that more than fifteen players on a side are taking part in a match, he must order a player off; though the onus is on a side to see that their opponents do not play more than fifteen men. —E.U.

There is no rule to prevent a team starting short making up its complement later. A player is justified in endeavouring to force down immediately on entering the field of play.—N.Z.

Can an injured player who has retired from the game, and stands on the touch line, come out of touch and tackle a player of the opposite side?—Yes, provided that he is not "off-side."—E.U.

Flags should not be less than 5 feet 6 inches from the ground.—E.U.

All grounds should be properly marked out, including the half-way, 25 yards, touch, goal, and dead-ball lines (unless other boundaries form these latter), in which case flags at the half-way and 25 yards lines are unnecessary; if they be used, they should be set well back from the touch lines. Corner flags should be used, and should be at the junction of the touch and goal lines. A player may himself be in touch-in-goal and yet play the ball with his foot if the ball be not touch-in-goal, or he may touch it down with his hand.—E.U.

A player cannot replace another injured.—E.U.

LAW 2.

If the ball be touched down on the line between touch-in-goal and in-goal, the ball shall be considered in touch-in-goal.—N.Z.

"A player with the ball in his possession touches a corner flag or a flag on the touch line." He is respectively in "touch-in-goal" or "in-touch."—E.U.

Touch.—If the ball cross the touch line, and is blown back into play before pitching, it is in-touch.—N.Z.

Should any part of a player who is running with the ball swing into touch or touch-in-goal, such player shall be considered in-touch or in touch-in-goal respectively.

Kick.—If the referee is satisfied that the player intended to propel the ball by the action of his leg, he shall consider such action to be a kick.—N.Z.

Tackle.—A player shall be considered to be tackled when an opposing player has a fair hold of him.—N.Z.

A player is fairly tackled when held by an opposing player. If the ball be not held by the tackler, the player tackled can play the ball. —N.Z.

Throwing Forward.—If a ball is passed back, but after alighting on the ground is blown forward, the pass is good, provided the ball did not alight in front of the passer.—E.U.

Tackle.—To constitute a tackle, the player carrying the ball must be held; so that a player thrown, or knocked over, is not necessarily tackled.—E.U.

A player from whose grasp the ball is snatched cannot claim that it has been held.—E.U.

The referee has sole control of the game, and therefore the right to put the ball in when a scrummage has been formed; but he should only use this right under exceptional cases, as, for instance, when a scrummage is formed near a goal line—when it is of the utmost importance that it should be put in with the greatest precision. The English Union Committee strongly disapproves of the practice of a referee at every point of the game using his powers in this matter.—E.U.

The referee may order the ball to be put into any scrummage from either side he may choose.—E.U.

Attention is called to the fact that a scrummage can take place only when the ball is "put down" between players who "have closed" round on their respective sides, and only one player on either side is necessary. A scrummage ceases to be a scrummage when the original formation is entirely broken up.—N.Z.

Try (note to law).—So as to press the ball on the ground.—N.Z.

A player touches the ball down behind an opponent's goal line, and picks it up again. Question: At which spot is the try secured?—Ruling: At a spot where it was first touched down.—E.U.

A and B represent opposing sides. A kicks the ball and strikes B on the chest, the ball rebounds, strikes the ground and bounces in the air; while in the air about 2 feet off the ground A kicks the ball over the bar. Is this a goal?—Decision: Yes. Read Law 2, "A goal, etc."

A player throwing the ball forward in an endeavour to kick, and missing the ball, is to be regarded as throwing forward.—N.Z.

If the ball be thrown in a direction at right angles to the touch line, and on striking the ground bound forward, it shall not be counted a knock-on.—N.Z.

If a player makes a fair catch, but instantly changes his mind and runs on with the ball, he should be compelled, if the whistle is blown for a fair catch, to return to take his kick.—E.U.

A "fair catch" must be a clean catch at the first attempt, and the mark must not be allowed unless made in accordance with the law. —N.Z.

If a player be on the ground (provided he makes a fair catch), can he claim a mark?—No.—N.Z.

A fair catch can only be claimed by the catcher making his mark after he has caught the ball; the mark, however, must be made as soon after the ball is caught as possible; and, in practice, referees might allow a claim when the mark was simultaneously made with the catching —E.U.

A rebound is not a knock-on, and therefore no fair catch can be made therefrom or penalty given. This is important, as some referees appear to regard a rebound as a knock-on.

In the case of a "drop-out" the kick must be a drop kick.—E.U.

"Ball not reaching 25 yards limit."—Opposite side may play the ball at once or claim, as Law 2 directs.

A referee whistled inadvertently: must the play be stopped?—Decision: Yes.

If a player goes beyond the 25 yards to drop-out, or if he punts, the referee must blow his whistle and order the player to take a new kick, which must be a drop within the 25 yards limit.—E.U.

Law 3.

Referees must appoint their own touch judges.—N.Z.

Suggestion to Referees.—To ask their touch judges to take a note of the time.—N.Z.

"A referee having given a decision after blowing his whistle cannot under any circumstances alter it."—E.U.

If the referee orders a man "off," he cannot let him take part in the play again, and must report him to the Union.—E.U.

A referee cannot order a player off the field for throwing forward. —E.U.

The referee solely has the right to report players for rough play. A bye-law permitting other persons to report is *ultra vires* of the laws of the game.—E.U.

In the case of a player being ordered off the field by the referee: Unions are strongly recommended to deal with the case within ten days of the occurrence; pending their decision the player is not to be prevented from playing.—E.U.

If the ball, not in possession of a player, strikes the referee when in in-goal, or strikes a touch judge standing in in-goal to assist the referee in deciding as to a kick at goal from a fair catch, a try should be scored for the attacking side if in the referee's opinion a try would undoubtedly have been obtained but for the ball touching the referee or touch judge; otherwise a drop-out from the 25.—E.U.

The English Rugby Union do not consider that the ball is out of play when the referee stops the game for an infringement of the laws. —E.U.

In case of a player being hurt, the whistle should not be blown until the ball is dead or out of play, unless continuance of play endangers the hurt player.—E.U.

The International Board have decided that in the event of a player being injured, the game shall not be stopped for more than three minutes.

Referees should insist upon the field of play being kept clear of spectators.—N.Z.

DUTY OF TOUCH JUDGES.

Touch judges are to hold up their flags "immediately" the ball has crossed the touch line, and go to the spot where the ball went out as quickly as possible.—N.Z.

In case of misconduct on the part of a touch judge, the referee shall report him to his Union.—N.Z.

It is advisable that touch judges should note the play along the lines from the corner flags to the dead-ball line, so as to assist the referee if applied to by him.—E.U.

Hukanui *v.* Konini.—The Hukanui Club appealed against the decision of the Makakatu Rugby Union (branch of the Bush Union) for ordering the above match to be replayed. The facts of the appeal were as follow:—During the first half of the game Hukanui obtained a mark in front of their opponents' goal line, and were in the act of placing the ball when the captain of the Konini team appealed. Simultaneously with the kick at goal the referee blew his whistle. A goal resulted, and on the referee finding the appeal was a frivolous one, he allowed a goal. Konini team appealed to the Makakatu Rugby Union, on the ground that when the whistle was blown the ball was dead (Law 3). As a result of this appeal, the goal was disallowed, and the game ordered to be replayed. The referee in his report stated that he did not understand the appeal when it was made, and blew his whistle to make inquiries; that the kicker was running to kick the ball when he blew the whistle, and that physically it was probably possible for the kicker to refrain from taking the kick, but mentally he thought it was almost impossible. Decision: The goal kicked by Hukanui must be allowed.

LAW 5.

"Kick-off"—(1) Ball not reaching 10 yards limit.—Law 2.—E.U.

The referee having sole control of the game, in the case of "kick-off" the ball pitches into touch, should he order a second kick-off, or wait an appeal?

Also, at "drop-out," under similar circumstances to question I., should the referee order a second drop-out or wait for an appeal?

Decision: The referee must permit the side to exercise their option.—E.U.

LAW 6 (a).

It is lawful to pick up the ball in any manner except by hand or arm.—N.Z.

The act of a player taking the ball off the ground with his feet in a scrummage does not constitute "picking up" in a scrummage within the meaning of Law 6.—E.U.

APPENDIX

Is the act of a player taking the ball off the ground after a tackle or the ball being fairly held to be considered picking the ball up in a scrummage?—No.—E.U.

LAW 6, AFTER SEC. (c)—("AT ONCE").

The words "at once" are to be interpreted very strictly.—N.Z.

I. On a player being brought to the ground, can he pass the ball to a confrère, or can the latter take it from him, always providing the ball has not been held by an opponent?—Yes, provided also the ball is not on the ground.

II. (a) Can a player kick the ball with his knee or leg?—Yes.
(b) If so, and an opponent makes a fair catch, is it a free kick? Or
(c) Is it a rebound?
(b) and (c) It is a free kick.

III. An attacking side, in a scrum, with the ball between the first and second rows, and pushing the defending side over the in-goal line, touches the ball down—(a) by the half-back, (b) by a forward in the scrum—is it a try?—The try should be allowed.—E.U.

LAW 7 (OFF-SIDE).

If the ball is heeled back out of a scrummage, and carried or kicked in again by a player outside the scrummage, his forwards are placed off-side.—E.U.

If a player on the line-out deliberately stands on his opponents' side, or amongst the opposing forwards, he can be penalised for being off-side. —N.Z.

A player may play in any position so long as he is on-side and does not obstruct his opponents; he may come up to a scrummage and attempt to hook the ball out with his foot, provided that his other foot is behind the ball.

A player must be in the field of play when he puts his men on-side after kicking the ball when behind them. Whilst he is not debarred from starting running up in touch, he must get into the field of play as soon as possible.—E.U.

A free kick is "a penalty kick" or "a kick after a fair catch."—E.U.

A goal from a penalty kick counts 3 points.—E.U.

A goal from a kick after a fair catch counts 4 points.—E.U.

A goal kicked from a free kick awarded through an opponent being off-side, under Law 8, shall count 3 points, as it is the result of a penalty kick awarded under Law 11 (e).—E.U.

LAW 9 (FAIR CATCH).

When a kick from a fair catch is being taken, if the defending side appeal because the wrong man is about to place the ball, the right man shall be allowed to do so.—E.U.

Unless the appeal is made before the kick is taken, the appeal shall not be allowed, as it was not made "immediately."—N.Z.

"Fair catch behind goal line, etc."—Read in conjunction with Law 19.—N.Z.

The ball must be held clean at the first attempt.—N.Z.

A player can intercept a pass, but can only mark if the pass intercepted is a forward pass.—N.Z.

A player may make a mark and claim a fair catch in his own "in-goal," and the opposing side may line up to such mark.—E.U.

In cases of players waiting to charge when a kick after a try, fair catch, or free kick is about to be taken, they must remain behind the goal line or behind the mark with both feet, and any standing over the goal line or over the mark with one foot shall be considered to have charged, and the referee shall blow his whistle and award no-charge. The referee shall also be particular that any side waiting behind a mark do not gradually creep up beyond the mark; such shall be considered as a charge. When a player is placing the ball he shall not wilfully do anything which may lead his opponents to think he has put the ball down when he has not; if he does, the charge shall not be disallowed. Even when a charge has been disallowed, the would-be chargers may, provided they remain behind the mark, jump up and attempt to stop or touch the ball; if they so touch it, no goal can be scored.—E.U. But if they cross the mark and touch the ball, the goal should be allowed.—N.Z.

Law 10.

If a referee whistles to allow a no-charge just as a kicker takes his kick, such kicker shall have the option of another kick—that is, if he has kicked a goal, he can allow it to stand; if he has not, he can take a second kick.—E.U.

In cases of tries and free kicks, any player may place or kick the ball; in cases of fair catches, the catcher only may place the ball.

After a charge has been disallowed, any player except the kicker may place or replace the ball, and he may alter the spot for the place kick.—E.U.

The charge should not be disallowed if the placer intentionally deceives the other side; for instance, if a player by his action make the opposite side believe that he is going to take a place kick, and then without warning takes a punt or drop kick, the referee shall insist that the place kick be taken.—N.Z.

When the ball has once been placed on the ground, the opposite side may charge at once.—N.Z.

"Must be in the direction of the opponents' goal line." NOTE.—If the ball be kicked in the direction of the opponents' goal line, but before pitching is blown behind the spot where it was kicked, the kick shall be regarded as fair.—N.Z.

APPENDIX

The kicker or any other placer may touch and arrange the ball in all cases in which "a kick at goal is taken after a try has been obtained," "a place kick is taken after a free kick has been awarded by way of penalty," and "a free kick is taken after a fair catch has been made."—E.U.

After the charge was disallowed the kicker placed the ball. It was decided to disallow the goal.—E.U.

In case a referee disallows a charge, the kicker may not touch the ball after it has been put on the ground. If he does so—(1) when a try has been obtained, a kick-out from 25; (2) when a free kick or fair catch has been awarded, a scrummage where the mark was made. The kicker and placer must be different persons.—E.U.

The Wanganui Union desired to know in regard to Law 10, whether a referee has power to disallow a kick in case of feinting by either the placer or kicker. Decision: The kick cannot be disallowed.—N.Z.

Law 11.

Section B.—Note the word "immediately," but the ball must be "held," not the player only.

Section C.—Players must early understand that the penalty will be inflicted if they interfere with the ball in any way while they are lying on the ground.—N.Z.

Section E.—In cases where two players of opposite side are running for the ball, a player overtaking another may not shove the overtaken player from behind; if he does, it is illegal, and should be penalised by a free kick.—E.U.

A player running at the ball may charge an opponent also running at the ball, but such charge may only be shoulder to shoulder.—E.U.

Section H.—Supposing a ball is coming out of a scrummage, and a half-back, seeing he cannot get away, shoves it back with his hands or foot, then the penalty of a free kick should be given.—E.U.

Section J.—This prohibits three-quarters and half-backs standing in front of the ball so as to mark the opposing backs, and should be strictly enforced.—E.U.

It was decided that the word "standing" must be read as meaning "wilfully" standing and remaining; therefore, in future, half-backs mus not be penalised for unintentionally overrunning the ball.—E.U.

When the ball is in the scrummage, every player, except those in the scrummage, must stand on his proper side of a line drawn through the centre of the ball and at right angles to the touch line, otherwise he shall be judged off-side; wing forwards are not in the scrummage.—N.Z.

Section K.—Unless the ball is put past the first man on that side of the scrummage that has the shorter front, it shall not be considered to have been put fairly into the scrummage.—N.Z.

Law 12.

Bouncing ball out of touch, Law 12 (*a*).—It is necessary that a player who has bounced the ball must have both his feet in the field of play when he catches it.—E.U.

If the ball be not properly bounced, should a throw-out be allowed, or a scrummage from 5 yards to 15 yards out?—The side to whom the ball belongs has the option.—E.U.

The thrower-out need not come up to the touch line to throw out. —N.Z.

If the ball is not thrown out at the right place, a second throw out must take place by the side to whom the ball belongs.—E.U.

If the ball has not been fairly bounded into play, or not bounded or thrown at the right place, the referee shall order that the same side shall bound or throw in at the proper place.—E.U.

NOTE.—"Opposite side shall bring," not "may bring."

The player throwing-in is not permitted to run into the field after the ball and play it before it has been properly bounded or another player has touched it.—E.U.

Law 13.

After word "brought" read as though the words "in any manner" were inserted.—N.Z.

In case of any dispute relative to a try, where it is possible an appeal may be made to this Union. Referees are recommended to allow a kick at goal, so that if this Union afterwards allows the try, the goal points may be added if the kick was successful.

The referee should see that players have reasonable time to get behind their goal line before the ball is placed.—E.U.

NOTE.—Duty of referee to see that the ball is taken out straight.

Law 15.

At "kick-out" it is the duty of the referee to see that reasonable time is given to the players to get into their positions before the kick is taken.—E.U.

Law 16.

A "fair catch" claimed for a "knock-on" or "throw-forward" takes precedence in every case, even though the referee had whistled or not for the "knock-on" or "throw-forward."—E.U.

A player crossing the opponents' goal line with the ball, and then touching the referee, should be allowed a try at the spot where he touched him.—E.U.

APPENDIX

A player running out from his own "in-goal" touches the referee, the ball is dead at the spot where he touches him, and a "kick-out" must be taken, except in the case of a player having run back behind his own goal line, and the ball must then be scrummaged at the spot whence it was carried back.—E.U.

A ball is not to be considered dead when it strikes a spectator, unless a special arrangement is made before or during a match that such should be the case.—E.U.

If, in the opinion of the referee, a try would undoubtedly have been scored but for the ball touching the referee or touch judge, he shall allow a try, otherwise a drop-out from the 25 line.—E.U.

LAW 17.

Heeling back over own goal line shall be considered as wilfully kicking back. If, when a ball is passed back, the would-be receiver fumbles it so that it goes over his own goal line, the referee shall decide whether such fumble were intentional or not, and decide accordingly.—E.U.

From a kick the ball is blown behind the kicker's goal line; can the attacking side touch the ball down and secure a try?—Yes, provided no appeal is made by them.—E.U.

Is it a try in the case of a player passing the ball back behind his own goal line, and the ball is touched down by one of his opponents?— Ruling: Yes.—E.U.

THE BRITISH TEAM IN NEW ZEALAND, 1888.

Full backs—J. T. Haslam, Yorkshire and Batley; A. Paul, Lancashire and Swinton. *Three-quarters*—H. C. Speakman, Cheshire and Runcorn; Dr. H. Brooks, Durham and Edinburgh University; J. Anderton, Lancashire and Salford; A. E. Stoddart, Middlesex, Rovers, and English International. *Half-backs*—W. Bumby, Lancashire and Swinton; J. Nolan, Rochdale Hornets; W. Burnett, Roxburgh County and Hawick. *Forwards*—R. L. Seddon (captain), Lancashire and Swinton; C. Mathers, Yorkshire and Bramley; S. Williams, Lancashire and Salford; T. Banks, Lancashire and Swinton; H. Eagles, Lancashire and Swinton; A. J. Stewart, Yorkshire and Dewsbury; W. H. Thomas, Cambridge University and Wales; T. Kent, Lancashire and Salford; A. P. Pinketh, Douglas, Isle of Man Club; P. Burnett, Roxburgh County and Hawick; A. J. Lang, Roxburgh County and Hawick; Dr. D. J. Smith, Edinburgh University, Corinthians, and Scottish International; and J. P. Clowes, Yorkshire and Halifax.

19 matches played; 13 won; 2 lost; and 4 drawn.

APPENDIX

THE BRITISH TEAM IN NEW ZEALAND, 1904.

C. F. Stanger-Leathes, Northern and Northumberland; W. Llewellyn, Newport, Wales, and Kent; P. F. McEvedy, Guy's Hospital and Kent; A. B. O'Brien, Guy's Hospital and Kent (manager); R. T. Gabe, Wales, Cardiff, and Middlesex; E. Morgan, Wales, Guy's Hospital, and Kent; J. L. Fisher, Hull and East Riding and Yorkshire; E. Jowett, Wales and Swansea; F. C. Hume, England, Birkenhead Park, and Cheshire; P. Bush, Cardiff and Glamorgan; J. Vile, Newport and Monmouthshire; D. R. Bedel-Sivright (captain), Scotland, Cambridge University, and West of Scotland; D. Dobson, England, Oxford University, and Devon; R. W. Edwards, Ireland and Malone; C. D. Patterson, Ulster and Malone; S. Beaven, Wales and Swansea; S. N. Crowther, Lennox and Surrey; D. H. Traill, Guy's Hospital and Surrey; R. H. Rogers, Bath and Somerset; F. McKay Saunders, Guy's Hospital and Kent; B. I. Swannell, Northampton and East Midlands; A. F. Harding, Wales, London, Welsh, and Cardiff; B. F. Massey, Hull and East Riding and Yorkshire; J. Sharland, Streatham and Surrey.

5 matches played; 2 won; 2 lost; and 1 drawn.

There was also an informal game played against fifteen Maoris at Rotorua on 22nd August, the Maoris winning by 8 points to 6.

This British team played fourteen matches in Australia, and won them all.

THE NATIVE TEAM IN ENGLAND, 1888–89.

This team was not sent out by the New Zealand Rugby Union. It was a private venture.

Backs—W. Warbrick, J. Warbrick, F. Warbrick, W. T. Wynyard, H. J. Wynyard, E. McCausland, W. Elliott, and C. Madigan, Auckland; H. Lee, Southland; P. Keogh, Otago; D. R. Gage, Wellington; Ihimaira ("The Smiler"), and Taare (Goldsmith), Hawke's Bay. *Forwards*—T. R. Ellison and G. Williams, Wellington; D. Stewart, W. Anderson, A. Webster, Alf. Warbrick, Arthur Warbrick, G. Wynyard, and R. Maynard, Auckland; R. Taiaroa, Otago; T. Rene, Wi Karauria, Nelson; W. Nehua, Hawke's Bay.

74 matches played; 49 won; 5 drawn; 20 lost.

THE NEW ZEALAND TEAM IN BRITAIN, 1905.

Heights, Weights, and Ages.

Backs.	Age.	Weight. st. lb.	Height. ft. in.
W. J. Wallace	27	12 0	5 8
E. Harper	27	12 7	5 11
E. Booth	26	11 10	5 7½
G. W. Smith	33	11 12	5 7
H. Abbott	23	13 0	5 10½
F. Roberts	23	12 4	5 7
R. G. Deans	21	13 4	6 0
J. Hunter	26	11 8	5 6
H. G. Mynott	29	11 9	5 7
W. J. Stead	28	11 4	5 9
G. Gillett	28	13 0	6 0
H. D. Thompson	24	10 9	5 8
D. McGregor	23	11 3	5 9

Forwards.	Age.	Weight. st. lb.	Height. ft. in.
D. Gallaher (captain)	29	13 0	6 0
W. S. Glenn	27	12 12	5 11
S. Casey	22	12 4	5 10
A. McDonald	22	13 0	5 10
W. Johnston	23	13 6	6 0
C. Seeling	22	13 7	6 0
G. Nicholson	26	13 10	6 3
G. A. Tyler	26	13 0	5 10
J. Corbett	25	13 9	5 11
F. Newton	23	15 0	6 0
F. Glasgow	25	13 3	5 10
J. O'Sullivan	22	13 7	5 10
W. Mackrell	23	12 7	5 10
W. Cunningham	29	14 6	5 11

These were their weights on landing in England.

The number of matches played in by the different members of the team was as follows:—Roberts, 29; Stead, 26; Glasgow, 24; Seeling, 24; Gillett, 24; Wallace, 23; Gallaher, 23; Hunter, 23; Casey, 22; Cunningham, 22; Tyler, 22; O'Sullivan, 20; Deans, 19; Mynott, 18; Smith, 18; Nicholson, 17; McDonald, 16; Newton, 16; Corbett, 14; McGregor, 14; Johnston, 14; Booth, 13; Glenn, 13; Harper, 10; Thompson, 9; Abbott, 7; Mackrell, 3.

Thirty-two matches were played.

APPENDIX

THE TEAMS IN THE INTERNATIONAL MATCHES.

SCOTLAND *v.* NEW ZEALAND AT INVERLEITH, NOVEMBER 18, 1905.

SCOTLAND.—J. G. Scoular (Cambridge University), *back*; T. Sloan (Glasgow Academicals), L. M. McLeod, K. G. McLeod (Cambridge University), J. T. Simson (Watsonians), *three-quarter backs*; P. Munro (Oxford University), L. L. Greig (Glasgow Academicals), E. D. Simson (Edinburgh University), *half-backs*; D. R. Bedell-Sivright, J. M. Mackenzie (Edinburgh University), W. P. Scott (West of Scotland), W. E. Kyle (Hawick), J. C. McCallum) Watsonians), W. L. Russell (Glasgow Academicals), L. West (West Hartlepool), *forwards*.

NEW ZEALAND.—G. Gillett, *back*; W. J. Wallace, R. G. Deans, G. W. Smith, *three-quarter backs*; W. J. Stead, J. Hunter, *five-eighths backs*; F. Roberts, *half-back*; D. Gallaher, S. Casey, G. A. Tyler, J. O'Sullivan, W. Cunningham, A. McDonald, C. Seeling, F. Glasgow, *forwards*.

Referee—Mr. Kennedy (Irish Union).

IRELAND *v.* NEW ZEALAND AT DUBLIN, NOVEMBER 25, 1905.

IRELAND.—M. F. Landers (Cork Constitution), *back*; H. Thrift (Dublin University), B. Maclear (Cork County), J. C. Parke (Dublin University), C. G. Robb (Queen's College, Belfast), *three-quarter backs*; E. D. Caddell, F. H. Robinson (Dublin University), *half-backs*; C. E. Allen (Derry), A. Tedford, H. G. Wilson (Malone), Joseph Wallace (Wanderers), H. J. Knox (Lansdowne), G. Hamlet (Old Wesley), J. J. Coffey (Lansdowne), H. S. Sugars (Dublin University), *forwards*.

NEW ZEALAND.—W. J. Wallace, *back*; G. W. Smith, R. G. Deans, H. G. Mynott, *three-quarter backs*; W. J. Stead, J. Hunter, *five-eighths backs*; F. Roberts, *half-back*; G. Gillett, A. McDonald, C. Seeling, F. Glasgow, W. Cunningham, J. O'Sullivan, G. A. Tyler, S. Casey, *forwards*.

Referee—Mr. Crawford Findlay.

ENGLAND *v.* NEW ZEALAND AT THE CRYSTAL PALACE, DECEMBER 2, 1905.

ENGLAND.—E. J. Jackett (Leicester), *back*; H. Imrie (Durham City), R. E. Godfray (Richmond), H. Shewring (Bristol), A. E. Hind (Leicester), J. E. Raphael (Old Merchant Taylors), *three-quarter backs*; J. Braithwaite (Leicester), D. Gent (Gloucester), *half-backs*; V. H. Cartright (Nottingham), B. A. Hill (Blackheath), C. E. L. Hammond (Harlequins), J. L. Mathias (Bristol), E. W. Roberts (Dartmouth), R. F. Russell (Leicester), G. Summerscales (Durham City), *forwards*.

APPENDIX 317

NEW ZEALAND.—G. Gillett, *back*; D. McGregor, R. G. Deans, W. J. Wallace, *three-quarter backs*; W. J. Stead, J. Hunter, *five-eighths backs*; F. Roberts, *half-back*; J. O'Sullivan, G. A. Tyler, S. Casey, F. Newton, F. Glasgow, A. McDonald, C. Seeling, D. Gallaher, *forwards*.

Referee—Mr. G. Evans.

WALES v. NEW ZEALAND AT CARDIFF, DECEMBER 16, 1905.

WALES.—*H. B. Winfield (Cardiff), *back*; *E. Gwyn Nicholls (Cardiff) (capt.) and *R. T. Gabe (Cardiff), *centre three-quarters*; *W. Llewellyn (Penygraig) and *E. T. Morgan (London Welsh), *wing three-quarter backs*; *Cliff Pritchard (Pontypool), *extra back*; *R. M. Owen (Swansea) and P. F. Bush (Cardiff), *half-backs*; *W. Joseph (Swansea), *C. M. Pritchard (Newport), *A. F. Harding (London Welsh), *J. F. Williams (London Welsh), *G. Travers (Pill Harriers), *J. Hodges (Newport), and *D. Jones (Aberdare), *forwards*.
* Old International.

NEW ZEALAND.—G. Gillet (Canterbury), *back*; D. McGregor (Wellington), R. G. Deans (Canterbury), and W. J. Wallace (Wellington), *three-quarter backs*; H. G. Mynott (Taranaki) and J. Hunter (Taranaki), *five-eighths backs*; F. Roberts (Wellington), *half-back*; J. O'Sullivan (Taranaki), G. A. Tyler (Auckland), S. Casey (Otago), F. Newton (Canterbury), F. Glasgow (Taranaki), A. McDonald (Otago), C. Seeling (Auckland), and D. Gallaher (Auckland) (capt.), *forwards*.

Referee—Mr. J. D. Dallas (Watsonians).

THE RECORD OF THE TEAM.

	G.	T.	P.		G.	T.	P.
New Zealand	*9	4	55	v. Devon	†1	0	4
New Zealand	4	7	41	v. Cornwall	0	0	0
New Zealand	7	2	41	v. Bristol	0	0	0
New Zealand	4	4	32	v. Northampton	0	0	0
New Zealand	5	1	28	v. Leicester	0	0	0
New Zealand	5	3	34	v. Middlesex	0	0	0
New Zealand	2	2	16	v. Durham	0	1	3
New Zealand	9	6	63	v. Hartlepool	0	0	0
New Zealand	2	7	31	v. Northumberland	0	0	0
New Zealand	7	3	44	v. Gloucester	0	0	0
New Zealand	†3	3	23	v. Somerset	0	0	0
New Zealand	3	2	21	v. Devonport Albion	*1	0	3
New Zealand	3	2	21	v. Midland Counties	1	0	5

* One penalty. † One dropped.

APPENDIX

	G.	T.	P.			G.	T.	P.
New Zealand	1	2	11	v. Surrey		0	0	0
New Zealand	*5	3	32	v. Blackheath		0	0	0
New Zealand	4	9	47	v. Oxford University		0	0	0
New Zealand	1	3	14	v. Cambridge University		0	0	0
New Zealand	1	4	17	v. Richmond		0	0	0
New Zealand	‡5	6	41	v. Bedford		0	0	0
New Zealand	0	4	12	v. Scotland		†1	1	7
New Zealand	2	4	22	v. West of Scotland		0	0	0
New Zealand	3	0	15	v. Ireland		0	0	0
New Zealand	*4	5	33	v. Munster		0	0	0
New Zealand	0	5	15	v. England		0	0	0
New Zealand	3	1	18	v. Cheltenham		0	0	0
New Zealand	2	8	34	v. Cheshire		0	0	0
New Zealand	5	5	40	v. Yorkshire		0	0	0
New Zealand	0	0	0	v. Wales		0	1	3
New Zealand	0	3	9	v. Glamorgan		0	0	0
New Zealand	1	1	6	v. Newport		*1	0	3
New Zealand	2	0	10	v. Cardiff		1	1	8
New Zealand	†1	0	4	v. Swansea		0	1	3

* One penalty. † One dropped. ‡ One mark goal.

31 matches won to 1.
830 points to 39.
103 goals to 6.
109 tries to 5.

INDEX

Abbott, H., 243.
Africa, South, football in, 232.
Alternatives in arrangement of side, 192.
Alternatives in tactics, 137.
Amateurism in New Zealand, 221.
America, football in, 232.
Angle kick, 97.
Arneil, J., 28, 117.
Association, Football, founded, 14.
Association game, comparative merits of, 229, 231.
Attack, 63, 126, 127, 141, 143, 145, 158.
Auckland, early football in, 18, 19; tour in South Island, 23; Rugby Union formed, 30; organisation in, 37; residential qualification in, 39; club system in, 40; system of promotion in, 42; common ground at, 44.
Australia, football in, 232.

Back-row men, 105.
Backs, 63, 68, 70, 79, 145.
Backing up, 142.
Basilikon Doron, reference to football in, 9.
Bedford, match against, 162, 261.
Beginning of Rugby Football, 1.
Blackheath, match against, 260.
Blackheath club founded, 13.
Bloxam, Matthew, report on origin of Rugby, 12.
Bluff, pure, in attack, 168.
Boldness in attack, 140.
Boots, 176, 208.
Brady, C., 110.
Bristol, match against, 253.

Cambridge, early football at, 13.
Cambridge University, match against 260.
Canterbury (N. Z.), football at, 23, 24.
Captaincy, 188–200.

Cardiff, match against, 141, 269.
Case law, 205, 304.
Changing places in team, 192.
Charterhouse, football at, 11.
Cheltenham, match against, 266.
Cheshire, match against, 266.
Code words, 75, 76, 202, 203.
Coles, Percy, 109.
Colonies, game for, 231.
Combination, 32, 55, 85.
Combined attack on the open side, 145, 157.
Companionship in training, 181.
Concentration of effort, 56.
Conference between London and Cambridge, 13.
Cornwall, match against, 252.
County championship, 283.
County qualifications, 282.
Country football in New Zealand, 50.
Coventry, R. G. T., 74.
Cricket, comparative merits of, 228.
Crystal Palace, match at, 265.
Cunningham, W., 104, 243.
Cutting through, 77, 90, 91, 152.

Dacre, 25.
Deans, R. G., 69, 92.
Deception, 61.
Defence, 63, 123, 170.
Definitions, 275.
Delegation of Union's powers, 286.
Development, future, 223, 225.
Devon, match against, 249.
Devonport Albion, match against, 258.
Diet, 183, 184.
Digestion, 174.
Doctor, seeing, 173.
Dress for referees, 217.
Dribbling, 81.
Drop-kicking, 98.
Drop-out by opponents, attack from, 164.
Dunnett, George, 22.

Ear guards, 176.

INDEX

Economy of force, 106, 107.
Edward II., Proclamation by, 4.
Edward III., objection to football, 4.
Elizabethan football, 7.
Ellis, William Webb, first to pick up ball at Rugby, 12.
Elyot, Sir Thomas, 7.
Embrocation, recipe for, 186.
England, International match against, 160, 265.
English Rugby Union founded, 14.
Equipment, 173.
Evans, Gil, 109.
Expansion, prospects of, 225-238.
Eyes, watching opponent's, 95.
Eyesight, 174.

Financial system in New Zealand, 47.
Findlay, Crawford, 264.
Fitness for play, 174.
FitzStephen, William, 4.
Five-eighths, 64, 73, 76, 156, 157.
Five-eighth's attack on the blind side, 106.
Five-eighth's variations of attack by cutting in, 152.
Follis, the, 4.
Following up, 209.
Football Association founded, 14.
Footwork, 81, 82.
Formation, changes in, 15, 16, 27, 28, 30, 31, 32, 62, 64, 66, 103.
Forwards, 63, 80, 138.
Foul play, 208.
France, Rugby football in, 227; match against, 269.
Free kicks for infringement of rules, 215.

Gallaher, D., 69, 243.
Gap movement, the, 128, 133.
Gillett, G., 69.
Glamorgan, match against, 268.
Glossary, 272.
Gloucester, match against, 257.
Gloves, 176.
Greeks and football, 3.
Ground, best kind of, 203.

Half-backs, 63, 71.
Harpastum, the Roman, 3.
Harper, E., 249.
Harrow, football at, 11.
Health of player, 173.
Heart trouble, 173.
Hill, Rowland, 221.
Hookers, 104, 108.

Hooking the ball out, 108, 110.
Hunter, J., 69, 91, 162.

Idea of the game, 53.
Ideas and inventions, new, 203.
Individual effort, 59, 152, 167.
Insurance against accident in New Zealand, 48.
International Board, Bye-laws of, 285.
—— Recommendations, 301.
Interpretations of rules, 205.
Injured players, 206.
Invercargill, 30.
Ireland, International match against, 130, 264.
Irish forwards, 82.

James I. condemns the game, 8.
James III. prohibits football, 5.
Jerseys, New Zealand, 174.
Jones, A. O., 254.

Keenness, 207.
Kicking up the field, 141.
Knee bandages, 175.
Knickers, 175.
Knocking-on, 82, 215.

Ladies, free admission for, 44.
Laws of the game, 272.
Leicester, match against, 254.
Line-out play, 83, 113, 122-134.
Lockman, 104, 176.
London sheriffs put down football, 5.
Loose rush, 134.
Losing game, the, 140.

McDonald, A., 249.
McGregor, D., 69, 160.
Mackenzie, W., 117.
Maoris and football, 29.
Mark, the, 204.
Melbourne rules, 19, 21.
Mercer, C. B., 26.
Middlesex, match against, 255.
Midland Counties, match against, 259.
Millton, W., 31.
Monte Video, 245.
Morgan, E. T., 90.
Munster, match against, 264.
Mynott, H. G., 92, 162.

Neilson, W. F., 24.
New South Wales, football in, 29; New Zealand tour in, 31; tour in New Zealand, 32; v. New Zealand, 242.

INDEX

New Zealand, development of football in, 17; team in New South Wales, 31; Union formed, 33; organisation in, 35; system of promotion in, 42; financial arrangements in, 47; training halls in, 49, 179; British tour promoted by, 220, 239; selection of team, 242; bye-laws of Union, 291; Referees' Association, 295.
Newport, match against, 268.
Newton, F., 104.
Newton Abbot, quarters at, 248, 250, 258.
Nicholls, Gwyn, 92, 94, 268.
Nolan, J., 25.
Northampton, match against, 253.
Northern Union, 15, 221.
Northumberland, match against, 257.
Numerical advantage by combination, 57.

Off day, 205.
Opponents, study of, 195, 204.
Opportunism, 59.
Otago, football at, 23, 27, 29.
Overtraining, 186.
Oxford, system of passing at, 15.
Oxford University, match against, 260.

Paris, visit to, 269.
Passing, 85, 86, 87, 149, 150, 155, 207.
Passing forward, 215.
Passing rush, 96.
Pass-in variation of attack, 161.
Penalties, 215, 216, 276.
Place-kicking, 96.
Placing the ball for place-kicks, 97.
Plan of the field, 271.
Plans, preconceived, 201.
Plymouth, arrival at, 248.
Practice of specialities, 202.
Pressing home an attack, 143.
Professionalism, 220–224, 287.
Provinces on tour in New Zealand, 51.
Public schools, Rugby at the, 11.
Punctuality on the field, 201.
Punting, 71, 99, 209.
Pushing in the scrum, 106.
Putting ball in scrum, 109.

Queensland, football in, 232.

Ranfurly Shield, 51.
Receiving the ball from a pass, 88.
Record of New Zealand tour, 317.
Rees, W. L., 19.
Referees and refereeing, 78, 211–219.
Reserve men, 56, 57, 142.
Return to New Zealand, 270.

Richard II., Proclamation by, 5.
Richmond, match against, 261.
Roberts, F., 69, 72, 162.
Robinson, W. W., 17, 22, 24, 25, 117.
Romans and football, 3.
Romans taught the Britons, 4.
Rosario, match against the, 18.
Rubbing mixture, 186.
Ruck, loose, 134.
Rugby, early football at, 11, 12.
Rugby Union Bye-laws, 279.
Rules, study of, 189.
Running exercise, 180.
Ruses, 60, 129, 168.

Scone, annual match at, 9.
Scotland, football prohibited in, 5.
Scotland, International match against, 220, 261.
Scottish Rugby Union founded, 14.
Scoular, J. G., 91.
Screwing the scrum, 110.
Scrum, the, 32, 83, 100, 106, 110, 114, 140, 170, 214, 223.
Scrum half, 63, 75, 126.
Seddon, Mr., telegram from, 256.
Selection of teams in New Zealand, 51, 242.
Shadowing the man, 125.
Sheffield, football at, 13.
Shin guard, 175.
Shrove Tuesday festivals, 11.
Side-row men, 105.
Smith, G. W., 69, 90, 91, 130.
Smoking, 185.
Soles of boots, polishing, 177.
Somerset, match against, 258.
South Island, Auckland's tour in, 23.
Speed, cultivation of, 182.
Spoiling game, 169.
Staleness in New Zealand team, 263, 267.
Stead, W. J., 69.
Stimulants, 185.
Stoddart's British team, 33.
Strategy, 58, 73, 168.
Strengthening the defence from the scrum, 170.
Strutt's description of the game, 10.
Stubbes and football, 8.
Studs on boots, 177.
Study of tactics, 136, 180.
Surrey, match against, 259.
Swerving, 89, 90.

Tackling, 58, 94, 96.
Tactics, 76, 77, 113, 135–171, 197.
Taipu movement in attack, 163.

INDEX

Talking on the field, 80, 206.
Taranaki, football at, 23, 29.
Teams, British and New Zealand, 313-317.
Temper, bad, 204.
Thames Goldfields, match against, 19, 21.
Thompson, H. D., 90.
Three-quarter backs, 63, 77, 78.
Throwing-in on the line-out, 125, 129.
Tonics, 204.
Training, 173, 177.
Training halls in New Zealand, 49, 179.
Training on board ship, 246.
Tries, methods of scoring, 55.
Two-three-two formation, 32.
Tyler, G. A., 110.

Unmarked men, the, 124, 125, 126.

Variations in attack, 152, 161.
Versatility, 69.
Voyage to England, 244.

Wales, International match against, 267.
Wales, development of the game in, 16.
Wallace, W. J., 69, 90, 97, 143.
Warbrick, Joe, 27.
Watching the ball, 202.
Wedge formation, 103, 106.
Wellington, football at, 23, 29; New Zealand v., 243.
Welsh Rugby Union founded, 14.
Welsh system, 67.
West Hartlepool, match against, 256.
West of Scotland, match against, 262.
Westminster, football at, 11.
Wet weather, play in, 98, 112, 123, 205.
Whitaker, F., 18.
Winfield, H. B., 107.
Wing forward, 28, 72, 100, 115-121.
Wing three-quarter's attack on the blind side, 158.
Winning game, the, 140.
Wood, J., 25.

Yorkshire, match against, 266.

Printed by MORRISON & GIBB LIMITED, *Edinburgh*

Lightning Source UK Ltd.
Milton Keynes UK
UKHW022115080223
416681UK00011B/2593